RETURN
— TO THE —
REICH

BOOKS BY ERIC LICHTBLAU

Bush's Law:
The Remaking of American Justice

The Nazis Next Door:
How America Became a Safe Haven
for Hitler's Men

RETURN
—— TO THE ——
REICH

A Holocaust Refugee's Secret Mission
to Defeat the Nazis

ERIC LICHTBLAU

Houghton Mifflin Harcourt
Boston   New York
2019

For information about permission to reproduce selections
from this book, write to trade.permissions@hmhco.com or to
Permissions, Houghton Mifflin Harcourt Publishing Company,
3 Park Avenue, 19th Floor, New York, New York 10016.

hmhbooks.com

Library of Congress Cataloging-in-Publication Data
Names: Lichtblau, Eric, author.
Title: Return to the Reich : a Holocaust refugee's secret mission
to defeat the Nazis / Eric Lichtblau.
Description: Boston : Houghton Mifflin Harcourt, 2019. |
Includes bibliographical references and index.
Identifiers: LCCN 2019009834 (print) | LCCN 2019011526 (ebook) |
ISBN 9781328529909 (ebook) | ISBN 9781328528537 (hardback)
Subjects: LCSH: Mayer, Frederick, 1921–2016. | Spies — United
States — Biography. | United States. Office of Strategic Services —
Officials and employees — Biography. | Jews — Germany — Freiburg
im Breisgau — Biography. | World War, 1939–1945 — Secret service
— United States. | World War, 1939–1945 — Underground
movements — Austria. | Espionage, American — Europe — History
— 20th century. | Freiburg im Breisgau (Germany) — Biography. |
BISAC: HISTORY / Military / World War II. |
HISTORY / Holocaust.
Classification: LCC D810.S8 (ebook) | LCC D810.S8 M337 2019
(print) | DDC 940.54/8673092 [B] — dc23
LC record available at https://lccn.loc.gov/2019009834

Book design by Chrissy Kurpeski

Printed in the United States of America
DOW 10 9 8 7 6 5 4 3 2 1

Photo credits appear on page 276.

Images taken from the interviews of Frederick Mayer (1997) provided by
USC Shoah Foundation. For more information: http://sfi.usc.edu/.
Excerpt from the poem by Hans Wynberg originally appeared in an email to
Marjorie Bingham dated March 9, 2009. Lines reprinted with permission.

To the "Zollers" — Leslie, Matthew, Andrew, Elliot, and Harold . . . who inspire me every day

CONTENTS

INTRODUCTION

This book grew out of an impromptu discussion about heroism
and the Holocaust. I was meeting at a Washington coffee shop
a few years ago with Eli Rosenbaum, a dogged Nazi hunter who
was a critical resource for my last book. Skimming the day's news
that morning, I came across the obituary of an obscure European
man who hid countless Jews from the Nazis seven decades earlier. I mentioned the obituary to Eli, admitting with some embar-
rassment that I had never heard of this man before. How was it,
I asked, that so many anonymous people did such heroic things

during the Holocaust, yet we only learned about them after they died?

Eli had no ready response. "Okay," I continued, "so tell me someone that I'll wish I had heard about *before* they die." This time Eli had an immediate answer. "You should meet Fred Mayer," he said. "A Holocaust survivor and a war hero. He lives in West Virginia. Well into his nineties now."

So began my introduction to Freddy Mayer, as Eli gave me a brief recap of his remarkable life: from Jewish teenager in Germany to Holocaust refugee in America to spy and war hero in Nazi-occupied Austria. After all these years, there was a campaign going on to award him the vaunted Medal of Honor, Eli said.

I wanted to meet Freddy. I had been writing about villains for years — Nazis in World War II, modern-day scoundrels in the US capital — and his story seemed like an inspiring respite. Eli helped me get in touch with him, and in February 2016 I drove the ninety minutes from Washington, DC, to Mayer's cottage in the woods of West Virginia, not far from a casino and a racetrack. I spent a moving afternoon with him. At the age of ninety-four, he had trouble with his hearing — the lingering effects of his treatment by the Nazis, I learned — but otherwise he seemed remarkably spry. Living by himself, he was still driving, still shoveling snow, still delivering Meals on Wheels to less independent elderly neighbors. And he could still tick off the names and dates associated with his war story in rapid-fire succession. He struck me as ageless.

We talked about what it was like for him to grow up as a Jew in Germany, a pleasant childhood turned toxic by the Nazis. He told me about his father's resistance to leaving a country where he had fought proudly as a decorated officer in World War I. We talked

about his life as a teenage immigrant in Brooklyn, and of course
we talked about his Nazi spy mission.

I had already read a bit about the three-man espionage team he
led into the Austrian Alps. I told him how inconceivable it seemed
that he managed to pose undetected as a German officer on the
ground in a Nazi stronghold for more than two months, gathering
valuable intelligence on military operations. He smiled and gently corrected me. The Nazi officer was just one of his disguises;
he had also transformed himself into a French laborer at a Nazi
factory — simply changing the pronunciation of his name to *Freh-
deh-REEK May-YEHR,* he told me in an exaggerated French accent. He laughed as he said it, flashing the wide grin that I would
come to learn was a personal trademark.

He turned deadly serious, though, as he recounted for me in
wrenching detail his eventual capture by the Gestapo. Standing
up from his chair slowly but determinedly, he showed me how
Nazi interrogators hoisted him onto poles and tortured him for
hours. In slow motion, he demonstrated the roundhouse punch
delivered to his chin as he reenacted the gruesome scene. Then he
revived his French accent to describe how he had kept his mouth
shut, telling his Nazi interrogators that he was just a simple workman who knew nothing about any American spy operations. "Je
ne sais rien!" *I know nothing!*

Telling reminders of the war dotted the house. On a kitchen
wall was a large photo of an airborne B-24 Liberator, the aircraft on which he'd flown back into the Reich; it was signed by
the members of his mission. By the door was a three-foot statue
of William Donovan, founder of the Office of Strategic Services,
the wartime intelligence agency that dropped him into Austria.
And in a glass-enclosed frame were a half-dozen medals he had

been awarded. Freddy wanted me to see another medal, too: the "golden eagle of Tyrol," which the Austrian embassy had given him four decades after the war. He rummaged through a dresser in his bedroom looking for it, then gave up in frustration. The medal, like his story, seemed to have been stashed away somewhere and largely forgotten.

I told Freddy I'd like to write about him — maybe for a book, or maybe for the *New York Times,* where I was an investigative reporter based in Washington. He shrugged, as if to say, *What's the big deal?* I would learn that the shrug, like his smile, was another of Freddy's trademarks. "Eh, what more is there to say?" he asked me. Over the last forty years, there had been several books and documentaries about his mission and other notable OSS spy operations targeting the Nazis. He pulled out one book from the 1970s to show me.

I explained that I thought there was still a lot left to say. Many people remained sadly unfamiliar with the wartime heroism of refugees like him, I said, and it seemed like a particularly ripe time to remind them. During the 2016 presidential campaign, then-candidate Donald J. Trump was vilifying immigrants as the central plank of his platform. At the same time, he had triggered a mystifying debate about the meaning of heroism when he said that Senator John McCain, who had spent more than five years as a POW in Vietnam, was "not a war hero" — because he had been captured. Freddy's story, from war refugee to war hero, fascinated me: too often it seemed that America had forgotten its true heroes and their origins.

At the end of a conversation that could have lasted all night, Freddy asked me to come visit with him again soon. Just two months later, in April 2016, he died after a sudden decline. As it

77

turned out, I did write about Freddy's heroism for the *New York Times*, but unfortunately, it was for his obituary. "Frederick Mayer, Jew Who Spied on Nazis After Fleeing Germany, Dies at 94" read the headline. Like the obituary I had read on my way to meet Eli Rosenbaum, it was a story of wartime courage long forgotten.

As I was writing up Freddy's obituary, I called John Billings, the pilot who flew him and his team over Nazi-occupied Austria and dropped them into the Reich. "I was in awe of him," said the ninety-two-year-old veteran, his voice emotional at the passing of his longtime friend. "He was born without the fear gene. He feared nothing."

A fitting epitaph for a man who fled the Nazis, only to return to help defeat them.

RETURN
— TO THE —
REICH

PROLOGUE

The snow-capped Alpine Mountains looked deceptively quiet, even peaceful, as Freddy Mayer, crouched in the back of a B-24, gazed down at the majestic peaks whizzing by in the frigid night air. Close your eyes and you could almost forget there was a brutal war being waged on the ground ten thousand feet below. Peering one last time through the narrow "Joe hole" on the floor of the plane's bomb bay, Freddy waited for the final signal from the cockpit.

Seven years earlier, when Freddy had fled Nazi Germany as a teenager, a return trip to the hellfire Adolf Hitler had made of Europe would have seemed unthinkable. Yet here he was now, at the age of twenty-three — a parachute on his back and a bulky bag strapped to his leg with a pistol, ammunition, and supplies inside it — preparing to dive back into the Nazis' stronghold in Austria. And he was doing it for the Americans, no less, on an improbable spy mission aimed at thwarting Hitler's feared "last stand" in the Alps.

This was the life-on-a-tightrope adventure that the barrel-chested refugee had been craving for months, pitting him against men he had once called countrymen. Somewhere below him, unseen amid the rugged mountain terrain, were Nazi soldiers armed with antiaircraft weaponry designed to shoot down planes just like this one. The chances of success for Freddy's tiny, three-man spy team were one in a hundred, an officer had told him glumly. That was good enough for Freddy. Anything to defeat the fascists, he said.

He had waited so long for this chance, and he was desperate to make the jump. The mission had already been scuttled twice in the last five days because of bad weather, and less than half an hour earlier the flight crew had almost been forced to turn back yet again for Italy. Freddy was determined to make this the night. The moonlit skies that separated him from the Nazis on the ground below now looked calm, even inviting. *Gorgeous*, he thought to himself. An odd feeling of tranquility washed over him.

The cockpit relayed the signal. "Ready, ready, ready, go!" the crewman yelled. Seated at the edge of the Joe hole, Freddy pushed away and jumped.

1

A German Boy

FREIBURG, GERMANY

Spring 1933

Freddy's world, nestled in the lush foothills of Germany's Black Forest, was collapsing around him.

The signs were subtle at first: a slight from a classmate, a sneering glance across the neighborhood pool, as if to say, *Stay on your own side.* Then the noxious changes in the air became too blatant to ignore, even for a rambunctious boy focused mostly on cars and girls. There were the venomous speeches spewing from loudspeakers in Freiburg's sun-splashed town square. The laws establishing Germany's "Aryans" as supreme. The mandatory salutes, the fervent shouts of "Heil Hitler!" from the boys of the Hitler Youth, the red-and-black flags emblazoned with the crooked arms of the Nazi swastika fluttering from balconies across the city. It was hard for Freddy — "Fritz," as everyone called the eleven-year-old — to look away. A place that had once seemed tolerant, even welcoming, was growing ever more menacing for his family and the other Jews of Freiburg, a tiny minority of scarcely a thousand scattered throughout the largely Catholic city.

One of Freddy's best pals in town had already fled the country for Switzerland with his family. The book burnings and Nazi boycotts of Jewish businesses had just begun in April of 1933, and his friend's father didn't want to wait to see what would come next; Freddy's boyhood playmate was gone in a matter of weeks. Other Jewish families were leaving as well. No one knew where this would all lead, or how much worse it might get.

Freddy's father assured him and his three siblings, again and again, that things would be okay for them. Heinrich Mayer was a decorated veteran of the Great War, after all, and he clung to his Iron Cross medal as a bulwark against anyone who might question his German patriotism. The cross, bestowed by the Kaiser two decades earlier for Heinrich's valor in World War I, became his shield. "They'll never come for me," Heinrich would say. "I was a *Frontkaempfer*" — a German combat soldier. "Nothing is going to happen to us."

The "gathering storm," as Winston Churchill later described the dark forces at work in prewar Europe, was already beginning to breach Germany. Heinrich, a dapper dresser with a bushy mustache and thin, round spectacles, spent his days focused on the family hardware business, keeping his head down and wishing the storm away. He wasn't about to let outsize fears lead him to toss away everything that he — and his father before him — had built over the better part of a century in Freiburg, in his home country of Germany.

Freddy's mother, Hilda, who kept the books for the hardware business, wasn't nearly so confident. They were Jews, after all, and Germany had a long and ugly history of turning against its Jews. They wouldn't get any preferential treatment, Iron Cross or not, she warned Heinrich. In Hitler's eyes, she feared, they would always be Jews first: inferior, subhuman. She was anxious and fretful, looking for a way out of a place that was turning increasingly hostile. Freddy could hear the fear in her voice. But that was a mother's job, wasn't it? To worry about her family. Freddy knew his father would protect them. That was a father's job.

Freddy himself was not the nervous type, but still, it was hard not to worry about the changes in the air. He was a scrapper, a mischievous boy who spoke with his fists. He wouldn't be pushed around. His ever-present smile — so wide that it seemed his ears might snap off from the strain — belied a fighter's spirit. One day a classmate on the playground called him "a stinking Jude," a phrase now heard with chilling regularity in the hills of Freiburg. The other Jewish kids would simply look away when the epithet was used. Not Freddy. Short but stocky, with lightning-quick hands, he slugged the name caller on the chin and readied himself for a round of fisticuffs as the boy hit the ground. A teacher sent Freddy to see the dean — a big, hulking Nazi official named Friedrich Ludin, who would walk through the hallways in his German uniform. Freddy braced for his punishment. "He called me a stinking Jew. I didn't like that," he explained matter-of-factly. Ludin eyed the boy. "I can understand that," he answered finally. Much to Freddy's surprise, the dean sent him back to class without even a reprimand. Nobody in class dared talk to him that way again.

Freiburg hadn't always been so hostile to its Jews. Freddy remembered a time — not that long ago, it seemed — when the city, in the southwestern German state of Baden, hugging the French and Swiss borders, was a place that seemed to have accepted his people as its own. In the early 1930s, not long before Hitler, it was the kind of place where a few dozen boys from a Jewish fraternity at the local university, dressed in their best blazers and ties, could take their girlfriends for an outing and pose for photos in the town square with no one bothering them. They didn't have to fear anyone knowing they were Jewish. The grand Gothic cathedral at the center of town, with a giant spire towering in the sky, seemed less a religious threat to nonbelievers than an architectural point of pride.

With the city's picturesque tree-lined hills as their backyard, children — Christian and Jewish alike — skipped across the tiny inlets that ran through town, where merchants' pushcarts rumbled along the centuries-old cobblestone streets. It was an idyllic childhood for Freddy: dinners with his family, with their own maid to serve them dumplings, goulash, and other delicacies; weekends at the movie theater, watching the new black-and-white films; trips deep into the Black Forest to go hiking or skiing with school clubs. As a boy, he led a life that had all the warm serenity of a landscape painting by Renoir or one of the other French impressionists whose works had become so popular across the border just twenty-five miles to the west of Freiburg.

Yes, Freddy knew that as Jews they had always been different, but they were Germans, too; proud Germans, as his father would often remind him. His family could trace its roots in the region back more than five hundred years, all the way to the thirteen hundreds, when the surrounding state of Baden was still in the hands of dukes and monarchs. In the 1860s his grandfather had started his own business, Julius Mayer Hardware, and became the first Jew since the Middle Ages allowed to purchase his own home in Freiburg: a handsome three-story brick townhouse in a leafy part of town known for its linden trees. That same year, in 1865, Julius and the other Jews in town formed a synagogue to call their own, the first in the city in generations. After centuries of rampant anti-Semitism in the region, a new era had begun.

Across Germany, in fact, the Jews were enjoying a remarkable golden age that continued on through the 1920s, as German leaders — ushering in a Second German Empire with grand economic ambitions — gave the Jews greater civil rights and opened doors long closed to them. While the vestiges of centuries-long persecution lingered, Jews managed not only to assimilate but to thrive in almost every walk of life. It was an era in Germany when a young Jew named Albert Einstein could become a world-famous scientist; a businessman named Adolf Jandorf could found an iconic Berlin department store; novelist Lion Feuchtwanger could enter the ranks of Germany's most respected writers; and a young political philosopher named Hannah Arendt could begin her storied career. By the time Freddy was born, in 1921 — the same year Einstein, living in Berlin, won the Nobel Prize for his groundbreaking work in physics — the cloud that had shadowed German Jews for so long appeared to have finally lifted.

Most of the goyim — the non-Jews — were civil and cordial, even friendly, to Freddy and his family. The Mayers' next-door neighbor, Herr Wagner, who owned an umbrella shop, was a trusted friend to Heinrich and helped with the accounting for his hardware business. Wagner had been Heinrich's sergeant during World War I — a Christian soldier answering to a Jewish officer — and the two neighbors built a bond that erased whatever religious differences separated them. Freddy would come to remember him as "a gentle Gentile."

At his hardware business, Heinrich was known around town for letting his customers — most of them Christian — buy their metals and hardware products on credit. It was a practice his customers came to appreciate. "It was not always possible for us to make payments to the Mayers in a timely fashion," the family of one tin buyer wrote years later, when Heinrich tried to reclaim some of the money the Nazis had taken from him. "Other suppliers kept pressuring us, but never the Mayers."

Freddy's father would sometimes give the children presents at Christmastime so they didn't feel left out of the holiday festivities. At his core, Freddy was a proud *Bobbele,* a term of affection for someone born in Freiburg — Christian or Jew. Being a Jewish boy in those years felt so unremarkable that it seemed almost an afterthought to Freddy. He never considered himself deeply religious, although his parents certainly were. The family kept kosher in the home, and he grudgingly went to religious school like almost all the Jewish kids in town; but that was his parents' choice, not his. He loved the Jewish holidays — not because of any deep religious connection, he admitted, but because he was allowed to skip school for the day. He identified culturally as a Jew, an oppressed people in Germany for centuries, but God and spirituality? That was never really Freddy's thing.

Nor was he a deep thinker. He was a mediocre student, by his own admission; his older brother, Julius, named after their grandfather, was the real scholar in the family, the "smart one," an accountant in the making. Freddy wasn't envious; he had no real academic ambitions himself, and he always admired his brother's intellect — at least until nightfall came. Julius would stay up for hours reading German books of all sorts in the bedroom they shared, and Freddy would plead with him to turn the light off so he could *please* get some sleep. Finally, Heinrich and Hilda reached a truce and put the boys in separate rooms to end the bickering.

If his brother was the thinker in the family, Freddy was the doer: his genius resided in an adeptness with his hands. He would spend his free time in his father's workshop tearing things apart and putting them back together — toys, gadgets, soapbox cars, engines, anything he could find. Or he would sit in the warehouse adjoining the house and watch his father's employees prepare hardware parts and wholesale metals to sell.

He loved nothing better than examining the newfangled automobiles from Mercedes-Benz and other German, and even American, manufacturers, which were becoming a more common sight on the streets. Freddy talked of building cars, or maybe airplanes, when he grew up. In the boy's eyes, no task was too difficult, or too dangerous — although some experiments did go awry. Freddy, as a boy of only five or six, had an idea to make the car his father bought, an American-made Ford, go farther with less fuel, so he poured a liquid concoction of his own making into the gas tank. The experiment did not go well. A few years later, still barely able to see over the steering wheel, he managed to start the car and take it out on the streets by himself for a brief ride, only to have a passing police officer stop him and drag him back home by the ear. Heinrich was not amused.

As much as anything, Freddy loved listening to his father regale him for hours with stories about the Great War — even in Germany's losing cause. Heinrich, a lieutenant in the German 110th Regiment, told the boy how he had fought for the Kaiser at the French fortress of Verdun in 1916, one of the war's bloodiest battles. It was his valor there that earned him the Iron Cross, the holy talisman that he kept stashed in a special place in the house. That Heinrich was a Jew never mattered to the Kaiser, he told the boy.

Freddy would parade around the house wearing his father's black military belt, the shiny German medallion on the buckle pulled so tightly that his belly bulged over the top. He imagined that he might get the chance to fight for Germany himself, perhaps as a pilot like the Red Baron, the country's famous World War I ace. This was his country, after all, and the boy was eager to defend it, not as a Jew but as a German, just as his father had done before him.

But neither Heinrich nor Freddy had anticipated the startling rise of Adolf Hitler and the Nazis. Few Germans had. Hitler was a political outlier in 1925 when he wrote *Mein Kampf,* his race-baiting jailhouse screed calling for the creation of a New Order and an Aryan master race. Yet by the early 1930s his Nazi Party was winning seats in the Reichstag with a campaign built on restoring German "pride" in the midst of the economic woes blamed on the Treaty of Versailles — and on the Jews.

Improbably, Hitler was now knocking on the door of the presidential palace in Berlin. Heinrich, five hundred miles away, noticed the Nazi Party's ominous rhetoric — how could he not? — but he was convinced that the party's vile brand of politics would not take hold. Hitler would never come to power, he told Freddy. The Nazis' views reflected an ugly, extremist strain, his father said; not the true German sentiment he had always known. Hitler wasn't even a native-born citizen. He had started adulthood as a low-ranking soldier in the *Austrian* army. What business did he have trying to run the country? "They're still a minority; nothing bad will happen," Heinrich told the boy, then just twelve, as Hitler prepared a bold bid for president of Germany in 1932.

His father was right — for the time being at least. Hitler earned barely a third of the vote in the national election. While it was a formidable showing for a onetime fringe candidate, he still lagged far behind incumbent president Paul von Hindenburg, who branded him a dangerous extremist and a "Bohemian corporal." What Heinrich and so many others hadn't foreseen, however, was the shrewd backroom maneuvering of Hitler and his top Nazi lieutenants; they succeeded less than ten months after the electoral defeat in striking a deal with Hindenburg to make Hitler the ruling chancellor of Germany — and setting off the Third Reich's twelve-year reign of terror in Europe.

Hitler's bold political coup triggered a panic among Germany's Jews. Tens of thousands fled the country within months of Hitler's rise to power in 1933. The Nazis were all too eager to see them go. Freddy's childhood playmate, eight-year-old Gerd Schwab, was among the early refugees. Like Heinrich, Gerd's father, David, was a Jewish businessman and a decorated World War I veteran; David and his wife were best friends with Freddy's parents, making up a regular foursome in bridge games at the house. That was before Hitler. After the Nazis took power, David Schwab feared the worst, but unlike the Mayers and many other of the city's Jews, he had an escape route in mind. His plumbing business had a second plant in Basel, Switzerland, about forty-five miles across the German border. Desperate to get out of Freiburg, the Schwabs gathered up as many of their things as they could and left, with Freddy's oldest friend suddenly gone overnight.

A year into Hitler's reign, Freddy became a bar mitzvah at his family's synagogue, the same one his grandfather helped found sixty years earlier, when the Jews' place in Freiburg finally seemed secure. Freddy's ceremonial rise to manhood coincided with the ascent of a Nazi madman in Berlin, but the boy walled off the outside demons, undertaking the ritual with his customary ear-to-ear grin. His brother, Julius, always the scholar, had chanted practically the whole prayer service for his own bar mitzvah a few years earlier, but Freddy was content reading a single *parsha* from the Torah; that was enough for him. The family celebrated with a party at the house in an ornate room reserved for special occasions. The room was normally off limits to Freddy, a boisterous boy always at risk of breaking the good china, but now he basked in the milestone. With his whole family around him — parents, siblings, grandparents — the place felt safe and protected from the unease swirling around them.

It was a brief respite. Not long after his bar mitzvah, the Nazi campaign of persecution hit Freddy straight on the first time, when he was forced to leave his public school in Freiburg. His offense: being a Jew. It was part of a series of Nazi education policies put in place nationwide, throwing nearly all Jewish children out of the public schools based on the pretense of "overcrowding." Ludin, the same Nazi dean who let Freddy off the hook for slugging his classmate, delivered the news personally. Ludin seemed apologetic; he didn't want to do this, he told Freddy, but it was a new era in the Reich and he had no choice. He sounded sincere to Freddy. For a Nazi, Ludin didn't seem like such a bad guy.

Freddy made the best of his abrupt expulsion, shrugging it off the way he did most problems once he realized he couldn't fight his way past them. For him, there were worse punishments than having to give up his schoolbooks. He quickly set to work on his first love — engines and automobiles — as an apprentice for a mechanic at a trade school. His father, meanwhile, talked the Ford auto dealer who had sold him his car into getting the boy a job at the repair shop in Freiburg. Freddy was content; he just had to hope that the Nazis wouldn't ban Jews from working on automobiles anytime soon.

Heinrich remained resolute. No matter what draconian policies the Nazis enforced, he would not be run out of his homeland. Not when Freddy was expelled from school. Not when a Nazi newspaper campaign demanded that Germans boycott Jewish businesses. Not when the Nuremberg Laws banned Jews from mixing with people of "German blood." Not when all his Christian employees and the family's maid had to stop working for him because he was a Jew, or when it became almost impossible for him to buy raw materials like lead and copper for his business. Not when he and Freddy, dismayed, watched the footage of Hitler presiding over the 1936 Olympics after banning "non-Aryans" from German squads. Not even when word began to spread that the Nazis were rounding up Communists, homosexuals, and other "undesirables" — and that the Jews might be next.

Even then, Heinrich stayed firm. "Nothing bad will happen to us," he kept repeating to his son as a matter of faith. His optimism sprang not from mere hope or delusion. In a particularly cruel bit of psychological warfare, in 1934 the Nazis sent certificates in Hitler's name to thousands of Jewish war veterans, honoring their service to Germany on the twentieth anniversary of World War I and promising them special treatment even in the face of sweeping anti-Semitic measures. On its face, it was recognition of Heinrich's standing. He was a leader in the Freiburg veterans' council, a volunteer in the local fire brigade, a citizen of standing, a good neighbor and friend to the Christians. He was even due a sizable German pension when he retired: 177 marks a month. If things got worse, God forbid, he was protected. Or so he thought.

As the man of the house, Heinrich made the decisions, but Hilda could at least ponder the family's potential escape routes. "Look, we better prepare," she told Freddy one day. They needed to make plans. Even if she could somehow persuade Heinrich to leave, she knew it would be difficult to find a place to take them in, and that would take time, regardless. They would need visas, transportation, a place to stay, money — all the elusive essentials necessary to get out of the country. She began contacting the few relatives she knew outside Germany, quietly at first, then with increasing desperation. Could they help? Somehow?

Even Herr Wagner, the "gentle Gentile" next door, was urging Heinrich to flee. He offered to manage the hardware business until the Mayer family could come back — *if* they could come back. Then it happened. In late 1937, more than four years into Hitler's reign, Heinrich's resolve melted. One day he announced to Hilda that he was ready to leave. There was no single trigger point, no final threat or frightful episode that made him reverse course. It was simply the end, the crushing weight of four years of Nazi edicts vilifying him and his people, sapping his business, making his family outcasts. He had no will left to fight for his survival in this oppressive new place called the Third Reich. It was time to get out.

If it wasn't too late already. Where could they go? The British had squelched emigration to Palestine, the ancestral homeland where so many frightened European Jews longed to resettle. And Heinrich had no real foothold elsewhere in Europe outside Germany, unlike his friend David Schwab, with business interests across the border in Switzerland.

They had one real hope — America. Although it was a faint beacon, barely flickering, they put in an application with the American consulate in Germany, knowing that getting a visa to the United States was difficult, and the gates of America remained closed to all but a lucky few. Many American leaders were oblivious, or willfully blind, to the plight of Europe's Jews and the havoc that Hitler was wreaking. The tight restrictions on visas reflected that gross misperception. The Nazis had shown "a desire to ease up on the Jewish problem," the American ambassador in Berlin, William Dodd, wrote optimistically in 1933 during Hitler's first year in office. A few months later, the ambassador met with Hitler himself and cabled Washington to report that he had come away more optimistic than ever for "the maintenance of world peace."

President Franklin D. Roosevelt, in his first term in the White House, remained largely a silent bystander to Hitler's threats of terror, as tens of thousands of German Jews were denied entry, even as American immigration quotas sat unfilled. Bureaucrats in the immigration service were indifferent to the refugee crisis, and the political perils of letting in Europe's Jews were too great for even a popular president like FDR to take bold action. Hatred for the "kikes" was blatant in many quarters; in 1934, a year after Hitler seized power, some twenty thousand American Nazi supporters held their first mass rally at New York City's iconic Madison Square Garden. A giant swastika banner hung between two smaller American flags at the rally, an onerous symbol of Hitler's support in America.

Not until Roosevelt won reelection in 1936 did his administration begin to lower the bars to immigration for those trying to flee Nazi persecution. Nearly eleven thousand Germans, overwhelmingly Jewish, began to enter the next year. It was only a tiny fraction of those seeking to escape, but it was something. With their prospects for getting out improved, Hilda tracked down relatives in the United States on her side of the family to vouch for them with the immigration authorities; they had to produce affidavits affirming that Heinrich had the character and money to come to America. Policy makers, with distorted images of immigrants as slothful, insisted that Jewish émigrés not become a "public charge" and a drain on Depression-era resources.

Hilda waited anxiously for any word from America. She didn't realize it, but their timing was fortuitous. In November 1937, just before a crush of new Jewish applicants made immigrating to the United States even more difficult, the notification came: the American consulate in Stuttgart had approved their visas — seven in all for the whole family and Hilda's mother. Hilda was jubilant; Heinrich less so. How they had managed to get so lucky was unclear. Freddy didn't know, and didn't ask. He had little sense of what to expect in America, but he accepted his newly approved visa for what it was: the chance at a new start in an exciting, far-off land.

Just as Freddy's family was finally planning its exit, Hitler was maneuvering to expand his tyrannical empire. The Führer convened secret meetings that same month with top military and foreign policy aides, laying out his brazen plans for Europe in what became known as the Hossbach Conference. Two weeks later, on the very same day that the Mayers' visas to America were approved, Hitler and his top lieutenants were wrapping up a series of meetings with Britain's Lord Halifax, a key aide to Prime Minister Neville Chamberlain, during an extravagant game-hunting tournament in Berlin. A rambling Hitler assured his British visitor that he "wanted no more wars," and an upbeat Lord Halifax came away believing that Hitler did, in fact, want peace, just as Ambassador Dodd had informed Washington four years earlier. Halifax had to concede that many of the Nazis' policies, including the onerous treatment of German Jews, "offended British opinion," but he recognized Hitler's accomplishments, too. "I was not blind to what he had done for Germany," Halifax wrote. Ten months later, Britain's ill-fated policy of appeasement toward Hitler would be formally enshrined in the signing of the notorious Munich Agreement, which allowed the Nazis to seize part of Czechoslovakia without fear of resistance from Britain or France.

As Hitler's ambitions grew more audacious, Heinrich realized that their American visas were worthless without the king's ransom needed to transport them across the Atlantic. After years of letting his hardware customers buy from him on credit, he counted up about ten thousand marks' worth of debts owed to him (more than $70,000 today). He tried to collect on them, but doors in Freiburg were now closing in his face. Many of his customers, once so grateful to Heinrich for the unofficial line of credit, knew that they couldn't be forced to repay a "Jewish debt" in the current Nazi climate. So most of them simply reneged.

Cobbling together money from savings, loans from friends, and the sale of valuables, a deflated Heinrich managed to come up with about three thousand marks to pay for transatlantic passage for the seven of them, as well as train tickets to get them to the port in France. He paid extra to ship some well-worn furnishings to America with them. Nothing new or terribly valuable, though;

the Nazis wouldn't allow it. At the start of Hitler's reign, the Nazis were so eager to force the Jews out of Germany that they had allowed them to leave with much of their money and property. But those days were gone. Now the Nazis were confiscating virtually everything of value they could grab: bank accounts, storefronts and businesses, artwork, jewelry, and generations' worth of family heirlooms and valuables, forcing the Jews out with little more than the clothes they were wearing.

Leaders of the synagogue in Freiburg, the one that Heinrich's father had helped found, bid farewell to Heinrich, thanked him for all his work, and gave him a book in German, *History of the Baden Jews* — now an endangered species under Nazi rule. Freddy himself insisted on working at the auto shop right up until the day of their departure, making sure to get a letter of reference from his boss before he left. On a mild winter's day in March of 1938, he put on his best suit and tie, stashed fifty marks in his pocket, and posed for a last family portrait before leaving the home that his grandfather had bought decades before. For the camera, Heinrich mustered a steely grin. Behind him, peering between his mother and father, was sixteen-year-old Freddy, now a hair taller than his father. His smile wasn't quite as broad as usual, but it was there. He was going to America. And finally, he thought, he could leave the Nazis behind.

2

Enemy Alien

BROOKLYN
March 1938

As the SS *Manhattan* sailed past the Statue of Liberty and docked in New York's bustling harbor, Freddy couldn't set foot on American soil fast enough. It had been a wrenching few weeks of global hopscotch for him and his family as they traversed three ports and four countries — more than four thousand miles by land and sea, as well as an ocean of swirling emotions.

His teenage exuberance was evident as the family piled into a couple of large yellow taxicabs at Pier 52 for the last leg of the journey to their new home in Brooklyn. He had never seen automobiles like these on the cobblestone streets of home. As Freddy eagerly pulled the cab door closed behind him, he accidentally shut it on the cabbie's hand. "Stupid son-of-a-bitch!" the man yelled at him. Freddy didn't know what the phrase meant; his English teachers at school in Freiburg had never taught him words like that, but he could tell from the cabbie's tone that he had been cussed out. He was going to have to study up on American slang in his new country.

Freddy laughed off the episode, unperturbed as usual. He figured the rude reception was a small price to pay for the safety and solace that America promised his family. He was happy just to be out of Germany. Every week seemed to bring more frightening news of Hitler's latest affront, making it clear how lucky he and his family had been to get out when they did. His mother was right. This was 1938, the "fateful year," as one Nazi document would call the Reich's escalating oppression of Jews at the time. If they had waited much longer, they might not have made it out at all.

Indeed, even as they had packed up the family home and begun their journey, they couldn't be certain of their fate. Freedom seemed elusive as they headed west by train through the Black Forest's rugged frontier toward the Rhine River and on to the French border. The Nazi border guards didn't need a reason to rough them up on their way out, or to seize the few valuables they had with them; hassling the Jews as they fled Germany had become blood sport for the Nazis.

Freddy and his family had waited anxiously with papers in

hand at the border crossing to leave their homeland for France. The boy stood motionless as the Nazi guard eyed the family's travel papers and clawed through their belongings, finally letting them cross without incident. Freddy let out a sigh. They were out. He hadn't wanted to leave Germany at first, not when his father was struggling so mightily to hold on to all that the family had, but once they had crossed the border, he was glad to leave it behind.

Then it was off to the port city of Le Havre in France's Normandy region to board the SS *Manhattan*. Just two years earlier, the same stately ocean liner had ferried more than three hundred American athletes to compete at the Olympic Games in Berlin. Now the ship was crammed with Jews from Germany, Austria, and beyond, fellow refugees fleeing the Führer. A butcher from outside Heidelberg, a merchant from Stuttgart, a baker from Budapest, a clerk from Vienna, a rabbi from Palestine: all designated "Hebrew" on the ship's passenger manifest. It was a rough crossing, so rough that rumors flowed back to the Jews in Freiburg that Heinrich and his family had perished en route to America. Grim news from the continent they had left behind, meanwhile, followed Freddy and his family relentlessly out to sea. Days after his family set sail came reports that Hitler's troops had invaded Austria with little opposition. Hitler, the onetime Austrian corporal, was coming home, and his imperial ambitions were now plain for the world to see.

Freddy could see the pain in his parents' eyes as they heard the news. To them, the threat posed by the Nazis was obvious, but the world seemed indifferent. On the very day they arrived in America, the front page of the *New York Times* carried a largely steno-

graphic account of a speech by Hitler, with the German dictator declaring that the Nazis' invasion of Austria had "saved many
lives."

The mere thought of his native land now riled Freddy. He and
his family had barely settled into their cramped new home near
Brooklyn's Flatbush neighborhood, not far from the famed ball-
park at Ebbets Field where the hapless Dodgers played, when he
made a defining decision. Named Friedrich at birth, he had gone
by "Fritz" his whole childhood, but he would no longer answer
to it. It was the puckish nickname of Prussian kings and emper-
ors, and it sounded too German for his tastes; he wanted nothing to do with it. From now on he was "Fred," or "Freddy" to his
friends. That sounded American, which was what he now considered himself. Likewise, his father abandoned "Heinrich" in favor
of "Henry," and father and son vowed never to speak German in
the house again. Their new language was English, complete with
all the gruff slang the young man picked up on the street from
assorted cabbies and street vendors. The Germans had forsaken
them, and Freddy was now determined to forsake Germany as
well.

His brother, Julius, ever the studious one, enrolled in college
in New York soon after their arrival. Freddy had no interest in
going back to school. Forgoing a high school degree for a voca-
tion wasn't a difficult decision for him. He wanted to keep working on automobiles, and anyway, the family was desperate for
money. American immigration authorities had made clear that
they didn't want any newly arrived refugees living on the public
dole. In Germany, the Mayers had lived the genteel life of a merchant's family, but now Heinrich — Henry — was scrambling just
to come up with rent money. The once-successful businessman

doubled up on jobs, working as a dishwasher and a night watch-man; to save a nickel in bus fare, he would trudge by foot across the last long stretch of bridge over the bay to Rockaway to scrub dishes. It was a desolate walk. He didn't complain, not in front of the children. He had escaped the Nazis, which was more than many Jews in Germany could say. But he was a broken man; he considered himself a "nobody" — a *Niemand* — in his new home-land. As badly as he wanted to abandon the German language, at fifty he found it difficult to learn English, and he struggled to fit into this strange new land of FDR, Fred Astaire, and Joltin' Joe DiMaggio. The Nazis had robbed him of both his past and his fu-ture, creating "impossible circumstances" for him and the coun-try's Jews, he said. Not only had he left his home and his family business in Germany, he had left his identity as well.

With a teenager's adventurous spirit, Freddy had a much eas-ier time of it. The reference letter from his former German Ford employer helped him quickly find work fixing and painting cars in Brooklyn. He was a curiosity at the auto shop, speaking Eng-lish with a combination of German and British accents, just as his teachers in Freiburg had taught him; the other mechanics found his speech and mannerisms amusing. Freddy laughed along with them. When he told them stories of the old country, they were surprised to hear that Germany had modern-day innovations like movies and cars. They thought of it as a backward place, the country that had lost the last big war.

But there was one topic he talked about only rarely: being a Jew. Once, overhearing one of his bosses at the shop slurring a Jewish customer, he confronted him, just as he had the student who had used an anti-Semitic epithet against him at school in Freiburg, and quit on the spot. But for the most part he didn't ad-

vertise his religion. He wanted to blend into Brooklyn life. Generations of Jews and other Ellis Island immigrants before him had
formed their own separate enclaves in America, transplanting the
roots of ethnic and religious identity from the homeland to their
new country. Freddy had no interest in that. He wanted to become what he would later describe as "the perfect American."

That included practicing American-style capitalism. He found
his skills as a German-trained diesel mechanic in high demand in
New York City, as automobiles became the new mode of transportation, and he parlayed one job into another, then another. As
a mechanic, as a cabbie, as an auto painter; anything that paid the
bills. If on a Friday he thought his boss wasn't paying him enough,
he would quit and by Monday find a better gig that paid him a
dollar more. He cycled through dozens of jobs in his first year or
so in New York — too many to count — with each earning more
than the last. He knew that his father needed every dollar.

But even as Freddy followed the classic path of the American immigrant, the Third Reich continued to shadow him. Eight
months after his arrival, in November 1938, came the most jarring
news yet from Nazi Germany. Kristallnacht, "the Night of Broken
Glass," brought a terror unlike anything the Jews remaining in the
country, some four hundred thousand of them, had ever experi-
enced. In an orgy of violence that was carefully planned by the
Reich's propaganda minister, Joseph Goebbels, to look spontane-
ous, Nazis and German rioters burned more than a thousand syn-
agogues, destroyed countless Jewish businesses and storefronts,
killed nearly one hundred Jews, and began imprisoning tens of
thousands more in camps.

The horrific reports from Germany reached Freddy and his
family in fragments, like the shards of broken glass in the after-

math of the attacks themselves. The frustration of not knowing what was happening in their homeland compounded the pain of the rampage itself. Why wasn't the vaunted American press telling the world more about the ravages of Hitler's regime? Freddy wanted to know. Why was the world not rising up against Hitler and the Nazis?

He could only wonder what had happened to the Jews who had stayed behind in Freiburg, friends and neighbors who hadn't been lucky enough to get out. What had become of the stately home where he had grown up, or of the Jewish cemetery where his grandparents were buried? He and his family had no way of knowing that Nazi mobs in Freiburg had destroyed the synagogue where he had celebrated his bar mitzvah; or that the mobs had looted and burned what was left of the city's Jewish businesses; or that the Nazi authorities had begun rounding up virtually all the remaining Jews in town to send them to near-certain deaths at concentration camps.

But improbably, the violent rampaging in Freiburg had yielded a glimmer of hope as well: the silver breastplate from the synagogue's holy Torah had survived the night of destruction, along with a pair of ornate wooden doors that had welcomed worshipers. Undetected in the bedlam of Kristallnacht, congregants had somehow managed to remove the sacred artifacts and hide them underground for safekeeping. If that wasn't a sign of resilience, what was?

Hitler seemed unstoppable to Freddy and his family as they followed the dire news out of Europe from afar. Months later, in the summer of 1939, the Nazis and the Russians signed their notorious "nonaggression" pact. "Strange bedfellows," his father observed when he heard about the agreement. "It'll make a hell of a marriage." No longer fearing Soviet intervention, Hitler invaded Poland barely a week later, with a massive attack force of 1.5 million smashing through the borders by land and sky. "Here's the next world war," his father told Freddy as they listened anxiously to the radio reports. Britain and France declared war on the Nazis two days later, and World War II had begun.

For now, however, it was a war for Europe to fight, not America. The strains of "America First" isolationism ran deep in the United States, fueled by the ugly strains of anti-Semitism from influential Americans like aviator Charles Lindbergh and auto magnate Henry Ford, each of whom accepted high-profile honors from Hitler, even as his policies grew more oppressive. Freddy had always adored Ford automobiles, whether he was tuning one up in Brooklyn or swiping his father's in Germany. He was unaware of the long-running vitriol of the company's famous founder, whose Michigan newspaper, the *Dearborn Independent,* had published a series called "The International Jew: The World's Foremost Problem" in a remarkable ninety-one consecutive issues beginning in 1920. On his seventy-fifth birthday, in 1938, Henry Ford beamed as a German diplomat pinned a golden cross with four small swastikas on his breast pocket, the first American to receive a medal created by Hitler himself to honor "distinguished foreigners."

Colonel Lindbergh, for his part, denounced "the Jewish groups" in America in 1941 for dangerously "agitating for war" against the Nazis. Freddy bristled when he heard such nonsense. The Jews were trying to *survive* a war, not start one. There were a few like-minded people among the Washington power-brokers who mattered most, but not many. Harold Ickes, FDR's longtime cabinet member, called out Lindbergh and Ford by name repeatedly — both for their "unworthy words" of isolationism and for their proud acceptance of medals from a "ruthless dictator who is . . . robbing and torturing thousands of fellow human beings."

FDR himself came to see war as inevitable against the Nazis and their menacing Axis partners, Italy and Japan, but short of a clear provocation he seemed determined to stay out of the growing conflict as long as possible. Even when a Nazi submarine torpedoed an American navy destroyer ship near Iceland in October 1941, killing eleven sailors, Roosevelt held his fire, and America waited.

The inevitable came seven weeks later, on December 7, 1941, as the Japanese bombing of Pearl Harbor brought America to war. It was a Sunday afternoon in Brooklyn when Freddy heard the news. Flooded with rage, he wanted to run down to the army recruiting station that very day to enlist, but since it was a Sunday, the office was closed. The next day, he was among the first swarm of young men at the recruitment office on Whitehall Street in Lower Manhattan. He could see the Statue of Liberty off in the distance, the reflection cascading off the water. Lady Liberty had ushered him into the country three years earlier when he fled Nazi Germany, and now she was beckoning him once again — this time to fight for his new homeland. Thousands of gung-ho recruits around New York had the same idea. All anyone in line at the recruitment office could talk about was Pearl Harbor, and many of the recruits spoke eagerly of shipping out to the Pacific to "fight the Japs." Freddy had a different agenda. Although the United States would not officially declare war against Germany until four days after the Japanese attack, he was already bristling to bring the fight to his old countrymen — the Nazis.

He could almost imagine himself in a fighter plane over Europe, or at least working on fighter plane engines, as he handed over his papers to the military recruiters that day.

Name: Friedrich Mayer.... Age: 20 years old.... Height: 5'7".... Residence: 651 East Fifth Street, Brooklyn, N.Y.... Place of Birth: Freiburg, Germany.

The formal response stunned Freddy: *Rejected.*

Some of the other would-be military recruits were turned away for being too heavy, or too sickly, or too old, or having too many children at home to support. Freddy—young, fit, and eager—had a different defect: he was considered an "enemy alien." As a German immigrant, he was banned from enlisting because the government feared he might work to assist the other side. He could turn out to be a German spy, or some sort of anti-American saboteur, the thinking went. No matter that he was a German Jew. He and his family had fled the Nazis, and yet now his adopted country thought he might be one of them. Freddy was dumbstruck. It seemed crazy. In Germany he was targeted for being a Jew. In America he was targeted for being a German. Which was it? No one standing in line in that recruiting office hated Hitler and the Nazis more than Freddy, and no one knew them better than he did. Yet here he was being denied the chance to fight them, just as America was going to war.

Freddy trudged home, disappointed but resigned to the decision. What else could he do? He didn't make the rules.

Up until then, Freddy had heard nothing about the urgent edicts issued by FDR's War Department on the subject of "enemy aliens." But in Washington, outsize fears of a possible "Fifth Column"—a supposed stealth force of 1.1 million American residents of German, Italian, and Japanese descent who officials worried might aid the enemy — were driving a crackdown on civil liberties unlike anything seen before in times of war or peace. Japanese Americans bore the worst of it, with more than 110,000 ultimately forced into internment camps on orders from President Roosevelt. But hundreds of thousands of Americans of German and Italian heritage, including many born in the United States, were targeted as well, not only prohibited from serving in the US military but sometimes arrested, put on watch lists, restricted in their travel, or forced to turn over their cameras, radio transmitters, and guns. So widespread were fears of a Fifth Column incursion that some young students of German American heritage were even barred from participating in a spelling bee.

Very few actual cases emerged of foreign-born Americans plotting acts of sabotage against the United States, and within months Washington began easing some of the more severe restrictions, including the ban on military service. Officials came to realize that they would need every able-bodied man they could find, not to mention women, in this new world war. But it was Julius, as the older of the two Mayer brothers, who got the first notice from the draft board to appear for duty, in the fall of 1942. Freddy saw his chance. Julius was close to finishing college by then, and through a bit of fast talking, Freddy appealed to the draft board to let him take his brother's place, so that Julius could get his academic degree as planned.

The plea worked, and that October, Freddy got his orders to report to Camp Upton on Long Island, then travel by train to Alabama for infantry basic training at Fort Rucker. Even before he was officially sworn into the army, he waited in line with the other new soldiers to learn his first assignment. He hoped to draw a slot that would let him work on engines — jeeps, tanks, maybe even aircraft. But an officer walking up and down the long line went looking for volunteers for a less glamorous assignment: "KP" duty in the kitchen. Seeing no hands raised, the officer barked at Freddy and two others in his line of sight: "You, you, and you: volunteer!" Freddy's first duties in the military would be fixing eggs, not engines.

His new home base in southeastern Alabama had been built hurriedly just five months earlier, as the United States began the biggest military mobilization in its history. It was less a formal army base than a massing of tents in the middle of a peanut field. After four years in Brooklyn, with the constant hum of trolley cars, baseball, hot dog vendors, and dance halls, Freddy had taken on a bit of northern big-city snobbery. This place seemed like a wasteland to him. There was a small town nearby — "a hick town," Freddy called it — and he would wander there on leave to get a Coca-Cola. The merchants made Yankee soldiers like him pay a dime, twice what they charged the locals. He couldn't wait to leave the place.

From Alabama, it was on to another base in Florida, then another in Tennessee, then another in Arizona. Training, downtime; more training, more downtime; and so on. "Hurry up and wait," as the soldiers liked to say. He finally got to work on a few engines after volunteering for a slot in the 81st Division's heavy-machinery unit, but after a short while, even that work seemed mundane. He was anxious for more; the war seemed agonizingly far away, and it was being fought without him. The Nazis were gaining ground through Europe with terrifying force, and Freddy found it hard to envision how all this stateside training was preparing him and his fellow enlistees to go overseas — back home, for him — to fight them. While stationed in Tennessee his restlessness got the best of him when he went into town with another soldier and missed a march — earning him an AWOL notice and a stint digging ditches six feet deep in rock-hard clay. "Fill it up!" the sergeant would yell as soon as he finished digging a ditch, then he would pile in the dirt and start all over again.

Freddy's disdain for military rules and regulations became his calling card. He didn't like waiting around — in a line of infantrymen or anywhere else. He seemed to fail more inspections than he passed, with his face rarely shaven quite closely enough, and his boots never shined quite brightly enough. That earned him more stints on KP duty, and fewer weekend passes, but beneath Freddy's irreverence, his commanding officers detected grit and tenacity, enough to stick with him.

In the summer of '43, in Arizona, Freddy got the chance to show his mettle on a battlefield — albeit a simulated one. It was there, in the searing desert heat, that he began to show off the traits that would later be documented in military assessments describing him as "a natural leader" and an "ingenious" soldier, with "remarkable stamina" and "a remarkable ability to improvise in unexpected situations." Camp Horn, where Freddy was stationed, was part of a sprawling, eighteen-thousand-square-mile base that spilled from the Mojave Desert in Southern California into the Sonoran Desert in southern Arizona in a never-ending sea of sand, rock, and cactus. General George S. Patton, who knew the region from his own childhood in Southern California, had handpicked this otherworldly terrain as a proving ground for a million war-bound infantrymen.

For Freddy, the assignment was as much a test of physical endurance as military preparedness. With temperatures reaching

110 degrees for six straight weeks, and soldiers crammed six to a tent, the men had to survive on rations of eight ounces of water a day — little more than the bottle of soda that Freddy bought for a dime in Alabama. Freddy maximized his rations as best he could, even swallowing the water he used for brushing his teeth. His unit trained to see how long they could last out in the heat and how long they could go without sleep. The scalding temperatures, the meager rations, and the exhausting regimen beat down many men; seven died during training, mostly from dehydration. Yet somehow Freddy, a Jew now truly wandering in the desert, seemed to flourish in the nomadic conditions. He actually gained a few pounds that summer, and he never seemed short of strength or stamina. He even found time to become an American citizen while in Arizona.

Freddy volunteered for the "Wildcat" Rangers, an elite reconnaissance group, and he rose to become "first scout" on training missions in the war game simulations pitting soldier against soldier. He loved the challenge. This was about as close to real-life warfare as a soldier could get on American soil, complete with fighter planes, tanks, freshly dug foxholes, and encrypted radio transmissions. In one days-long exercise, Freddy broke away from his troop and managed to sneak behind "enemy" lines, slithering on his squat frame with a .45 pistol in hand — alone and unseen — along the rock-hard desert floor. The goal was to capture the "blue" enemy soldiers and seize their territory, bit by bit, but Freddy had bolder ambitions. Spying the headquarters where the 81st Division's top officers were huddled, he burst in with gun drawn and demanded their surrender. This wasn't in the Wildcat playbook. "You can't do that!" yelled the stunned commander, General Marcus Bell. The private was undeterred. "The rules of war are to win," Freddy responded matter-of-factly in his German accent. The general put his hands in the air. Freddy had taken down the enemy, rules be damned.

The very next day, General Bell called Freddy into his office at division command — not for a reprimand or another ditch-digging stint, but for a possible promotion. He had to admit that the kid had moxie. "You're wasting your time in the infantry," the general told him. "Would you like to do something more daring?" Freddy's eyes widened. The general explained that OSS was looking for soldiers — especially foreign-speaking men from Europe — to penetrate enemy lines in secret espionage missions. Was Private Mayer interested?

The general didn't need to sell him on the idea. Freddy was anxious to do anything to escape the tedium of being just "another body" in the infantry. He had shucked his misbegotten status as an enemy alien, and this new assignment promised him the prize he had been chasing: return passage to Europe to take the fight to the Nazis.

Freddy had just one question for the general: "What's OSS?"

3

The Cloak-and-Dagger Brigade

BETHESDA, MARYLAND
December 1943

By the time he had dropped his sun-bleached duffel bag inside the gates of a converted country club outside Washington, DC, Freddy knew exactly what OSS was. He was joining up that winter with a brand-new American spy outfit aimed at sussing out the enemy's plans — and filling a gaping void in American intelligence. It was an elite spot, and dauntingly dangerous, even by the standards of warfare. But for Freddy, anxious to escape the monotony of the Arizona desert, it was precisely where he wanted to be.

"Espionage" had become something of a dirty word in American foreign-policy circles in the run-up to World War II. In the 1930s, amid the isolationism of the Fords and Lindberghs, many war-weary government leaders in Washington had soured on the messy business of breaking secret radio codes and spying on enemies. President Herbert Hoover's secretary of state, Henry Stimson, was furious when he learned in 1929 of a covert American code-breaking program known as the Black Chamber, which targeted foreign diplomats both friend and foe. Stimson promptly shut it down. "Gentlemen do not read each other's mail," the buttoned-up lawyer declared primly. Peace was secured through trust, not trickery, Stimson believed. "We will do better by being an honest simpleton in the world of nations," he said, "than a designing Sherlock Holmes."

The dramatic pendulum-shift away from foreign snooping left deep fissures in America's intelligence operations. The military was still gathering intelligence on foreign enemies, but as Hitler's Panzer tanks began ransacking Europe in 1939, it was a fractured effort, with little ability to target the biggest threats or piece together the fragments of information that had already been collected. The closest the United States came to a centralized intelligence agency in those years, some observers scoffed in the sexist tone of the era, was a group of a half-dozen matronly secretaries at the War Department who stood watch over a few file cabinets marked SECRET.

A celebrated World War I hero named William Donovan, an Irish lawyer with a brash swagger and a nickname — "Wild Bill" — to match, was determined to change what he saw as the dangerous, see-no-evil approach in Washington. Donovan had gone to law school with FDR at Columbia University, and despite their political differences, the retired colonel — a conservative Republican — became a confidant to the president on matters of war. As Roosevelt's unofficial emissary, Donovan made two long trips throughout Europe and northern Africa in 1940 and early 1941 to survey the darkening wartime landscape.

Donovan had met Hitler by chance seventeen years earlier in a foreboding evening they spent at a Bavarian resort, when the Nazi Party's charismatic young leader told him of his grand aspirations, comparing himself to Christ in "driving the Jewish moneylenders from the temple." Now Donovan was returning to Europe to witness the destruction that the Führer had wrought in the interim.

In the British leg of his travels, Donovan dined with King George VI, strategized with Prime Minister Churchill, and spent days alongside the country's master spies to study how even their famed intelligence services were struggling to keep pace with the Nazis. He returned to Washington with a blunt warning — not only for FDR but for the American public. In a remarkable call to arms that was broadcast by all three existing television networks in the United States, Donovan — still with no official role or title in the government — warned that war was at hand for America, whether the country wanted it or not. In his travels, he had come to the grudging conclusion that "Germany is a formidable, a resourceful, and a brutal foe." Donovan "Says Nazis Seek to Rule the World," warned the front-page headline of one US newspaper reporting on the speech.

Privately, he offered FDR a plan of action. It would take the United States two years to build a military machine capable of challenging the Nazis' intimidating arsenal, he predicted, and the Americans still might not win in a straight fight. The nation needed to create a commando-style spy force and start playing dirty: "Play a bush-league game, stealing the ball and killing the umpire," he told FDR. He formalized his proposal in a memo that June. In the face of "immediate peril," America's fractured approach to wartime intelligence had left it dangerously exposed, he wrote to FDR. The bottom line: "It is essential that we set up a central enemy intelligence agency."

Rivals inside the government like J. Edgar Hoover, the always turf-savvy FBI director, had their knives out for Donovan, fending off what they saw as a reckless power grab by the cocky Irishman. Hoover, who had built a vast counterespionage operation of his own and didn't want competition, even opened a dirt dossier on Donovan at the FBI. Henry Stimson, who had now become FDR's war secretary a decade after famously turning up his nose at the reading of "gentlemen's mail," didn't like Donovan's brash presidential pitch either. His nemeses were beginning to resent Donovan not only for his growing influence, but also for the colorful public persona of a man who would get his own comic strip, "The Exciting Adventures of 'Wild Bill' Donovan," in the *Washington Star*. "I have greater enemies in Washington than Hitler in Europe," Donovan once remarked.

The man who mattered most was ultimately persuaded by Donovan's warnings about America's foreign-intelligence void, and Roosevelt gave approval in June 1941 for the creation of a fledgling US intelligence service. Not surprisingly, he tapped its inventor to lead it, giving Donovan the vague title of "coordinator of information." The new agency was a scaled-back version of the one Donovan had planned, without the muscle and reach he had imagined, but it was a win for the decorated war hero none-theless.

Less than six months later, with his spy group still jockeying with other agencies to find its place in the crowded federal bureau-cracy, Donovan's warnings about America's fractured intelligence system proved tragically prophetic when the Japanese launched their surprise attack on Pearl Harbor, bringing the United States to war. On the night of December 7, 1941, as sporadic reports of the scope of the death and destruction in Hawaii streamed into the White House, Donovan rushed back to Washington from a football game in New York and met with a shaken Roosevelt to map out the next steps for his fledgling spy force. "It's a good thing you got me started on this," FDR told Donovan as he left.

Even as the country went to war, national security officials in Washington agonized over the question of whether a better-prepared intelligence apparatus could have averted the noto-rious "date that will live in infamy." Ultimately, a string of gov-ernment reviews would demonstrate that American military cryptographers had managed to break Japan's encrypted "Purple" code-making system long before the surprise bombing, offering tantalizing glimpses of Japan's intentions in the Pacific, but the in-formation was splintered across so many levels — from the army and the navy to the FBI and the White House — that no one fore-saw what was coming. "We might have had the genius to break the Purple code, but in 1941 we didn't have the brains to figure out what to do with it," bemoaned Henry Clausen, a military lawyer who conducted an extensive postmortem on the attack on orders from Stimson. The surprise strike would rank, one scholar said, as "certainly one of the greatest intelligence failures in history."

OSS grew out of the embers of Pearl Harbor. Six months after the bombing, President Roosevelt formally rebranded Donovan's intelligence brigade as the Office of Strategic Services, with a broadened new mandate to train American spies and commandos in a way the country had never tried before. Now on wartime footing, Donovan's spy service profited from more of almost everything: more money, more soldiers, more training sites, more weapons, and more political might. The one constant was Donovan, who as head of OSS wanted his growing band of "glorious amateurs"—thousands of agents strong—to wage "unorthodox warfare" against the enemy.

This was to be "the cloak-and-dagger brigade," as Donovan called his team; or, as his rivals inside the federal government sniped, "Donovan's private army," a "Tinker Toy" outfit among real military men. Donovan wanted his agents to employ not only the traditional tools of spycraft, like surveillance and undercover work, but also psychological tricks, propaganda, sabotage, and even guerrilla warfare and assassinations. While the military was readying for traditional, head-on attacks with fighter planes, battleships, and tanks, Donovan's idea was for his agents to penetrate enemy lines undetected, just two or three at a time, by parachute, submarine, tunneling, or any other means they could devise. Imagination was the only limit, Donovan would say. One favorite mantra—"Let's give it a try!"—would have sounded trite had it not come from a war hero who had famously refused to be evacuated from battle after being wounded multiple times, insisting instead that his men carry him from one foxhole to the next.

His break-the-mold concept for OSS would mean sending some men to near-certain deaths in the hopes that a few might complete their missions and make it out alive with prized intelligence. They would create a new brand of spies and saboteurs:

before America deployed Green Berets in the Vietnam War in the 1960s, or Navy SEALs in Afghanistan after the terror attacks of September 11, 2001, or Delta Force soldiers in Syria after that, it unleashed OSS and Donovan's brigade of covert agents.

Freddy got his orders while stationed in Arizona in December 1943, traveling by train to OSS headquarters in Washington, DC, then up the road twelve miles to a secret location in rural Maryland known only as Area F. Freddy and the other OSS trainees weren't allowed to disclose their destination to anyone, but Area F was a hard place to hide: a postcard-worthy landscape on four hundred acres of rolling greens, swarming day and night with armed men in camouflage uniforms. Curious cabbies and well-heeled neighbors soon got wind of what was going on inside the gates. The idyllic setting was almost as unlikely as the OSS mission itself. Until just a few months before, this had been home to Congressional Country Club, which for years had catered to American elites with names like Coolidge, Rockefeller, Carnegie, Hearst, and Du Pont. But the country club's Shangri-La veneer was fading badly by the late 1930s, and shrinking membership and the Depression had left it broke. The war proved a boon for both the club and for Bill Donovan. The club got a financial lifeline, renting out the entire property to the military for four thousand dollars a month in the name of wartime patriotism, and Donovan got a sprawling new training facility for his spy brigade.

The bucolic club was soon transformed into a military proving ground, with a missile range near the eleventh and sixteenth holes of one of the golf courses, climbing ropes hanging from the towering oak trees, a makeshift deck high above the pool for parachuting, and barbed-wired fences splicing through the grounds. Nighttime "compass runs" required the men to navigate their way through darkened woods and six-foot-deep creeks where errant golf balls had once landed. The only place that was off limits to the soldiers was a room in the clubhouse converted into a laboratory, where scientists were working on secret weapons for the American arsenal; among the sci-fi ideas that OSS scientists entertained were training bats to drop bombs and injecting Hitler with female hormones to make him less aggressive.

Donovan would stop by Area F to show the place off to generals and senators over drinks on a terrace overlooking an obstacle course or at lavish dinners in the clubhouse, featuring fresh Gulf shrimp and broiled porterhouse steaks. The soldiers themselves missed out on many of the club's amenities. Life for Freddy and the other OSS agents was much more austere, with food tightly rationed and men crammed six to a tent or in temporary huts. Training was constant, as they learned everything from parachuting to picking locks and intercepting radio signals. A former police chief from Shanghai taught them dozens of different ways for a man to kill an enemy with his bare hands. The unvarnished goal was "to make young Americans adore wringing the necks and breaking the spines of Gestapo officers, SS men, and all Nazis in European countries occupied by Germany," one instructor crowed.

A brand-new, pristine nine-hole golf course was soon torn to shreds by bazooka fire and errant missiles, with land mines and hand grenades buried in the sand traps for the trainees to defuse. Golf divots turned to craters, and the club's caddy shack was destroyed. Besides paying the monthly rent, the government wound up reimbursing the club $187,000 for the unexpected damage. Three men were killed in training mishaps, and many others ended up in the hospital, with broken bones, burns, and bruised egos. The men figured that if they could survive here, the real war couldn't be much worse.

Area F brought Freddy one step closer to fighting the Nazis. In training, he was often the first to volunteer for the mission of the moment, whether it was learning to fight a black belt in jujitsu or planting a live bomb in a sand trap. For Freddy, any chance to impress his superior officers was a chance to stamp an early ticket for his return to Europe.

Not everyone was so eager. Watching quietly from the back at many training demonstrations was a tall string bean of a kid named Hans Wynberg. A gangly six foot two, the twenty-one-year-old trainee towered over most of his fellow soldiers, but Hans's unassuming manner helped him fade into the crowd. He was a loner. When he did speak, it was with a foreign accent that sounded vaguely Dutch. He had an air of baby-faced innocence, remarked one of his military supervisors, who questioned whether Hans was tough enough for what lay ahead. "Young and requires direction, but 100 percent willing and gets results," another military supervisor would write in his file.

Hans never considered himself much of a leader, and he had no real desire to be one. In the chaotic environs of Area F, he had been bumped up in rank a few times during training only to be bumped down again for various infractions. Yet if anyone at the country club could have mastered the practice of building bombs and detonating explosives, it was Hans. A prodigy in chemistry, he had worked in a New York lab before the war and had science in his blood. His grandfather and his father had developed a special glue process to repair bicycle tires in his native Netherlands; in his bicycle-crazed homeland, just about everyone seemed to have one of their black-and-red Simson repair kits.

Hans carried a science book with him almost everywhere he went, and there were few chemical reactions that he hadn't mastered as a boy, at least on paper. Real-life chemical explosions were another matter. He'd always aspired to be a scientist or a professor, not a soldier or a spy. Hans was glad to leave the detonation drills and derring-do to others. There were days he wondered why he was among the recruits at Area F at all. He did his training tasks capably most of the time, but the truth was that he would rather be playing chess or poring over his books than setting off a grenade in a transformed golf bunker.

Freddy and Hans soon picked each other out of the crowd at training. Yin and yang in personalities, the two young soldiers were drawn together by the eerie parallels that had brought them to this makeshift spy-training site. Each was born to a successful Jewish businessman in Europe; each fled the Nazis as a teenager before the war; and each wound up in Brooklyn, just a few miles apart in an immigrants' enclave, although they had never actually met there.

Like Freddy, Hans had embraced the refugee's life in Brooklyn as a teenager after coming to America. Looking back, he would call it "the greatest time of my life." He became a die-hard Brooklyn Dodgers fan, sitting in the cheap seats in the bleachers at Ebbets Field as he screamed his lungs out for Pee Wee Reese, Leo Durocher, and the hapless hometown "Bums." He finished near the top of his class in high school; he got a part in the school production of *Julius Caesar*, yelling "Hark, hark!" onstage in a Dutch accent, alongside the native-born students; and he came to adore Hollywood starlets like Bette Davis and Joan Crawford.

Hans liked to say he had become "more American than the Americans." He would venture into Manhattan on Saturdays to watch the city's most famous chess players in the park, and he found a restaurant in the basement of Grand Central Station that served Dutch-style raw herring just the way he liked it. Even better, he had met a girl named Elly — a Dutch immigrant like himself, and brainy, too — and he thought she might be the one. Home on leave from military training soon after a promotion, Hans took Elly to New York's iconic Tavern on the Green restaurant, and he wrote her a poem for the occasion: *The sergeant and his lady / They went and saw the town / He had a brand new uniform / She had an evening gown.*

Brooklyn hadn't brought Hans and Freddy together, despite their proximity as refugees there; Hitler had. Training together at OSS, and grumbling about the endless exercises, the two young men developed a deep kinship born of exile. "My little brother," Freddy called Hans. Freddy's own brother, after finishing college, had enlisted in the army and shipped out for the Philippines, but in the bookish Hans, he found a worthy stand-in. If it weren't for the army's "lights out" rules, Freddy might have been yelling for Hans, instead of his brother, to quit reading and turn the lights out at night so he could get some sleep.

Though Hans was nearly a head taller and outranked him, Freddy played the role of domineering drill sergeant in the pairing. Hans revered him for his brashness and sheer chutzpah, and he tolerated his bossiness. Hans could be headstrong himself, chafing at times under military rules, but he was no match for his newfound OSS partner. Freddy had bent the rules with abandon his whole life — whether it was "borrowing" his father's car as an eight-year-old in Germany or getting a general to surrender in an army war game in the Arizona desert. He was an agitator, an innovator, and nothing seemed to rattle him as far as Hans could tell. And boy, could he talk. That riled some people — colleagues described him as "a windbag" and a "talkative braggart," noted one military review — but Hans loved listening to Freddy spin his yarns about his old homeland and their new one.

Freddy and Hans stood apart at OSS. Many of the agents who passed through the spy agency during the war were well-connected blue bloods, Ivy League professionals who would come to steer American intelligence for decades: men like Princeton-educated William Colby, who trained at Area F and was one of four OSS men to become CIA directors. Or Harvard-trained scholar Arthur M. Schlesinger Jr.; major-league baseball player Moe Berg, who graduated from Princeton and spoke eight languages; and famed movie director John Ford. Donovan's spy crew at OSS was dominated by men who had been noted lawyers, writers, businessmen, and academics before the war, and the tony grounds of the Maryland country club were, at least before the bombing drills started, just the kind of place many had frequented in civilian life. The joke at the agency, in fact, was that "OSS" actually stood for "Oh-So-Social."

But Freddy, the German-born mechanic, and Hans, the nerdy Dutch science whiz, were a different breed, refugees who were in high demand by OSS more for the foreign languages they spoke and their experience with other cultures than the people they knew or the schools they attended. Donovan and his aides understood that the United States couldn't hope to gather needed intelligence on its wartime enemies in Europe and Asia if it couldn't understand them. Ironically, Donovan himself had stirred fears before the war about the possibility of German émigrés worldwide secretly helping the Nazis — the dreaded Fifth Column. But now that he was running OSS, he was anxious to find immigrants who spoke German, as well as Dutch, Italian, Japanese, and other war-zone languages — even though many, like Freddy, had never finished high school much less gone to elite institutions.

Freddy and Hans were assigned to an "OG," an operational group made up of about thirty men. The *Mission: Impossible*–style mandate out of Washington for these groups was to train foreign-speaking soldiers "skilled in methods of sabotage and small arms" and launch them "in small groups behind enemy lines to harass the enemy." That so many of the spies-in-training were foreign-born Jews was not lost on the higher-ups. Despite the prejudice that many Jewish Americans faced before the war, and even during it, more than a half-million Jews ended up serving in the US military in World War II. Among them, thousands of Jewish immigrants from Europe returned to fight the Nazis for their adopted country. Out of that group came the smallest and most elite subset of all, numbering only a few dozen or so: Jewish immigrants who had fled Hitler and volunteered to be dropped behind enemy lines for OSS.

That Freddy had been banned from the army as an "enemy alien" just two years before didn't matter now. Nor did it matter that in peacetime, he and Hans would have had trouble even getting on the grounds of Congressional Country Club, which had few minorities or Jews as members. What mattered now, in the view of Donovan and his top officers, was that they had the background, the language skills, the training, and the indefinable "guts" to confront the enemy at almost incalculable risk. If the ideal OSS spy was "a PhD who could win a bar fight," as agency leaders liked to say, then Hans's brains and Freddy's brawn combined those elements in a tag-team pairing.

For Hans, like Freddy, OSS was a way out of the traditional army. He had already served a stint in the infantry after enlisting, but he felt like he never quite fit in. He wasn't an army grunt; he was an individualist, a scholar who wrote poetry, listened to Bach, and dabbled in the philosophy of Socrates and Plato; he resisted the "groupthink" of his army days, of marching in formation and working en masse. Just the thought of large numbers of people reminded him of Hitler and how he riled up a crowd. He found the whole notion of mass manipulation deeply unsettling.

Hans also chafed against the army's rules and rigidity. He often thought he knew better than the people above him — not a good trait in the military, he admitted. Once, marching in the Texas heat during basic training, he had asked his drill sergeant if maybe they could take it a bit slower. That did not go over well, and the whole company got KP duty because of his insolence. The lanky kid from the Netherlands was not a popular man that day.

Hans got his chance for something different when he was called into base command in Texas one day. A lieutenant had an unexpected question for him. A new agency called OSS was looking for European-born soldiers, the officer explained to him. He spoke Dutch, right? Yes, Hans said. "So," the lieutenant asked, "do you want to liberate Holland?"

What a question, Hans thought to himself; of course he did. After war had first erupted in Europe, the Dutch army had drafted him to return to fight, but he had decided to stay put in America. Now the thought of going back to the Netherlands with the Americans to fight the Nazis energized him, and not just because of his Dutch loyalty. He was also drawn back to his native land by a wrenching burden, a piece of his life story that he had hidden from almost everyone. The truth was that, as much as he loved his new life in Brooklyn, he had left his parents and his little brother behind in the Netherlands, and he had no idea what had become of them under Nazi rule.

The agonizing separation from his family had not been Hans's choice. Four years earlier, in 1939, his father, Leo, alarmed by the growing Nazi menace in Europe, had sent him and his twin brother, Luke, to America at the age of sixteen. They couldn't all leave yet, Leo told the boys. Leo stayed behind with Hans's mother, Henrietta, and their youngest son, Robbie, then twelve, and waited for their chance. Money, visa problems, family obligations — all kept them in the Netherlands for the time being. Leo's friends and relatives in the Netherlands were baffled when he first told them he was hatching an exit plan to send the twins away by themselves. Hitler was not the Netherlands' problem, not yet at least, and sending a pair of teenage boys to live alone in America — in the land of the "cowboys and Indians," as they called it — seemed rash, if not downright foolish. *Gek,* they called him: "Crazy."

But Leo was a determined man. Always politically minded, he had become alarmed by Hitler's piercing, anti-Semitic rhetoric soon after hearing one of his very first speeches as German chancellor in 1933. The man was "a maniac," he told Hans and anyone else who would listen. He started a political group not long afterward opposing Nazi-aligned political candidates in the Netherlands and the spread of fascism in Europe, and he went door-to-door to make his case. When civil war broke out in Spain three years later, he told Hans that he wished he could go there himself to fight Franco and the Nazi-backed fascists, but his family and his business kept him where he was. Meanwhile, he watched with dread as more and more Jews from Germany began to stream into the Netherlands to escape Hitler's reach.

Leo wasn't going to wait any longer to see how far Hitler's territorial ambitions would extend. With Europe on the verge of war in 1939, he managed to snare two prized visas to America for Hans and Luke. He mortgaged the family tire-patching business, booked passage for them on a transatlantic ocean liner, deposited $3,600 at Chase Manhattan Bank in New York for their support, and sent them to stay with a kindly Polish businessman there, a diamond cutter whom he barely knew. He was desperate to find a refuge for his family, even if it meant breaking them up and sending them away in stages.

Hans didn't question the decision, as difficult as it was to leave his family, even temporarily, for a foreign land. He trusted his father's judgment. Leo had always been a successful, charismatic, and dapper figure in the twins' lives. When Hans wasn't making model planes on his own or inspecting his stamp collection, Leo would be taking him and Luke out on the weekends to go fishing in one of the local canals or to look at Dutch ships and trains.

On the day the twins left for America in May 1939, Leo and Henrietta held a farewell party for them in their yard on a bright morning. Hans's parents were determined to put on their best face; they wanted this to be a celebration, not a wake. Leo chronicled the event in a black-and-white home movie, with Hans and

Luke preening for the camera. Everyone was dressed in what even the Dutch Jews called their "Easter best"; Hans had on his fanciest suit, with his tie knotted tightly under a sweater vest. He kissed his grandmother on the cheek, hugged the family dog, and tussled playfully with his little brother, Robbie. With an American flag flying from the house for the occasion, Hans unfolded a giant map of the United States and searched for their destination in New York. Robbie, in knickers and knee-high socks, did handstands on an antique chair, and the three brothers competed in a spirited footrace.

As the twins prepared to leave on their long journey, Leo reminded them of an expression that emphasized family bonds: "Family," he said, "are the people who can call you by your first name without having to ask permission." Leo assured the twins that he and the rest of the family would follow them to America later, as soon as they could.

Hans and Luke made it to Brooklyn, settled in together in a small room in the diamond cutter's apartment, and enrolled in public school. But Leo's promise to join them "soon" turned to weeks, then months, then years, and still Hans's parents and his little brother were unable to flee. Leo would write long typewritten letters to the twins every week or so, asking about their faraway new life in Brooklyn, pushing for them to give him more details in their letters home about their schoolwork, and dutifully updating them on the mundanities of daily life back at home: a shipment of tire tubes that just arrived; a new train station nearby that finally opened; an infuriating car tax that he was contesting.

What weighed more heavily than ever on Leo's mind, though, was the madman Adolf Hitler, who was holding court barely four hundred miles to the east in Berlin. In one letter in the fall of 1939, five months after Hans and his brother had left for America, Leo wrote of how a Nazi U-boat had sunk a British aircraft carrier in one of the first naval skirmishes of the European conflict; he was worried about the strength of England's vaunted military, which he considered "the most important defense against Nazism," not only for the British but for all of Europe. Nor did he have any faith in Britain's Neville Chamberlain, a Nazi appeaser always walking around with his silly umbrella, Leo said.

His friends and neighbors in the Netherlands were finally beginning to see the grave danger that the Nazis posed, Leo reported. But too many others, he observed, were still painfully slow to recognize it. Like Mr. Buttinger down at the metal company, he wrote, who "continues to believe that Herr Hitler is a swell guy for the Germans!!" Leo couldn't fathom how people in the Netherlands, and even in America, could support Hitler and the Nazis. "That guy Lindbergh, he is so transparent," he wrote of the famed aviator, who was feted by Nazi leaders on trips to Germany. Such Nazi sympathizers "are the true traitors of the causes of freedom and humanity." More people were trying to go to America, he noted, hinting that the family might make it there soon, too. How and when, he didn't say. He made no promises. "OK boys, I will leave it at that for today," he wrote. "Kisses and all the best from your Pipa."

Leo's dire predictions were realized seven months later, in May 1940, when the Nazis invaded the Netherlands. The Dutch army was little match for Hitler's mobilized Panzer tanks, and five days after the invasion, the Dutch were forced to surrender. The German occupiers, greeted with Nazi salutes by some Dutchmen, soon began jailing many of the Jews who had fled Germany for the Netherlands and instituting their own brand of Nazi rule.

Just as Leo had tried to warn, Herr Hitler was now in charge. A Nazi "civil service" was now running the Netherlands, with its own handpicked mayors, judges, and police commissioners, but writing to Hans and Luke in the fall of 1941, Leo still tried to give the twins the most reassuring view of the situation that he could. At least the Netherlands didn't have it quite as bad as France or Belgium, where the full weight of the occupying German military enforced the hammer of Nazi law, he wrote to them. He explained that the occupying Nazis viewed the Dutch as "tribal kin," with hopes that they would eventually adopt the Nazi approach willingly. "But the Dutch masses are stubborn and opinionated. They have yet to be convinced that the old was so bad, compared to what has been visible of the new so far." People were upset about the daily necessities that they cared about, which were being redirected to the occupiers. Many foods — milk, cheese, beer — were hard to come by now, and it was difficult to find the materials for the cigars that Leo smoked.

No one knew how it would all turn out, Leo wrote. Separated from his sons for more than two years now, he loved to receive their letters with the news of their lives in America, land of the "cowboys and Indians." He was thrilled to learn that the twins had re-created a puppet show that the family used to put on in the Netherlands, complete with a hissing devil, and he read excitedly about all the activities and sports they were doing at school. Just don't overdo it with the swimming and the "excessive exercise," he cautioned Hans; there was no reason to risk an injury. "You are already the representative of the chess players," Leo wrote. Wasn't that enough?

There was no talk of any imminent reunion. But Leo looked forward to joining them in all the new pastimes they had picked up in America, once the family was together again. "Thankfully I'm still young enough so that once we are reunited in good health, I can join you for swimming, rowing, fishing (if you haven't become a vegetarian yet), and whatever else. You can rest assured I would take at least six weeks off for everything, as soon as this rotten war is over," he wrote.

At the very bottom of the letter, Robbie, now a teenager, added a note of his own in careful, cursive handwriting. "Dear brothers," it began. "Just now I was studying piano. I dream a lot of you guys lately (I know, what a surprise). Good luck! A punch from me! Rob."

By early 1942, there was no further talk in the letters of the Nazis or the war, much less a reunion. The Nazi censors might be screening the mail, and Leo was still intent on putting a bright veneer on their life in the Netherlands, writing of ice-skating outings and family birthday parties. It had been a cold and brutal winter, Leo wrote that February; more snow than he had ever seen. But everyone was healthy, he wrote, and missing the twins very much.

Hans received each new letter in the mail with a mixture of relief and expectation: relief that his parents and Rob were okay, and expectation that the latest letter might contain word that they had found a way out. It was too painful to read most of the letters himself, so he would let Luke read them and share what they said. In his father's absence, Hans clung to the memories of all the stories Leo had passed on to him as a boy: stories about science, about Dutch history, about life. One that always stuck with him was about a Dutch naval commander in the eighteen hundreds who found a way to blow up his own ship rather than turn it over to foreign invaders. "I'd rather ignite the fuse in the dynamite!" his father would shout at the story's climax. It was a story with an element of chemistry in it, a subject father and son both loved; but more than that, it was a story about bravery and heroism in wartime, topics that now seemed more relevant than ever for Hans.

In mid-1942, without explanation, the letters from his family simply stopped. Hans and Luke could only speculate, grimly, about what had happened. They knew that the news from the Netherlands, like much of Europe, was growing bleaker with every headline. "Nazis Execute 150 Jews; Netherlanders Taken to Poland Reported Machine Gunned," read one wire-service report from his homeland in the summer of 1943, just as Hans was entering the US army. Jews throughout the Netherlands were now in hiding. In Amsterdam, less than fifteen miles from the Wynbergs' home in Overveen, a young Dutch girl named Anne Frank was hidden away with her family in an attic. Hans's own family was "believed to be living in Holland," the American military noted in his file that year, but the truth was that no one knew for certain. Hans certainly didn't. In his mind, his parents and his little brother were neither dead nor alive; they were simply gone — taken from him in the moment by the Nazi menace his father had feared for so long.

Hans hoped that, wherever they were, they weren't suffering. But in darker moments, hope and faith collided with the reality of war. He was raised in an orthodox Jewish home, where his mother kept a kosher kitchen, his father followed the Jewish tenets, and he himself celebrated his bar mitzvah two years before coming to America, just as Freddy had. Yet the agonizing silence from his father tested his faith in God, and he became distrustful of religion. With Hitler creating such mayhem, terrorizing the Jews in the name of a Christian god, it was difficult to believe there was a higher power at work.

The military training he received at OSS was a welcome distraction for Hans. Although he might have lagged behind others in physical strength and endurance, the sweat and strain of the regimen gave him something to focus on apart from his family in the Netherlands. Where he excelled, however, was in more cerebral tasks: radio operations and secret codes, where his facility for science and mathematics came into play.

He and Freddy would travel a few hours with their units to rural Virginia, where they were tasked with sending coded radio messages from remote mountain areas with unreliable signals. OSS, with the help of a navy engineer from the RCA electronics company, was working to develop a wireless radio-transmission system to evade German ground radar. In the meantime, OSS's radio operators had to lug around the system's erratic, suitcase-sized predecessor. Freddy was lucky if he could transmit thirty words a minute in coded messages, while Hans would be tapping away furiously at twice the speed; it was one area where Hans could claim bragging rights over him.

Freddy's own passion was always for war games; quick, strong, and crafty, he thrived under the stress and physical demands. On one training mission, his group trucked up to Baltimore after hours to the offices of a major defense contractor; once there, instructors challenged them to find a way inside to pilfer top-secret military blueprints without getting caught. Most of the men were "captured" on the way, but not Freddy. He broke into the place without being detected and stealthily snagged the prized documents. On another training excursion, this one all the way out in

Southern California, he learned to scuba dive and detonate explosives underwater, then raided an island and shot a steer for food in a test of survival skills. Once he had captured his target, he and his small team — three of them Jewish refugees like himself — posed shirtless on the beachhead for a victory photo, rifles raised and muscles flexed, looks of elation on their faces.

For Freddy, success was a momentary rush, fun but fleeting. These were still war games, not the real thing — he was fighting phantoms, not Nazis. Much of the training was "piss poor" anyway, he would complain. In his opinion, these were skills he could have taught himself. In one session, Freddy and Hans even had to watch films on the venereal diseases they might contract in their foreign travels if they weren't careful. But they weren't going anywhere. Freddy felt stuck. He couldn't understand why Donovan and the agency brass wouldn't send them overseas to fight the real war. After two months of the constant "hurry up and wait" mind-set of military training, Freddy groused that the Area F officers were "wasting our time, not fighting a war." He felt useless: just one of the masses, "another body in the infantry." If he really wanted to see action, he might have been better off staying in Arizona with the 81st Wildcats, who at least were heading off soon to the Pacific theater.

His restlessness was infectious. Early in their training, Hans hadn't seemed to be in much of a rush to get back to Europe. Yes, he was ready to fight for his new country whenever he was called upon, and the prospect of somehow liberating his homeland — and finding his family — held deep personal meaning. But until the time came to head somewhere, he was content reading his chemistry books and playing chess in the country-club setting.

As training wore on with no end in sight, however, Hans grew frustrated, too. He still had no word about the fate of his family in the Netherlands, and chilling new reports from Europe in the spring of 1944 indicated that hundreds of thousands of Hungarian Jews had become only the latest Nazi victims sent to their deaths at Auschwitz and Birkenau. Who would stop the genocide? Hans now longed to go somewhere — anywhere — to see action. Liberate Holland? No one in the military even talked to him about that anymore. The way things were going, he complained to Freddy, they might not even make it out of Area F.

But the tide of the war in Europe was shifting in the spring of '44. Allied military leaders were mapping out secret plans for "D-day" — the Normandy invasion on June 6 — with Donovan at OSS closely involved in American strategy. His spy agency already had secret agents planted inside France, working side by side with French Resistance fighters to provide intelligence on Nazi troops in advance of the Allied landings. Donovan, never content as a desk manager, flew to Europe to be there in person for the massive invasion, aboard an American destroyer ship, and he went to France ten weeks later in hopes of witnessing the liberation of Paris from the Germans. Under occasional Nazi gunfire, he made his way to the French capital in a jeep with a noteworthy guest in the backseat: war correspondent Ernest Hemingway, armed with a submachine gun as bullets flew past them.

Donovan's hope was for the Normandy invasion to clear the path for OSS to expand its surveillance operations, allowing American agents to penetrate enemy lines in Nazi strongholds throughout Europe — Germany, Austria, Italy, and the Balkans — and priming the way for General Eisenhower's troops. That would require dozens, perhaps hundreds, of his "glorious amateurs" at OSS, trained and ready to go. The call went out to Area

F, the call that Freddy and Hans had doubted would ever come. Their units got their new orders that spring: another round of parachute training—always more training, they grumbled—and then they would sail across the Atlantic Ocean to northern Africa for points unknown.

There was talk that they would be parachuted into France after they landed in Africa, but their exact mission, and even their ultimate destination, was unclear. No matter. The details weren't of much concern to Freddy and Hans. They were finally going back across the Atlantic—this time not to flee the Nazis, but to fight them.

4

The Third Man

The Nazis were on the run in Italy, but inside POW Camp 209 in Naples, the Führer's men stood loyal. Day after day, the Allied military police hauled in German soldiers captured in battle and locked them up inside the gated compound. One prisoner, a Nazi sergeant still clad in his swastika-emblazoned uniform, would greet the newly arrived German POWs with a jarring command: when his fellow Nazi prisoners answered to one of the American jailers in the camp, the sergeant barked, "It's still 'Heil Hitler!'" It was a sign of defiance and loyalty; they might be imprisoned, but the Nazis weren't beaten yet, no matter what their Allied captors were telling them.

Franz Weber, a twenty-three-year-old prisoner from the Alpine region of western Austria, saluted Hitler on command, just like his fellow POWs. He wasn't about to invite trouble. Franz looked every bit the proud, unbroken Nazi: trim and fit, with the confident manner of the Wehrmacht officer he had once been. Franz had fought for the Führer across Europe — first in Poland and Russia, then Yugoslavia, then on to Italy — and had risen to company commander as a Nazi lieutenant in the Baltics.

But in reciting his Nazi credentials for his fellow prisoners, Franz left out the rest of his story: how he had become disillusioned with the Nazis; how he had been bumped down in rank for not toeing the party line; how he had slipped away during a bomb-laying mission near the Italian front that September and made his way through the vineyards to the Allied side to surrender; how Franz was, unknown to his fellow prisoners in Camp 209, a Nazi deserter.

If the truth got out, there was little doubt what the other prisoners in the camp would do to him. In the Reich's twisted moral code, deserters occupied a bottom rung near other undesirables like the Jews, the Communists, and the gypsies. Franz kept to himself in the tent that served as his jail bunk. His fellow POWs left him alone for the most part. But a few months after his imprisonment, a new Nazi prisoner, still in his German uniform, arrived at the barracks and soon after offered Franz some of his Spam. Any offer of food — even a strange, American-made meat concoction — was a surefire way to make an introduction to a hungry German prisoner. The new man was short and stocky, with a swarthy complexion, and he spoke in the Swabian accent of Germany's southern region. He had been captured in battle in northern Italy, he said. He was quick to smile, despite his confinement. He dutifully gave the "Heil Hitler" salute on command, but he seemed to be watching the other prisoners, almost studying them.

The new man and Franz got to talking over bites of Spam — small talk at first about the dreariness of prison life, and then weightier concerns about the flailing state of the war. Out of earshot of the other prisoners, the new man confided to Franz that he had no great loyalty to the Nazis; he just wanted the fighting to be over. He struck Franz as sincere, and Franz revealed his own bitterness over what the Germans had done to his Austrian homeland. "I have no use for the Nazis," he confided; Hitler, he said, was a "son of a bitch." If it weren't for the Führer, "I could be home now," he grumbled. "Where's home?" the new man asked. A small town in Tyrol, Franz answered; a place called Oberperfuss.

It was just a few days later that Franz's newfound confidant was gone from POW Camp 209, ushered out by the Allied guards. What had become of him, Franz didn't know.

A free man once again, Freddy Mayer was escorted from Camp 209 back to a secret OSS base clear across southern Italy on the Adriatic coast. Posing as a German POW for three days amid a swarm of Nazis, he had made it safely through his first big assignment for OSS.

He gave his commanders a buoyant debriefing. His German, though rusty, was still passable enough for him to have gotten by in the Nazi barracks without any obvious stumbles, Freddy told them. Some of the German military expressions that his father had taught him all those years ago in Freiburg had come back to him, and none of the Nazi prisoners seemed skeptical of his cover story.

Even better, he had identified a possible German collaborator, the third man they needed for a would-be mission OSS was in the process of planning. "He was very anti-Nazi," Freddy reported, and he hailed from the same part of Austria that they were looking to target: the Austrian Alps in Tyrol just north of the Italian border. He could make a perfect point man for them on the ground, Freddy said.

The Nazi's name, he said, was Franz Weber.

"The Alpine Fortress," the Americans called the scenario. The Nazi battleground they envisioned was a chilling one indeed. If Hitler was going to lose a war that he himself had begun, he was determined to mount one final, epic stand and go down in flames: at his country home in Bavaria, the birthplace of the Nazis, against the idyllic backdrop of an Alpine mountain range booby-trapped with explosives. And he wanted to take as many Allied soldiers down with him as he could.

That, at least, was the great fear of General Eisenhower and American leaders in Washington, as the collapse of the Third Reich began to look more and more likely by the winter of 1944– 45. Warnings about a last-stand Nazi "fortress" in the Alps were piling up in top-secret intelligence reports, becoming what General Omar Bradley called "an obsession." Newspapers at home were raising alarms over "Hitler's Hideaway" as well, with stories about an enormous network of underground tunnels and caves that were mined with bombs and could, with the push of a button on SS chief Heinrich Himmler's desk, blow up oncoming invaders. The "Alpine redoubt," military planners dubbed the plan. At OSS, Donovan wrote to FDR himself to warn of reports that stalwart Nazis under Himmler were stockpiling weapons and organizing "a German resistance army of between 35,000 and 40,000 men" trained in guerrilla warfare to mount a final siege.

Some skeptics saw the reports of an impregnable Nazi hideaway as exaggerated, if not fanciful. But American intelligence officials gave them credence — and were so desperate to avoid the disastrous scenario that they were willing to take ethically treacherous steps to do so. Donovan's top OSS man in Europe, Allen Dulles, met over a bottle of scotch in Switzerland with Nazi general Karl Wolff about the prospect of a surrender by Nazi SS in Italy, including parts of Tyrol. Wolff was a brutal and notorious figure: Himmler's onetime "bureaucrat of death," the man who set up the rail system that took trainloads of Polish Jews to death camps. Yet Dulles, disregarding a vow by FDR not to negotiate with the Nazis, was willing to treat Wolff favorably in an effort to work out an agreement. In secret cables back to Washington, he portrayed the Nazi war criminal as a "moderate" and well-intentioned Waffen SS man; he was "no ogre," Dulles wrote of him.

After softening up the Nazi leader's image, Dulles worked to protect him from war-crimes charges at Nuremberg once his SS men in the region laid down their arms in a war that Wolff feared he had already lost. It was an unsettling Faustian bargain that was justified in part, Dulles said, by the desire to avert the dreaded "Alpine fortress" scenario. Victory over Hitler seemed finally within reach, and Dulles was willing to help one of the Nazis' top generals to try to avoid a violent last stand in the Alps.

From their new OSS base in Italy, Freddy and Hans were anxious to join the fight, but they were not there yet — and they were losing hope that they ever would be. They had spent months training and traveling, shuffling aimlessly between military camps in Africa and Europe. They were inching closer to the fighting, yes; but it made little difference to them whether they were biding their time four hundred miles from the war at a remote Italian villa, or four thousand miles away at a Maryland country club. In their minds, they were still nowhere.

Their inauspicious reception on foreign soil months earlier might have been a harbinger. Their ship from America docked in Algeria, in northern Africa, in June 1944, and Freddy and Hans, along with another thirty or so men from Area F, showed up at the Allied base in the historic seaside city of Oran, which had been occupied by the Nazi-aligned French Vichy forces until the Allies seized control eighteen months earlier. Private First Class Fred Mayer and Sergeant Hans Wynberg from OSS were reporting for duty, awaiting their new assignment. Except that none of the army and navy men at the base knew who they were or what they were supposed to be doing; they didn't even seem to know what "OSS" was.

Freddy and Hans were issued cots and sheets, then went in search of their unit. But with linens in short supply in town, a swarm of Algerian youngsters near the train station grabbed the sheets out of their hands, tossed them some francs as payment, then scampered away. The boys were out of sight by the time Freddy and Hans figured out how little a local franc was worth and realized they had been swindled. They would have to go without sheets for the night.

They finally found their OSS team, but what they were supposed to be doing in this far-off African land still remained a mys-

tery. Day after day, they went through more training in spycraft
— but toward what end they didn't know. The wait seemed unending, as they trekked from one military installation to another
with no final destination in sight. From Oran, they went up and
around the northern African coast to Algiers, then across the
Mediterranean on a British transport to the southern heel of Italy.
Hurrying, waiting; hurrying, waiting. More training, then more
waiting for weeks at a time.

For that whole summer and into the fall of 1944, no assignment came. It was maddening for the pair. Seventy-three thousand American soldiers had just stormed the beaches of Normandy in June, while they were counting their days aimlessly in
Africa, resigned to reading about the action from afar in *Stars and
Stripes*. Hans chafed as his own twin brother was sent into France
with the army after Normandy, fighting for his adopted country.
But Hans and Freddy were stuck at another way station. They
were killing time, not Nazis. The inaction grated on them.

Hans used the time to master Morse code, but he wrote off
most of the other exercises as silly. He was struck by the advice of
one of his OSS instructors, who had fought in the Spanish Civil
War a few years earlier. "Hans, the only thing you have to do every morning," the instructor told him sardonically, "is this exercise with your pistol: Point it at a Nazi and pull the trigger. That is
all you have to do." Hans figured he could remember that much.

. Beyond marching and doing drills, they passed the time as
best they could. Hans had his radio codes and chemistry books
to occupy himself, but Freddy was always looking for a diversion.
Once, they drove a jeep up the steps of the historic Casbah in Algiers — just to see if it could be done. They played in craps games,
selling their blood to the local Red Cross to make up for one costly

gambling loss. To avoid a long, hot march in the desert, Freddy hot-wired a military truck he found at a British salvage yard; the tires blew out, so the men ended up having to walk the last leg anyway. In one town, Freddy spent his downtime with a lovely young French-Spanish woman he had met named Fernande. But when the young woman grew too attached to the American soldier with the mischievous smile, Freddy passed on word through another soldier that PFC Mayer was officially "missing in action."

Freddy and Hans had become unwitting characters in a World War II movie, but this wasn't the epic John Wayne drama they had envisioned; instead, it was one of those slapstick military films with Dean Martin and Jerry Lewis, where high jinks and hilarity combine with interminable bouts of boredom and frustration.

The closest Freddy came to glimpsing the violence of war firsthand was during a training exercise. They were hiking through the mountains of Algeria when a white shroud billowing in the distance caught his eye. It seemed like an apparition. As he and his unit moved closer, he realized there was a body underneath. And then the body jerked suddenly. Freddy didn't scare easily, but the sight jolted him. The man, apparently a soldier from the local area, was still alive. He appeared mortally wounded, and he was lying next to a freshly dug grave. Someone had dug it out for him, a makeshift funeral plot in the middle of nowhere. The man squirmed, then signaled to Freddy. He didn't want help; he just wanted a cigarette, just one last drag. Someone in the group handed him one and lit it. The man seemed content.

Freddy wasn't sure who the man was, how he got there, or whom he was even fighting, but the image stuck with him: a man at war, lying next to his own grave, just waiting to die. For all of Freddy's craps games and carefree joyrides of late, the scene was an opaque reminder that people were actually dying in a war around him. It was easy to forget sometimes.

An assignment finally came their way: Freddy and Hans were scheduled to parachute into southern France with an OSS unit to help the Maquis, rural bands of French Resistance fighters on the ground. Donovan's people had begun sending commando teams deep into Nazi territory in France a year earlier — even before the invasion at Normandy — to work with the Resistance in organizing sabotage missions. Hans and Freddy, who both spoke French, were supposed to help the Maquis blow up bridges. They readied themselves excitedly for the mission and reported to the airstrip at the appointed hour with parachutes on their backs and hand grenades on their belts. They were finally getting their chance. But just as they were about to board the military flight for France, the notification came: the mission had been scrapped. There was no official explanation, but word filtered down of a rift between the Americans and the Maquis fighters, who reportedly thought the OSS captain overseeing all the operations was "an absolute ass." Freddy and Hans were grounded, left once again to hurry up and wait for another chance, even as OSS moved them to another base — this one in Naples, Italy.

"I've had enough of this crap," Freddy finally declared in frustration. He threw out a radical proposition to Hans and three other OSS agents at the base — all three of them Jewish refugees as well, and all of them out of patience. If OSS wouldn't give them a real assignment, the five of them were ready to demand one for themselves, and they would go around their commanding officers to do it. So Freddy and his cohorts simply walked off the base in Naples one morning — without getting approval, without talking to their captain, without even having a concrete plan in mind.

OSS was looser about the rules than other branches of the military, but even so, Hans realized as he followed Freddy out, that what they were doing amounted to desertion. Desertion with a twist: traditional deserters were trying to get out of the war; they were trying to get into it.

They hitched a ride twenty miles up the road from Naples to the historic Italian province of Caserta, where OSS had set up headquarters in an enormous eighteenth-century royal palace. They talked their way inside and went looking for a lieutenant colonel named Howard Chapin. Freddy and Hans had first met Chapin back at Area F in Maryland, and they figured maybe he could get them off the hamster wheel they seemed stuck on. Chapin was always full of ideas: a Dartmouth man, he came to OSS by way of Madison Avenue, where he was a top advertising executive for General Foods. Like many of Donovan's "glorious amateurs" at OSS, Chapin was expected to adapt his peacetime skills for wartime use on the fly. More accustomed to pitching advertising campaigns for Jell-O and frozen peas, he was now pitching secret espionage plans to Donovan and his top aides in the effort to help quash the Nazis.

It had been a brutal time for Chapin and the OSS command in Italy, with missions blown, men lost or killed, and friction building with other branches of the American forces and their allies. One team of covert agents, led by a navy officer who was an orthodontist in Los Angeles before the war, had been captured by the Gestapo after parachuting into northern Austria; he was imprisoned at the Mauthausen concentration camp. The leader of another mission, meanwhile, shot himself to death when the Gestapo found him in bed with a local woman, a rendezvous that OSS noted dryly was not part of his assignment.

Now into Colonel Chapin's office marched, uninvited, five OSS men — all of them European refugees, all of them Jews — who had just deserted their base. Freddy, the self-appointed platoon leader, pleaded their case, a note of urgency piercing his guttural German accent. He told the colonel about all the training they had done at OSS, all the man-hours they had put in, all the far-flung places they had traveled at home and abroad — all to prepare for a mission that had still not come. "Our talents and time are wasted here," Freddy said, still smiling despite his obvious aggravation. "How about something a little more interesting?"

"This has now gone on for a year," Hans added, inspired as usual by Freddy's brashness. "I was promised that I'd liberate Holland. Now I am sitting in this goddam replacement depot in Naples. We've got to *do* something."

Freddy already had a plan in mind, and he laid it out for the colonel: Drop him and a small team of men into southwest Germany, back into the Black Forest near his hometown of Freiburg, where he could gather advance intelligence for the Allied troops that had started coming ashore on D-day. "I'm very familiar with the Black Forest," he told Chapin. "My brother and I used to bicycle there. Parachute me in there. I can be of more use than sitting around waiting for something to happen."

Not an option, Chapin told him; the Black Forest was well behind enemy lines, and OSS wasn't running any operations in the region. But Chapin had to admire Freddy's zeal. With all the trouble he was having finding competent agents, he certainly wasn't going to turn away five eager young men who spoke the enemy's language. He would find them a spot, Chapin assured them. With General Eisenhower's sign-off, OSS had recently created a new "special reconnaissance" battalion for parachuting as many as a thousand agents behind enemy lines into parts of Austria, Italy, and Germany itself. Chapin would try to get them assigned to this new group. He made no promises, but Freddy and Hans felt confident that their forced meeting had dramatically improved their chances of getting into the action, and soon.

Officially, Freddy's new supervisors at OSS papered over the matter of desertion and instead labeled Freddy and his crew as "brown offs" — military parlance for men who had, supposedly, gone through proper channels to request a transfer. Whatever it was called, their coup had paid off. The men got their orders to report to Bari, a port city along the Adriatic Sea abut 160 miles to the east. OSS had a base there that was used mainly for hazardous air operations over Nazi-held regions in the Balkans, and the mere existence of the place was a tightly held secret. None of their family or friends could know where they were going or what they were doing, the men were told. OSS would strictly censor their letters home to keep out any hint of their whereabouts, and anyone who disobeyed faced immediate discharge. Breaking the rules this time would have consequences, they were warned.

Freddy and Hans bunked in a spacious Italian villa surrounded by rolling green lawns: almost like the country club at Area F, but without the golf courses. A Yugoslavian woman in the kitchen cooked them more variations of Spam than they ever knew existed. Her concoctions were good enough for most of the men, but not Freddy. Always adept at working the angles, Freddy persuaded one of OSS's official document forgers at the base to draw up papers making him the supply sergeant for a ghost unit, and he parlayed his new assignment into extra rations of beef, turkey, ham, and other hard-to-find delicacies for his team. A man couldn't live on Spam alone. Freddy would need a refrigerator to store all the food, too, so he requisitioned one and put it in his new boss's office, helping to get in his good graces. About the only thing they lacked for a time was electricity, but Freddy convinced the MPs to loan him an unused weapons carrier, and he brought back a generator to rig up lights and a movie projector to pass the time.

There was still more training in Bari. But their main OSS instructor there, a tall, wily young lieutenant named Dyno Lowenstein, was not like their other instructors. Dyno was a German Jewish war refugee himself, for one; his father was a prominent Social Democrat in Berlin in the early 1930s who was chased out of the country by the Nazis when Dyno was a boy. Freddy could tell that Dyno knew intelligence matters — and that he knew the Nazis; he liked him right away. Dyno's philosophy was that a man who was about to risk his life parachuting behind enemy lines should have some say in what the mission looked like. That attitude played well with his new crew; Dyno sensed that Freddy, in particular, thought that his past instructors were, to put it bluntly, "a bunch of idiots."

Not long after their arrival in Bari, Dyno, often leading instructions with a cigarette drooping from his lips, asked Freddy what kind of mission he thought he could pull off. Freddy had already given the question some thought. He was undeterred by Colonel Chapin's rejection of his proposal to return to his home turf in Germany's Black Forest. So he came up with an even more audacious idea for Dyno: parachuting down into a different part of Germany, 250 miles to the east, at a place that had become notorious: a place called Dachau. Freddy and his team would bring a cache of weapons into the Nazi concentration camp, he told Dyno, then arm the Jewish prisoners and overtake the guards before they could be marched to the gas chambers. Freddy was "going to start a revolution that way," he declared with no lack of aplomb.

Just a few months earlier top officials at the War Department in Washington had considered, but quietly rejected, the idea of bombing the rail lines to Auschwitz in Poland in an effort to prevent more mass killings there. One member of Roosevelt's War Refugee Board had even raised the far riskier idea of dropping guns into the camps or parachuting commando teams inside. The proposals went nowhere. The raids were unlikely to work, military officials reasoned, and even if they did, the Nazis would simply build new camps.

Freddy knew nothing of these secret internal discussions as he sat with Dyno in an upstairs room in the villa and talked about potential missions. All he knew, based on a smattering of media reports in *Stars and Stripes* and on the BBC, was that the Nazis were killing Jews in horrific numbers at Dachau, and that America needed to do something to stop it. Why shouldn't he do what he could?

Dyno didn't know quite what to say when Freddy finished pitching his plan. He thought the proposal was nonsense, a senseless sacrifice. "Look," he said, "this has no chance of succeeding anywhere." He gestured outside at the ground below them. "Why don't you jump out the window now? It would be cheaper and more practical." Dyno loved Freddy's gumption, and his desire for vengeance against the Nazis was certainly apparent, but he knew he would need to rein him in.

Some of the other men at OSS thought Freddy was just a glory hunter, a man looking for a "spectacular" mission that could earn him some medals. Dyno didn't think so. The man's motives seemed righteous, he believed; his shortcoming, or maybe his strength, was that he didn't know any limits. He thought he could do anything, and he was always willing to try. There was nothing nuanced about Freddy, no shades of gray when it came to the war against the Germans. "Honest guys versus crooks is about the way Fred looks at civilization," as another OSS supervisor put it.

The wait for an assignment dragged on; only the Italian villa where they now bunked had changed. The frustration bubbled over in a letter that Hans wrote from Italy to his girlfriend Elly's parents in the Bronx. With all the starts and stops they had endured without yet seeing any action, Hans wrote, "it seems to me we are not nearly as vital to this war as we might be inclined to believe."

Hans had so much downtime on his hands that he decided to go to France anyway in November '44 — not on a mission with French resisters, but on leave. He hitched a ride with an OSS flight crew and went to Normandy to see his twin brother, Luke, stationed there with the army. The Allies were firmly in control of the coastal region by now, and Hans and Luke had time to relax for a few days together and catch up on army life after nearly two years apart. Hans met Luke's girlfriend — his twin had a French girlfriend! — and he got to explore some of the countryside, with a full-length winter coat keeping him warm in the winter chill. The atmosphere among the American troops seemed practically buoyant.

But there was one bleak topic that hung over Hans and Luke, almost unspoken. Neither one of them had heard anything more from the Netherlands about their parents and Robbie. Gently,

Luke mentioned them to Hans, and he waited. There was only silence. Had Hans even heard him? Yes, he had heard. There was just nothing to say. Their family members' fate was unknowable, and talking about the void offered Hans no promise of filling it. So he didn't.

By the time he returned to Italy, OSS had another assignment in mind for him and Freddy. Dyno had been trying to bring Freddy around to a more realistic target than Dachau. The agency's focus at the moment was "mostly Austria," he explained. As American troops advanced, the military was in particularly desperate need of intelligence about the Nazis' "Alpine fortress"; about their battle-hardened troops in the Tyrol region under Marshal Kesselring; and about their operations through the Brenner Pass dividing southern Austria and northern Italy for some sixty miles. The Brenner line had been a critical passageway through the Alps since Roman times, and it now provided the Nazis with a lifeline for transporting weapons and troops. US fighter planes had been bombing the train tracks and rail yards along the pass relentlessly, but somehow the Nazis always seemed able to get the rails up and running again quickly after a raid. The Americans couldn't figure out how they managed it. They needed help.

The more he heard, the more Freddy warmed up to the idea of a mission into the Austrian Tyrol. It wasn't Germany, but it seemed about as close as he could get: barely twenty-five miles to the south of the border in Bavaria. He would be the team leader, Dyno said, and he would have free rein on the ground to get the intelligence the Americans needed any way that he could. He would need to devise a cover story, perhaps several, and he would need a radio operator with him to pass information back to the base in Italy; Hans was the obvious choice for the job. "Completely loyal and devoted to Fred," an OSS officer wrote of Hans in one operational plan that February.

But there was a critical piece still missing. Neither Freddy nor Hans had ever been to Austria, and they would be parachuting in "blind"; in OSS terms, that meant there would be no anti-Nazi resisters on the ground to map out covert plans with them ahead of time, meet them at the landing spot, or find "safe houses" where they could hide out. In southern France, the site of their scuttled jump, the resisters in the towns vastly outnumbered those who backed Hitler, according to OSS's intelligence on the ground; a virtual greeting party of Maquis fighters was supposed to be there when they landed. In the Austrian Alps, however, Dyno expected no such reception: the Tyrol region was considered fervently pro-Nazi — 90 percent, by OSS's estimate — and it was controlled with violent zeal by Franz Hofer, a Hitler acolyte who was the Gauleiter, the Nazi Party leader, in the Austrian city of Innsbruck. If anyone at all was there on the ground to greet them, it would most likely be Gestapo men with rifles drawn and execution orders set on the spot.

Against those formidable odds, Dyno and Freddy realized that they needed to bring someone onto the team who already knew the area — both the treacherous mountain terrain and the people themselves. As improbable as it sounded, they needed a tour guide through Hitler's heartland. Dyno talked with American and British officials at Nazi POW barracks in Italy to scout possible candidates — prisoners who seemed disloyal to Hitler and might be willing to cooperate with the enemy. "DVs," he called them: deserter volunteers. American military policy, not to mention the Hague Convention of 1907 on the treatment of prisoners of war, frowned on the practice of using POWs as conscripted sol-

diers. But Dyno interpreted OSS's mandate from General Eisenhower quite broadly: practically anything short of flagrant war
crimes, he figured, was allowed.

For months the task of finding Nazi defectors for OSS's mission in Bari had fallen mainly to Dyno; his bosses thought that
a "hyphenated American" like him — a European-born American who spoke perfect German — was the ideal recruiter. Dyno
would drive to POW camps up and down Italy to look for Nazi
deserters he might be able to convert into OSS agents, talking first to the American jailers about their prisoners and then
to prisoners themselves to suss out candidates. Some deserters
seemed eager to work with the Americans — sometimes too eager
— in hopes of getting out of prison, and maybe even make some
money in return for their cooperation. Dyno interrogated them
about what they did during the war, why they deserted, and how
they felt about the Nazis, and sometimes, just to test their reac-
tion, he let them know in dramatic fashion that he himself was
a German Jewish refugee. "You know what you guys did to my
race?" he would ask angrily. If the prisoner revealed any defiance
at the remark, or displeasure at sitting across from a Jew, Dyno
quickly dropped him.

Dyno thought that Freddy might prove a helpful scout. "What
do you think," he asked, "if we both went out to find the third
man?" "The third man": just a few years later it would become the
name of a classic postwar film, also set, coincidentally, in Austria.
But for now, it was simply their most glaring need for the mission
ahead: someone who could plow the Alpine ground for them.

Thus had Freddy become a "prisoner" at POW Camp 209 in Naples. Part of Dyno's thinking in planting him inside the barracks

in Nazi garb was to determine, first of all, if Freddy's German was good enough for him to pose as a Nazi in Austria, six years after he had immigrated to America and stopped speaking the language on principle. There were bound to be Nazi expressions he had never heard on the streets of Freiburg, and being surrounded by German prisoners for a few days would help prepare him.

Freddy figured that his test run in the Nazi lockup could also help solve the bigger problem: finding their elusive third man. Indeed, by the time he left Camp 209 in Naples, Freddy was convinced he had found their Austrian expert in Franz Weber. Not only did the Nazi prisoner's disdain for Hitler seem sincere, but he came from a small town only about ten miles outside the Tyrolean capital of Innsbruck. After hearing Freddy recap his clandestine conversations with the prisoner, Dyno quickly arranged another meeting with Franz, pulling him out of his barracks to make him a proposition. Freddy came, too, but dressed in an American uniform this time. He kept a low profile, and in such a starkly different setting, Franz didn't seem to recognize the man now sitting with him as the same one who had been his fellow Nazi prisoner. Dyno, speaking in his native German, quizzed Franz about his background and why he had deserted, then cut quickly to the central question: was he willing to cooperate with the Americans and go back to Austria on an espionage mission?

Dyno didn't expect an answer right away. Think about it, he told Franz. This was an enormous decision for both sides. The Americans were taking a leap of faith with the young Nazi prisoner sitting in front of them. What if it was all a con? Franz had certainly sounded the right notes when he talked of hating what the Nazis had done to his Austrian homeland. He was horrified, Franz said, by the grotesque things he saw in Poland as an offi-

cer candidate in early 1941: He remembered arriving at the railway station in Warsaw to the jarring sight of haggard, deathly thin
people with yellow, starred bands on their arms, just lying in the
street in a snowstorm. "Who are these people?" he asked another
Nazi soldier. "They are Jews," came the answer. He had never seen
a Jew before. "What will happen to them?" he asked. "They will
be taken to a collection camp."

He had watched as the Jews were herded inside the ten-foot-
high walls of the Warsaw Ghetto; only watching, he insisted,
never participating. "It was a terrible scene . . . It wasn't normal
anymore." Of course, that was what all the Nazis said once they
were captured, wasn't it? Dyno had seen the ploy before. They
had heard things, but they never took part in the atrocities themselves, they would insist. It could all be a ruse by Franz to save his
own skin, to get leniency from the Americans after doing whatever unspeakable things he might have done in Poland without
admitting to them. Or worse, the earnest young man sitting in
front of him could be a Nazi plant who had surrendered not to
help the Americans, but to infiltrate them.

Dyno had little but his gut instinct to guide him, but his gut
told him Franz was really on their side. He wanted desperately to
be right. The Austrian's knowledge of Innsbruck and the Alpine
region could determine the success of the mission. But if they
were wrong, if Franz was just talking his way back into a free plane
ride home or worse, Dyno realized how damaging the miscalcu-
lation would be for him, for OSS, and for the American military.

There had already been too many costly miscues out of OSS
in Italy, and Dyno and his boss at the base in Bari, Alfred Ulmer
Jr., a navy lieutenant, were under intense pressure to score some
intelligence wins. Just a few months earlier, OSS had dispatched

Ulmer to take over the German-Austrian commando operations run out of Bari. He was another in the string of Princeton men at the spy agency; a "typical, clean-cut American naval officer," as Freddy would describe him. Ulmer was not optimistic about his new assignment. On first inspection, he felt as though he had been brought in to run "a circus." He thought many of the missions were poorly conceived, many of the agents and crew were badly trained, and many of the Nazi defectors were untrustworthy characters looking to get on the winning side in the war. One team of commandos was supposed to parachute into southeastern Austria, but instead was dropped more than twenty miles off course in Yugoslavia by mistake. A former Nazi POW on a mission in the Balkan Peninsula had buried a stash of gold OSS had given him for the operation and returned home to his farm in what Ulmer called "a fiasco." Most devastating of all, the Nazis executed a dozen OSS agents who were captured after parachuting into German-occupied Slovakia east of Vienna. The brutal executions had practically wiped out OSS's presence in that region.

Despite the travails, Ulmer developed complete confidence in Freddy — "our most aggressive and ingenious" agent, he called him. He recognized his penchant for taking shortcuts and his disregard for rules, even on the base, like the time he stole an army jeep to get around town. ("We had no transportation whatsoever," Freddy explained unapologetically.) But those same qualities, Ulmer believed, would make him a deft spy behind enemy lines.

Ulmer became sold on Franz as the point man for the mission as well. The Austrian seemed committed and reliable, or at least as reliable as a Nazi defector could be. Still, he wanted to make sure that Hans, as the radio operator, was comfortable with the prospective "third man." OSS missions had been undermined before by a personality clash, and Ulmer and Dyno didn't want to risk seeing another mismatch in Tyrol. But once Hans met the defector, he too was impressed by his demeanor. "A good anti-Nazi," Hans called him. Franz came across as solemn, even repentant, and he spoke of his *Gewissen* — his conscience as a Catholic. It was an odd word to hear from an officer with the Third Reich. Hans never thought he would meet a Nazi, current or former, whom he actually liked, but he might have just found one.

Dyno went back to POW Camp 209 in January to size up Franz one final time. So, Dyno asked, was he in? Yes, the Austrian said; he was in. He didn't want to be seen as just a deserter, a man who turned and ran, he said. A Nazi victory would be a disaster for everyone, he believed, and if he was truly opposed to this war — and truly opposed to the Nazis — then he reasoned that as a devout Catholic, he should actually do something to help end it. He did have some reservations, though. He was reluctant to pick up arms against his onetime cohorts, even Nazis. But if his role was to be simply a guide and a point man, working logistics in the Alps for his partners, then he would do it, Franz said.

"Okay," Dyno said finally, "you go with us." With that, Franz left the prison unit for good and headed with the Americans for the long drive back to Bari. He was no longer Franz Weber; he was now officially "Frank Winston," Nazi defector and new OSS agent. They had found their third man.

The mission was on, and OSS set a date for late February — a month away, in the dead of the brutal Alpine winter. Ulmer and Dyno knew they needed to move quickly with the final planning. Warnings about Hitler's Alpine fortress were growing more dire through the winter; "the Nazi redoubt was going to happen," Ulmer believed, "and we had to have some very crafty sleepers in there." While Allied forces were gaining ground throughout Europe, the Nazis had proven surprisingly resilient in staving off defeat. Just weeks before, Hitler had personally ordered a desperate but deadly blitzkrieg in the Battle of the Bulge, claiming more than eighty thousand American casualties. It was clear that the war was not over yet. The Nazis would fight on.

Back at the base in Bari, the newly formed spy team — Freddy, Hans, and Franz — was sequestered in private quarters away from other personnel to keep the details of their assignment secret. They would not know about any other OSS operations being planned at the base, and no one except the top officers would know about theirs. Freddy and Dyno questioned Franz for days about the Alpine area, and they briefed him on the information they hoped to get on the ground. They told him of reports that Hitler was preparing a violent last stand in the Alps, a fear they captured for him in a single word: *Festung,* or "fortress." Their most pressing priority was to identify a landing spot in the jagged mountain range — a flat ridge, maybe, or an iced-over lake where they could drop down outside the Nazi perimeter of powerful antiaircraft weapons. That would not be easy to find, especially with banks of snow thirty feet deep or more. OSS had asked an air force reconnaissance team to obtain aerial photos to help pinpoint a landing spot. But with a constant churn of storms affecting the region, the air force was dubious about being able to get them any photos, and the maps that OSS had for the area were badly outdated.

That left Franz as the only real eyes of the operation. He had grown up in a small farming town just ten miles from Innsbruck, with the Austrian Alps as his backyard, and he became an expert Alpine skier, learning every peak, ridge, and gulley of the Inn Valley. He "has expert local knowledge and contacts in 50 mile radius," Ulmer wrote optimistically in seeking approval for the plan, and the men "should be able to 'live off the land' for weeks at a time."

Yet as many times as Franz had crisscrossed the mountains, there was one thing he had never done: he had never once thought about jumping down onto them from an airplane. He had no experience in parachuting, and Dyno realized that he needed to have him trained quickly so he could get in some practice jumps before the real thing.

It looked like the mission might really be happening. Freddy and Hans memorized the secret code names they had developed for their communications on the ground; the capital city of Innsbruck became "Brooklyn," in honor of their adopted hometown. But the pair remained skeptical of ever needing them; they had been down this road together before, only to find themselves stranded on the runway en route to France.

Anxious about the thought of another scuttled mission, Freddy grew angry when he learned that OSS was scheduling a separate parachuting operation — weeks before theirs — on the opposite end of Austria, to the east; it was going to be carried out, in fact, by two of the same Jewish refugees-turned-agents who had accompanied him into the colonel's office at OSS headquarters to demand a transfer. "Why are you sending them out before us?" Freddy demanded of Ulmer. Freddy was the one who had led the revolt that day, and after all the waiting around he had done, he felt he had earned a spot at the front of the jump line. Ulmer assured him that there was no reason for alarm; Freddy's time was coming soon enough.

The men put together lists of all the equipment they would need: food rations for seven days, winter clothes, uniforms, counterfeit documents, compasses, maps, radio equipment, code-books, pistols, ammo, and more. They would need money, too — for bribing willing locals and paying for essentials — so OSS head-quarters approved fifteen hundred dollars in American money, ten thousand marks in Austrian currency, and sixty gold pieces. They packed the bulk of the supplies into giant metal drums that were to be dropped in parachutes from the sky just moments after the men themselves. Most of the equipment was standard stuff, but Freddy made sure to add one irregular item to his list: a package of condoms, just in case. Whatever it took for him to get information on the ground, he wanted to be ready.

Hans packed up his own rucksack to take with him. An OSS officer noticed him cramming a big, bulky book inside his bag. It didn't look like military issue, and the officer questioned him about it, since every extra pound of baggage mattered. Hans smiled and said, "That's my chemistry book," as if introducing a firstborn child. As the radio operator, Hans explained, he was expecting a lot of lulls between the transmissions that he would be relaying from Freddy to the base in Italy. "I'm going to have to lie low, so there will be a lot of time on my hands," he said.

As part of the subterfuge, meanwhile, Dyno and Ulmer directed Freddy and Hans to write batches of innocuous-sounding letters to their family members, dated weeks and months ahead of time; OSS, he said, would mail the letters home for them while they were gone. There was no way of knowing just how long the agents would be on the ground, and OSS didn't want to arouse any suspicions at home with a prolonged silence. So they wrote, and wrote, and wrote. When their hands got tired, Dyno helped them write. Freddy made sure to have Dyno send a birthday card to his father in a few months if he wasn't back by then. Hans still had no correspondence from his own parents, nor any word of their whereabouts, but he did have a devoted pen pal back in New York: he was now engaged to Elly, the same young lady he had taken to the Tavern on the Green on their first date, and he had plenty of letters he wanted to send her in his absence. "Tell Elly not to worry!" he instructed Ulmer.

But with the mission date quickly approaching, OSS still had not found time to schedule parachute training for Franz, and now there was simply no time left. Freddy, with his usual nonchalance, had spoken briefly with Franz about the basics of parachuting — just jump from the plane and pull the strap — but that was about as close as the mission's third man would get to formal training. It looked like Franz's first "practice" jump would come in the skies over Nazi-occupied Austria.

Ulmer still had an overarching question he needed to ask of the men as they gathered for final planning: Were they really prepared to go through with this? It wasn't a rhetorical question. The mission would take "superhuman courage," Ulmer believed, and he wanted to make sure that they knew what they were doing. The odds of success were depressingly slim: maybe one in a hundred. As pep talks went, this was not an inspiring one.

He reminded them that they couldn't expect much support on the ground. This wouldn't be like France. There weren't many Nazi opponents in Austria in the first place, "and damn few who would do anything about it," even if they did dislike the Nazis, he said. The area was swarming with Wehrmacht and SS troops, and it looked like "Tyrol would have to be fought and bled for." Once they were dropped, Ulmer warned, they would be on their own, with little help from the OSS base in Italy, and if they were captured, they shouldn't expect the Nazis to treat them as prisoners of war under international conventions. He told them the gruesome story of the dozen OSS agents summarily executed just weeks before by the Nazis in Slovakia.

"You fellows are Jewish," Ulmer said to Freddy and Hans. "You know what's going to happen to you?" Freddy stared back at Ulmer as if the very question offended him. The Nazis had chased him out of his boyhood home in Germany, seized his family business, crushed his father's spirit, and done God-knows-what to the Jews left behind in Freiburg. Hans's family in the Netherlands had been torn apart as well. Ulmer was a Waspy Ivy Leaguer from Florida — a nice enough fellow, but not a Jew, and not a European refugee, either — and here he was asking Freddy if he understood the stakes?

"This is our war," Freddy told him. "It's our war more than yours."

5

The Drop

AIRBORNE OVER THE ITALIAN-AUSTRIAN BORDER
February 25, 1945

The roar of the fighter plane's four engines pierced the cold night air high above the Austrian Alps. The B-24 Liberator, painted a sleek black to fade into the night sky, carried no American insignia on its tail, nor any other markings to identify its origin. Its human cargo — two Jewish refugees and a Nazi defector, oxygen masks cupped over their faces — huddled in a small hideaway in the back of the plane and waited.

Finally airborne, Freddy, Hans, and Franz were approaching their target — their designated "pinpoint" — in a rugged mountain region teeming with Nazi soldiers and stalwarts. Freddy was eager. Hans was calm. Franz was terrified.

In the pilot's chair up in the cockpit, walled off from the trio, Army Lieutenant John Billings didn't like what he saw beneath them. Through the dense cloud cover, his flight crew couldn't get a decent line of sight on the drop zone. Even in good weather, this would be a treacherous run, so treacherous that Britain's Royal Air Force, which flew many OSS missions, had refused to fly this one. "At this time of year, it would be extremely difficult to locate the area and make a successful blind drop," a British aviation officer, polite but firm, had cabled the agency weeks earlier.

Billings was willing to do it. A tall, redheaded New Englander, he had wanted to be a pilot from the time he was three years old, when his father paid for a ten-minute plane ride for the two of them over a rocky field outside Boston. Billings was now all of twenty-one, and his flight crew liked to say that he would give up eating before he would give up flying; the more challenging the assignment, the better. Billings had learned to pilot the B-24 just seven months earlier in South Carolina, but he had already flown dozens of missions across enemy skies in Europe — sometimes dropping five-hundred-pound bombs; sometimes food, weapons, or supplies; and sometimes secret agents for Bill Donovan's cloak-and-dagger brigade. Billings would describe himself, self-deprecatingly, as a glorified "taxi driver" on these missions; the OSS agents making the jumps, he said, were the ones doing the really hazardous work. He was just glad he got to stay inside the plane.

Billings didn't hesitate when he was asked to fly the Austrian mission. "If they're willing to jump, we'll take 'em," he told his crewmen. This mission was different from many of his earlier ones. For one thing, he had rarely dropped men inside Nazi-occupied Austria before; few Allied pilots ever had. For another, he had spent the last few days in the company of the motley crew of agents who were at that moment shivering in the back of his plane. That wasn't normal procedure. OSS demanded such intense secrecy for its missions that the crew in the cockpit was not supposed to even lay eyes on the agents who boarded the aircraft. Billings and his crew would ready the B-24 for takeoff, and only then would the agents climb into what was once the plane's gun turret — specially adapted to carry OSS agents instead of weapons. Billings only caught sight of the agents when they parachuted out hours later. OSS was so worried about security threats that Billings and the men in the cockpit knew the agents they flew only by the anonymous name of "Joe" — or, in the case of a lone female agent, "Jane."

But from the beginning, nothing had gone quite as planned on Freddy's mission. The air force hadn't gotten OSS the aerial photos of the Alps beforehand, Franz hadn't received his requisite parachute training, and bad weather had already forced the crew to scrap the mission twice. Five days earlier, Billings had flown Freddy's team on this same route; they got all the way to the drop zone, deep in Nazi territory, before Billings made the grudging decision to abort. The area was completely closed in by fog; crewman Walter Haass reported that Billings "could see nothing." In his own leather-bound flight log, Billings wrote later: "3 Joes . . . Bad weather." The crew turned the plane around and headed back to Italy. As close as they had gotten, the six hours in hazardous skies didn't even count toward the crew's military flight credits, since it hadn't actually been completed. The only solace Billings could take was that he had cruised hundreds of miles, flying dangerously low and near the mountain walls to evade German radar, without drawing any attention from the Luftwaffe's notorious antiaircraft fire.

More than two hours later, Billings and his crew landed right back where they had started: at a new Allied air base in the coastal city of Rosignano in Italy's Tuscany region. The Allies had set up the base only recently as their forces surged north toward Austria and Germany, hurriedly laying down six-inch-thick strips of asphalt for runways. Freddy was dejected to find himself back at the base; six hours in the air, hunched so tightly in his small cocoon in the back of the plane that his legs ached, and all for nothing. He trudged off the plane with Hans and Franz in tow, then disappeared behind the back wing, heading for a military vehicle waiting to take them to their quarters for the night. From the cockpit, Billings peered out the window to get a look at the mystery Joes, but they were nothing but shadows in the dark.

Billings and his flight crew gathered for breakfast the next morning under a tent that served as a temporary mess hall. The three Joes appeared as well, and now, in the light of day, they had faces. One was tall and skinny. Another had a prim, serious Germanic look. The third man, who acted like the leader, was short and squat and smiled a lot. They sat by themselves at a rickety picnic table and conversed in German, chowing on the day's serving of mystery meats, powdered milk, and an egg concoction drizzled in something called "jungle butter," which never seemed to melt.

Billings glanced over at them, unsure what to do. One of his crewmen, who spoke German, decided to approach the trio to introduce himself. It might be a violation of normal protocol, but the latest weather forecast indicated they had nothing but time on their hands. They were stuck together for a while. His curiosity getting the better of him, Billings soon wandered over as well. He wanted to see for himself what sort of men these agents were. Freddy introduced himself. "Joe," he said with a mischievous laugh.

The first thing Billings noticed was their clothing. The tall one and the short one were each wearing olive-drab American aviator uniforms. The serious-looking one had on a heavy trench coat; it was unbuttoned, and Billings could see a Nazi officer's garb peeking out from underneath. "He's the German," Freddy said, pointing at Franz. "He'll lead us to safety."

Freddy explained the thinking to Billings with a jarring nonchalance: they planned to ski down the Alps once they landed, but if Nazi soldiers spotted them and confronted them, their cover story would be for Franz, the Nazi, to say that he had captured two crashed enemy aviators. Franz was dressed as an Alpine ski patrol captain, and assuming he outranked any Nazi soldiers they met up with, he would insist on taking his prisoners to the Gestapo himself to earn the credit for their capture. And if he didn't outrank the soldiers? Well, Freddy would worry about that scenario later.

The American uniforms were the brainchild of the OSS planners in Bari; they believed that if Freddy and Hans were captured, the Nazis might treat them somewhat humanely as "regular" soldiers and POWs under international treaties, rather than executing them on the spot as spies. So the thinking went. OSS didn't want them carrying forged German papers for that same reason. Pure foolishness, and naive, Freddy and Hans thought; Americans caught with gold, radios, and code books, but they were just regular soldiers, not spies? They didn't like the idea, but they had little choice but to go along with it, American uniforms and all.

As for the actual purpose of the mission, Freddy was cryptic. A shrug of his shoulders told Billings that he wasn't willing to get into the details. Top secret; operational security and all that. Billings gathered that it had something to do with ferreting out intelligence about the Nazi train lines. FDR had just met with Churchill and Stalin a few weeks earlier at Yalta, with victory in sight, and the Alpine operation was designed as a critical part of that last push. Freddy talked big, but how exactly he planned to gather all this secret information on the Nazis in their Tyrolean stronghold, he didn't say. It all sounded implausible and almost suicidal to Billings as he listened, but Freddy was stoic. "We'll go down the mountain and handle whatever comes up," he said with another shrug.

Freddy reached into his pocket. "See this?" he asked Billings. He pulled out a tiny camera — a black 16 mm Minolta about the size of his index finger. Billings had never seen a camera so small. Freddy explained that he might need it to secretly photograph documents. He reached into another pocket, this time producing a loaded .32-caliber pistol. "This is just a 'scare' pistol," he said. "If I have to use it," he added with a sly grin, "I'm finished." He also showed Billings how OSS had taught him to pick locks. The pilot and his flight crew were now soaking up the wily agent's every word, waiting to see what he would do next. Joe, or whatever his real name was, seemed less a soldier to them than a magician.

Freddy, in his aviator's uniform, then got to talking about flying and his own experiences as a pilot. He told Billings how he had trained to fly airplanes as a teenager in Germany before the war; how the Nazis had sent him to Spain to help Franco in the civil war; how he was piloting a German plane there when he was shot down over the North Sea. A fisherman pulled him out of the water, he said, and he went to the Allies' side. That was how he wound up fighting the Nazis for OSS.

Billings listened to the tale, fascinated; the smiling German-American soldier seemed able to do just about anything. Almost none of the story was true, of course. As a teenager in Germany, Freddy had taken a glider lesson — once — but that was the limit of his experience as a pilot. Billings and his flight crew, experts in aviation, were buying it all. Another disguise, another facade for Freddy. If he was going to ultimately fool the Nazis, he figured he would try his disguises out on his fellow Americans first to see which ones worked.

After their aborted mission the night before, Freddy was anxious to get back in the air, but the storms weren't letting up. He thought they might be able to use the delay to their advantage. If nothing else, it might buy them time to obtain the aerial photos that could help them determine a suitable drop point. He and Hans sent a short cable back to the OSS base in Bari. "Last night's flight unsuccessful [on] account of weather," Freddy wrote. "Have pictures arrived?" True to form, he ended the military dispatch with an unlikely sign-off: "Love Freddy."

As it turned out, an American P-38 surveillance plane had managed to get the aerial photos the day before, and the air force phoned Bari to let them know — but by then Freddy's team was already in the air. "We got your pictures today, and we'll try to develop them tonight," an air force lieutenant reported to OSS. "Tell him it's too late," a supervisor yelled across the room; Freddy and his team were outside of radio contact, and Bari couldn't reach them. "No, don't," interjected another officer. If the operation was delayed for some reason, he said, "we might have the chance to get the pictures to the team tomorrow."

Ulmer and his people were elated to learn from Freddy's cable the next day that they were still in Allied territory in Italy. Ulmer convinced the air force to rush another plane to Tuscany, secreting the long-sought photos inside a mail bag. The aerial views were crisp and clear, providing a snapshot of the mountaintop barely a day old. As OSS feared, the pictures revealed few flat or navigable areas amid the rugged terrain that could be considered for a landing spot. But Ulmer and his people had circled for Freddy, in red crayon, a pair of small frozen lakes sitting side by side at an altitude of about eleven thousand feet. It was a tiny target, but it gave Freddy more to work with than he had the day before.

As the storms let up the next night, the Joes got off the ground and managed to fly into Austria almost as far as the drop zone once again, but there was virtually no break in the cloud cover. Restless, Freddy relayed word from the intercom at the back of the plane that he wanted to make the drop anyway. Billings overruled him. They were turning around. Again. "Bad weather," Billings wrote for a second time in his flight log, right below the first entry.

Freddy felt cursed. He could tick off all his military travels like postcards from a stale road trip that had dragged on far too long. From the peanut fields of Alabama to the unforgiving desert of Arizona. From a posh country club in suburban Washington, DC, to the tip of northern Africa and on to a villa in southern Italy. And now he was stuck again for four more days at another military base in Italy. For what? The ultimate payoff was still taunting him, still out of his grasp. The air base at Rosignano was certainly a nice enough place — another picturesque setting, in the heart of Tuscany's wine country, just twenty-five miles down the coast from the famed Leaning Tower of Pisa — and there were plenty of comfortable beds for them at the villas converted into military quarters. They got to sleep late, too. But the place lost even its small bit of luster after their second night stranded there. Their hosts at the base from Company D grew tired of their unexpected visitors after an ugly spat — something about untidiness, but no one seemed sure — and they kicked them out of their villa. Freddy and the whole crew had to camp in tents for the next two nights.

While they waited in Rosignano for a break in the weather, Billings's crew decided to take the plane out to run some tests on the instrument panel. Billings invited Freddy and Hans to go along with them for the ride — in the cockpit this time. It was an upgrade, if only temporary. Freddy jumped into the copilot's seat next to Billings, while Hans took the bombardier's spot ahead of them in the nose of the plane. They began cruising around the bay, and a few minutes into the flight, Billings remembered Freddy's own supposed training as a pilot. "Do you want to fly a little bit?" he asked his passenger. "Oh, yeah!" a surprised Freddy said.

Freddy grabbed the control-wheel yoke in front of him before Billings could change his mind. He showed no hint of nervousness. He had always been someone who lived for the moment, but his moments lately had been filled mainly with frustration. Now he was at the helm of a B-24, the biggest bomber plane in America's fleet. This wasn't exactly the way he imagined the scene playing out when he was a boy in Freiburg, when he would march through the house in his father's military belt, turning Heinrich's Iron Cross over in his hands and dreaming of someday becoming a German pilot. Even so, the adrenaline coursed through him to the rhythm of the Liberator's four propellers, as he steered the aircraft across the bay off the Ligurian Sea.

Freddy was just a hundred feet in the air, practically skimming the water below him. The plane's belly buzzed the roof of the villa that served as base headquarters for the 885th Air Squadron, rattling the officers inside. Then he sped straight for a small gap in the mountainside nearby. Billings thought for a moment that he might have to intercede and reclaim control of the plane as it neared the mountains. But just as they approached the ridge, Freddy yanked the yoke back hard toward his chest and began an abrupt, ninety-degree turn straight up the side of the mountain. Then, almost at a stall, he rolled the plane upside down and reversed course in the exact opposite direction, toward the base. Billings stared at his young copilot in disbelief; Freddy had executed a perfect "Immelmann Turn," an aerial acrobatic feat named for a German flying ace in World War I. And he didn't seem to even realize what he had done. He relied on pure instinct. *This kid really is quite a pilot,* Billings thought to himself.

To Freddy, the whole business of flying a thirty-six-thousand-pound fighter came with beguiling ease. He already figured that he knew everything there was to know about engines, and he remembered enough about aeronautics from what the Germans had taught him in that gliding class in high school years ago. What other training did he need? If anything, the bulky B-24 was a little slow for his liking; he wished he could crank the engines a little harder as he skimmed along the Italian coast.

"Okay, that's enough. Thanks," Freddy said, yielding control back to Billings to land the aircraft. He'd had his moment in Tuscany, and he was done for now. On an otherwise hapless trip, the impromptu joyride left Freddy and Hans almost giddy. The two

OSS men "had [a] good time" on the flight, Haass noted in his report. The base officers weren't nearly so pleased. Back on the ground, Billings was summoned to headquarters to explain to the colonel why his B-24 had buzzed their building so closely. An apologetic Billings took the heat for the episode himself, covering for his onetime copilot.

The next night, the men prepared for yet another run. The weather was still ominous, but it looked like there might be a break in the storm clouds over the Alps just before midnight. "We're going to do it tonight, one place or another," Freddy said to Billings. It was less a prediction than a demand; Freddy was acting as if he were in charge — not only of the mission, but of the airplane as well. Billings brushed aside the bravado; in a few short days, he had already learned that "Joe" was nothing if not confident.

They took off at ten o'clock that night, hoping the third time might actually be the charm that had eluded them. Once again, they hit storm clouds above their target. There was no way they could make the drop. Billings was now growing almost as frustrated as Freddy. He decided to try a second target about three thousand feet lower within the valley, below the rim of the mountains. Just as the plane dipped below the ridgeline, it jerked downward without warning and began screaming straight toward the canyon floor nearly ten thousand feet below them.

They were in free fall. Billings stared at the control panels but saw no sign of engine trouble, and no sign of Nazi flak hitting the plane, either. He quickly realized they were caught headlong in a ferocious windstorm that was particular to big mountain ranges, especially here in the Alps. He had heard about the notorious storms, called *foehns*, but had never actually been trapped in one. The warm winds were now crashing over the back side of the mountain and down on top of the B-24 at speeds measuring two hundred miles an hour. The aircraft was plummeting nose first toward the ground. One thousand feet down in just a few seconds, then two thousand feet. Billings cranked the turbo control power, but it was no match for the monstrous winds.

Now three thousand feet down; four thousand feet. The needle for the horsepower was tilting clear off the instrument panel, with the plane now generating even more thrust than Billings had needed at takeoff, and the engine was revving at an alarming twenty-seven hundred revolutions a minute. Yet still they were going down, and Billings was helpless to stop it. Five thousand feet down, then six thousand feet. Slammed downward by the overhead winds, they were now dropping even faster than a plane in an all-out nose dive: well over a mile in just eighteen seconds. Billings braced for the crash. His men were silent. In the back of the plane, the three Joes sucked oxygen from their masks and gripped the thin ledges of their seats. With no windows to reveal what was going on, Freddy peered outside through a tiny open flap in the back of the fuselage at the huge plumes of black exhaust and flames shooting into the sky. He couldn't see what was happening in the cockpit, but he didn't have to be a legitimate pilot to know that they were in trouble.

Then, almost as suddenly as the *foehn* winds started, they stopped. Billings and his crew had only a few moments to regain control of the plane. They struggled to slow their descent and level off the plane, then snaked their way slowly upward foot by foot, making one wide turn at a time, dangerously close between the canyon's narrow walls. "Turn, turn!" his navigator yelled, so close to one wall that they could almost count the pine-branch needles jutting out of the snow.

The agonizing climb, thousands of feet back up the canyon, took a full twenty-two minutes. As the aircraft lifted its nose over the rim of the mountain and toward the night sky, Billings could finally manage a deep breath. Out of danger for the moment, he thought about heading back to the air base in Rosignano yet again. No one would have blamed him. It was now after midnight. The white-knuckled dive down into the valley had sapped his crew's energy. Still, Billings knew how badly the lead Joe in the back of his plane wanted to make the drop. After all their starts and stops, Billings himself was invested in making it happen tonight, too. The plane had plenty of fuel left, and he wasn't returning again with his cargo if he could find another way.

Billings told his crew he wanted to make another pass. They headed back to their original target from days before: those iced-over lakes, ten thousand feet high, now looming in the distance. He veered down toward an opening in another mountain range; it was so narrow that the crew kept on the wing position lights for fear of scraping the mountain walls. They made it through unscathed, but another mountain ridge awaited them on the other side, blocking Billings from getting low enough to drop his passengers. They couldn't see the lakes that had been so prominent, circled in red, in the photos that OSS had rushed to them. It was as if they had disappeared. Billings wasn't giving up yet. Almost immediately, he and his crewmen spotted what looked like a clear, flat area several miles to the south. Like an eagle reversing course to swoop down on a fish, the B-24 pivoted toward its latest target. Three thousand feet below them was what looked like a glacier ledge about a mile or so wide, frozen but flat. They had a good look at it, with a clear pathway down. The bombardier relayed word to the Joes: *Prepare to drop.*

Cruising now at a low speed of about 110 miles an hour, Billings dipped down toward their new pinpoint target. This figured to be their last best hope. He had to decide how close the plane would get to the glacier before he dropped the men. Billings remembered Freddy's spirited protests back at the base over that very question. Safety regimens demanded a height of no lower than 600 feet, but Freddy, always negotiating for an edge, pushed Billings to drop him just 150 feet above their target; that would give any Nazi snipers in the area less time to shoot at them, Freddy argued. Billings demurred; a drop that low risked crashing a plane that heavy, and their parachutes wouldn't even deploy all the way in such a short range, he pointed out. Billings wasn't used to negotiating this way with his Joes — typically he had no contact with them whatsoever — but this time he compromised. "I'll give you three hundred feet, but no less," he told Freddy finally, hoping to shut him up.

Billings now zeroed in on the glacier poking out from the mountain, about ninety-five hundred feet aboveground. In the back of the plane, the Joes readied themselves, while Haass — who had escaped Nazi Germany himself as a boy — stood behind them to serve as jump master and time the choreography. The Joes took off their oxygen masks and removed the plywood board over the Joe hole on the floor, the only thing separating them from the sky below.

The opening was the size of a large manhole; a huskier man might have to wiggle his way through it, but the three of them would have no difficulty. They lined up in position — Freddy first, then Franz, then Hans. They needed to jump in quick succession; a delay of even a second or two could mean missing the ledge of the glacier and drifting thousands of feet farther down into unknown terrain. Back at training at Bari weeks before, Dyno Lowenstein had warned them of the risks. "The slightest hesitation when you jump, it counts for a few miles," he said. It wasn't just the timing of the men that mattered; their supplies needed to reach them on the ground, too. In rapid sequence, the flight crew would have to release the cargo-filled drums and hit their mark closely enough for the men to find them all on the ground.

Freddy sat down on the edge of the Joe hole, his legs dangling, like a kid on a swing set. He could still remember the pain in his father's face that day aboard the SS *Manhattan* seven years earlier, as they were fleeing Germany, when they learned that Hitler had taken over Austria. Now here he was, dropping into that very place to try to help free the country from the Nazis. Freddy double-checked the straps on his back; they held a single parachute that, unlike those of other paratrooper units, had no emergency backup if something went wrong. The parachute was tethered to the plane so it would rip away automatically once he began his descent. Strapped to his legs was a heavy bag with essential supplies the team would need immediately after they landed — including water and food rations for three days, flashlights, compasses, maps, a radio transmitter, and a specially designed fountain pen with a tiny piece of film hidden inside containing OSS's secret radio codes. The leg bag was supposed to hold just the essentials — but Hans had slipped in another chemistry book before they left the base. Freddy objected. A chemistry book? Just needless extra weight, he'd said. But to Hans, that qualified as essential, and Freddy wanted to keep his partner happy. So the book stayed.

"Here we go!" Freddy said, perched on the edge of the Joe

hole. He smiled. This was the moment. Finally, finally. He was two hundred miles inside Nazi territory, two hundred miles from the nearest Allied troops in Italy. The danger of the moment enthralled him; there were no last-minute nerves, no hesitation.

Freddy had made it all sound so easy when he was trying to ease Franz's jitters over his first-ever parachute attempt: *Just jump down and hang on to your harness,* he told the Nazi defector now waiting behind him at the Joe hole. Freddy had done it himself a million times, he assured him. But for all of his talk and self-assurance, Freddy left out one thing: he had never actually jumped out of an airplane before, at least not one that was moving. Sure, he had done practice jumps at the Maryland country club, but those were from a mock plane sitting safely on the ground on what used to be the putting green, as he strapped into a harness — with no parachute — and tumbled into a landing pit just a few feet below. And he had done practice jumps at North Carolina from a high tower — with a parachute that time. But jumping off an actual plane flying more than 110 miles an hour? In the dead of night, over Nazi skies, onto the biggest mountain range in all of Europe? No, never. Not once. But Franz didn't need to know that part; Freddy just needed his Nazi tour guide to stay calm and make it to the ground.

The cockpit relayed the final signal to Haass in the bomb bay. "Ready, ready, ready, go!" he yelled. Freddy thrust himself through the Joe hole and dropped down effortlessly. His parachute unfurled on cue moments later, and the rope line attaching him to the aircraft broke away neatly, leaving him alone and untethered in the Alpine sky. He was free.

He had no interest in solemn reflection or prayers about what might await him on enemy ground below. Freddy was not the praying type. He simply floated. All he could think about as he drifted down was how beautiful the night sky looked from his vantage point, with the moonlight cascading off the ice-capped mountain ranges all around him. The night was still and quiet save for the rumbling of the Liberator, which was now growing quieter in the distance.

With no hint of Nazi flak fire, it all felt so peaceful. After being hunched for hours once again in the back of the plane, with the heavy supply bag pinching off his circulation, it felt good just to stretch his aching legs. Time seemed to stand still for those eternal few seconds of weightlessness — until the moment that his army boots met the cold, hard embrace of the glacier. He rolled onto the ice and snow to brace his fall. He had made it. As cold as the snow felt, it was warmer than the freezing holding area in the back of the plane.

As soon as Freddy had dropped, it was Franz's turn, but he wasn't nearly as eager. Haass, the jump master, gave him the signal, but Franz wasn't moving. "Go, go, go!" Haass shouted. The mission's third man seemed frozen. One second passed, then two, then three. Hans, standing behind him and waiting for his turn, was getting anxious now. They had to stay in sequence. He gave Franz a gentle shove from behind, and the Nazi defector, willing or not, disappeared into the night sky to return to his homeland.

Hans stepped up quickly to the empty hole himself, not bothering to sit down. He wanted to make the jump standing up. He was eager to reunite with Freddy on the ground, eager to finally start their mission, even if this wasn't the mission he had envisioned. He wasn't parachuting back into his homeland in the Netherlands as the intrepid son, as he'd once imagined. No, this wasn't the place that the military claimed, all those months ago in Texas, that they would send him to help liberate — an empty inducement, he was now convinced. This wasn't where his family had gone missing. His Nazi-occupied homeland in the Netherlands, if his parents and Robbie were even still there, was more than five hundred miles north of here through the heart of Hitler's Reich. That trip might come another day, he hoped. For now, he was dropping down from the skies of Austria, one of the last major battlegrounds of the war, and the chance to fight the Nazis here for his adopted country instead felt like a noble substitute.

Hans stood tall as Haass gave him the "go" signal, as tall as he could without hitting his head in the cramped quarters. He took a single step and dropped his long, skinny frame through the Joe hole with plenty of room to spare, following Freddy down into the Alpine Mountains.

With the last of their human cargo now unloaded, Billings circled above the glacier and waited, while his crew searched for any signal of life on the ground — from the Joes, they hoped, not from the Nazis. The minutes passed slowly. Then from the ground came a beam through the darkness, faint but unmistakable. It was a solid green light. Whoops broke out on the plane. That was it, the signal from Freddy for a safe landing. "Everything OK," it meant.

All the men on the ground needed now were the supplies. Billings circled back to the drop zone again and zeroed in on the green light. The flight crew untethered their cargo in sequence: first the large metal drums filled with reams of supplies, and then, with some difficulty, the long packages of skis meant to get the men down the mountain. In case OSS should ever again get the idea to drop its agents onto a mountaintop, a crewman noted in his after-action report that "skis are hard to get out — too long and unwieldy in plane."

Moments after the cargo was dumped, the parachutes deployed, floating down toward the green light. With their mission finally complete after all the starts and stops, Billings began his ascent. The green beam of light shone in the distance as the plane climbed higher, but a crewman noticed that it was now flashing. Another message, it seemed; different from the last one. Was there trouble on the ground? If there was a sequence to the flashing lights, a code of some sort, the crew couldn't make it out. They had no way to tell what it meant, if anything. The Liberator's work was done, in any case; there was nothing more they could do now. Godspeed to the Joes.

Billings and his crew headed south back to the base in Rosignano, nearly four hundred miles away. "We never dropped a team in worse country," Haass, the jump master, would marvel. Billings summed up the final leg of the trip even more succinctly. In his flight log, just below the two entries for their failed attempts, he wrote simply: "Success."

6

===

The Glacier

SULTZTALER GLACIER, AUSTRIA,
ELEVATION 10,500 FEET
February 26, 1945

The skis. Where were the damn skis?

The three Joes had been trudging in the dark, through snow that was waist-high in spots, for nearly four hours now, struggling to gather up the supplies the B-24 had rained down on them from all directions. It was almost six o'clock in the morning; Freddy could see the sun just beginning to peek over the ridge of the Alps to the east.

This had been pristine ground when they first tumbled down onto it just after two o'clock in the morning. There was no sign that the snow and ice had been disturbed by human activity in weeks, maybe longer; even the Nazi Alpine patrols hadn't ventured this far up in the mountains in the dead of winter. But as the three OSS men crisscrossed the mile-wide glacier for hours in search of their supplies, the untouched landscape soon became pockmarked with boot prints and trenches. Every few steps sank them deeper into what seemed like an unending sea of cold, white quicksand.

In the pitch-black night, Franz wasn't even certain where exactly they were on the mountain range: somewhere very high up, he knew, but he didn't have to be an Alpine ski master to know that. With all the changes in the drop site and his own last-minute jitters, Franz seemed to have lost his bearings on his own home turf. It didn't help when he realized that he had forgotten to pack his flashlight in the bag of essentials. At least Freddy and Hans had theirs.

They continued traipsing through the dark to look for any foreign objects in the snow. Billings's flight crew thought they had hit a bull's-eye when they dropped all the gear down by parachute. Word filtered back to OSS at Bari that the packages "dropped almost on top of Freddy's green ground signal." But that would be news to Freddy. With the Alpine winds whizzing through the valley, the cargo drop was more scattershot than bull's-eye. The men had found each other on the ground quickly enough, with Freddy's green light acting as a beacon, but finding their cargo, spread across the wide glacier, was proving to be a much more exhausting task.

Short of breath from the altitude, they barely spoke as they traversed the cold ground one slow, sunken step at a time. They eventually stumbled onto one of the metal canisters, then another, then a long, skinny package with two pairs of wooden skis and poles inside. They began unpacking and gathering up their supplies. But they realized they were still missing one package — containing two more pairs of skis. They needed all four pairs: one set for each of them to ski down the mountain, and the fourth for Franz to use as a sled to transport their supplies.

They kept looking. Still, nothing. They had looked everywhere. They were frustrated and freezing; all their winter gear, including giant white snow capes meant to camouflage them in the snow, could provide only so much warmth after they had been rummaging around on an Alpine glacier for four hours. They snacked on Spam for sustenance and tried to figure out what to do. Peering up at the daunting mountainside, Freddy surmised that the final package might have gotten caught in a gust of wind and sailed over the ridge entirely. The missing skis could be in Italy now, for all he knew.

Freddy faced a dilemma. It would be daylight in another hour, which would certainly make their search for the skis easier, if they were anywhere to be found on the glacier. But the light of day would also make it easier for any Nazi patrols across the valley, or mountain hunters, to spot them on the open glacier, even in their camouflaged capes. Freddy decided to cut their losses and keep moving down the mountain any way they could. They needed to find a temporary refuge; maybe they would stumble onto one of the Alpine ski huts that Franz had said were common on the mountain.

Together, they decided that Franz would use both pairs of skis, one for himself and one to carry the supplies, just as planned. That left Freddy and Hans to walk down the mountain in Franz's path. Or slide. Or belly-crawl. There were no skis for either of them. *Just as well,* Freddy thought. Back in Bari, Hans had told the officers at OSS about all the skiing he had done as a boy. Freddy suspected that Hans, hailing from the flatlands of the Netherlands, was bluffing — just to make sure he got himself a spot on the Alpine mission. It was a maneuver that Freddy himself might have tried if he hadn't skied as a boy in Germany. In truth, Hans had as much experience with skis as Franz did with a parachute. If they put the lanky Dutchman on skis for the first time in his life, who knew what might happen to him speeding down an Alpine cliff? He might be better off walking, Freddy thought.

In Italy, OSS had assigned their mission a secret, random code name: Greenup. But their supervisors christened it the "Gulliver mission," as in *Gulliver's Travels,* the eighteenth-century classic about an Everyman who jumps blithely from one dangerous and improbable predicament to another, squaring off against gentle giants and menacing miniatures. The name seemed apt, especially at moments like this, with the three men finding themselves on a remote Alpine mountain in Nazi Austria, looking haplessly for the equipment they needed to descend it. Jonathan Swift's satire skewered the senselessness of war, attributing conflicts between nations to "difference in opinions ... cost[ing] many millions of lives," yet Hitler considered *Gulliver* a personal favorite and kept it in his library.

Freddy and his small team of Gullivers began tying their bags of equipment to the tops of the skis designated for supplies. They couldn't fit everything, and had to decide which items would be left behind. In a crevice at the foot of the glacier, deep in the snow, they buried a heavy battery, one of their radio transmitters, and some of the extra food rations they had packed. They buried their parachutes and other packing supplies in a second spot. Freddy marked the area with an extra ski pole, hoping the men would be able to retrieve the items later.

Hans and Freddy used some of the leftover straps and packing material to cobble together makeshift snowshoes, rigging them over their boots. They set off down the mountain, with Franz on his skis and Freddy and Hans on foot, sloshing and sliding their way down the steep, jagged incline. The improvised shoes helped a bit, but every three or four steps, Hans's long legs would sink deep into the snow, and he would have to summon all his energy to extricate himself. All the obstacle courses and training exercises at OSS hadn't prepared him for this.

An hour later, the sun was up, and they realized they had barely crawled a few hundred yards. They could still see the glacier, not far behind them. Exhaustion was setting in. They trudged on. Another hour, another few hundred yards, and still no sign of shelter. Franz, skiing ahead, stayed close enough to keep them in sight and make sure they were still heading in the right direction, difficult as that was. Hans needed to rest more often. The thin air was making him woozy. "Go on without me," he told Freddy; he would catch up. Freddy slapped him in the face, hard enough to jolt him. He wasn't going to leave Hans there in the middle of a snowbank in the Alps. They needed to keep moving, keep their blood circulating; Hans would freeze to death just lying there. Hans knew better than to defy Freddy when he wanted something; he had followed his team leader this far, all the way to the Alps in the dead of winter on what seemed more and more like a fool's mission with every frigid step. Hans stood up and kept moving down the mountain.

For hours they slogged on, until night descended on them once again. Thirteen hours after they had left the glacier, Franz spotted something in the distance below them: a large building with an A-frame roof. He recognized it even in the darkness. It was the Amberger Hütte, a popular Alpine sporting hut frequented by Austrian skiers and outdoorsmen since the late 1800s. Franz knew the place well. He signaled to Freddy and Hans to keep going; they were almost there.

At ten o'clock that night, a full twenty hours after they had parachuted down from the B-24, the three American agents in their white snow capes finally made it to the hut. From the outside, the sturdy, two-story stone enclave appeared uninhabited. Franz approached the door hesitantly. German soldiers from Wehrmacht Alpine units — wearing uniforms just like his — were known to use winter huts like this one on their patrols. If he was confronted, Franz had worked out a cover story for why he was out in the middle of nowhere — with two American aviators in his custody. The story had seemed plausible enough in theory when they were back at the Italian villa with Dyno, hashing out ideas. Here in the harsh, real-world environs of the Austrian Alps, Franz wasn't anxious to find out whether the story — his "fairy tale," he called it — would work in practice.

Franz peered inside the hut and tried the door. Locked. Glancing around, he smashed a hole in a window, reached inside, and unlocked the door. The three walked in cautiously and searched the place to confirm they were the only guests. They saw no sign of any occupants, but what they did see convinced them that they had come across a nirvana in the land of the Nazis: a fireplace with neatly stacked wood beside it, a kitchen stocked with canned goods and foodstuffs, working bathrooms, more than a dozen beds, and even a closet filled with clean wool blankets and linens. They seemed to have finally caught a lucky break. Hans, in particular, was desperate for one. He and Freddy had covered some two and a half miles on foot since they had set off from the glacier that morning. It was an agonizingly slow pace, barely the length of a football field every hour, yet in his current state, Hans marveled that he had managed to make it that far.

What the three Joes craved more than anything was heat and sleep — and food; anything besides Spam. They threw some kindling wood in the fireplace and started a fire, stripped off their sopping-wet layers of clothing, and sat motionless in front of the flames, soaking in the warmth. They wouldn't worry about their next move yet. For now, they just needed to rest. Freddy rifled through the food in the pantry and opened a can of green tomatoes, gulping them down ravenously. They didn't have the energy for much conversation, but at one point Franz pondered aloud what might happen to him after the war — as an ex-Nazi and now an American spy. "When it's over," Hans assured him, "you will get the Legion of Merit award!" Assuming they survived, of course.

They slept so soundly that night, they weren't completely sure what day it was when they finally awoke. Tuesday, or maybe Wednesday. Hans knew that Bari would be expecting a radio transmission very soon. OSS in Italy would be monitoring their designated radio frequency round the clock for a coded message advising the agency on their status. If Bari didn't hear anything within four days, they had warned Freddy, they would have to consider the team lost, or dead. OSS didn't have the manpower to stay on the open line indefinitely. It was a depressing scenario. The whole purpose of their mission was for Freddy to send back Nazi intelligence in Tyrol, and if OSS stopped listening for their transmissions, they would become useless, risking their lives to relay secret intelligence into a black hole. For nothing.

Hans unpacked the various parts of his shortwave radio from the cache of supplies. The military billed the 44-pound transmitter-receiver, called the SSTR-1, as "light, compact, and durable," but none of those qualities was apparent to Hans at the moment, especially after their mountainside journey. He connected all the components, the heavy battery unit, and an antenna. Then he flipped the power switch and searched for a signal. There was nothing but static. He tried again. Still nothing.

Hans was in this frigid no-man's-land for one reason: to make radio contact with Italy. That was his main job — in some ways, his only job — and now he couldn't get through. Frustrated, he began taking the transmitter apart, finding what he thought might be a faulty electronic tube inside; perhaps it had been damaged during the drop to the glacier, he thought. He went to swap it out only to discover that the replacement parts that OSS's supply people in Italy had given him — the same people who had managed to get Freddy a working fridge — had packed the wrong type of tube in his backup supplies. He was stuck. Finally he managed to get a signal allowing him to send out a "blind" message to a generic frequency; he hoped that someone in the American military, somehow, would receive it. But the signal went unanswered. He would have to find another way to get the transmitter working, and soon.

Freddy was having his own problems. The canned tomatoes he had gorged on did not sit well with him, and he was spending much of his time running to the bathroom. One of the few things he couldn't find in the well-stocked cottage was medicine to ease nausea. He tried baking some bread with the ingredients at hand; it was easier on the stomach than the green tomatoes.

Franz studied their maps. Now that he had found a point of reference at the Amberger hut, he determined that they had landed at a glacier called the Sultztaler Ferner — about 10,500 feet above sea level in the eastern Alps. That meant they were still some forty miles from Freddy's ultimate target in the heart of Tyrol: the city of Innsbruck. But they were near a tiny farming town on the mountain called Gries, with a trail leading there. Franz had been to Gries before, and he knew the area well enough to get around — but not so well, he hoped, that anyone in town would recognize him. They would head there, Freddy decided, and then look for a way to complete their descent. They could worry later about how to get to Innsbruck. One snowy step at a time.

Hans tried again to fashion snowshoes for the next leg of their journey — this time utilizing pieces of metal and rubber from a doormat in their mountain refuge. The new shoes were an improvement over his first try. But what if a Nazi Alpine patrol should stop off at the camp after them? They didn't need the Nazis out looking for interlopers who had ransacked the place, smashing a window and pilfering the doormat. That would only arouse suspicion. So to cover the damage they had caused, and the food they had eaten, Franz left 250 marks — real marks, not the counterfeits they had brought — along with a note of apology. He hoped the gesture of civility would suffice.

A snowstorm slowed their departure by a night, but after three restful days at the hut, they set off for Gries, their supplies in tow. The trek took them only six hours this time, a relief after their last adventure getting down from the glacier. Entering the small mountain town, they braced themselves for their first encounter with actual Austrians, as they spotted a tiny café. They walked in and ordered some hot tea, anxious to see how their guise would go over with the locals. Franz was in his Wehrmacht officer's uniform, but Freddy and Hans had ditched their American aviator suits for civilian attire, covered by their giant snow capes; they never liked the idea of the American uniforms anyway. "Ja, Herr Oberleutnant," Hans answered crisply whenever Franz addressed him at the table. The woman who served them showed no hint of suspicion. A Nazi was a Nazi.

When Franz asked where he might find the village leader — the Ortsbauernführer — the woman directed him to a nearby farmhouse. Franz took a deep breath. The village leader would be a Nazi loyalist, he knew, and he knew, too, that if their true identities were discovered, he would be treated even more harshly than Freddy or Hans, as an ex-Nazi who had dared return to Austria as an American spy. Steeling himself, he knocked on the door. A husky, middle-aged man, the de facto mayor among the farmers of Gries, answered it. Franz introduced himself with his alias — *Leutnant Erich Schmitzer* — and showed him his Nazi *Soldbuch* identification with his name, his Alpine unit, and his photo. Once again, there was no sign of suspicion; the OSS counterfeiters in Bari had done a good job with his papers. Franz explained his predicament: He had become separated from his unit along with two Dutch collaborators under his command — he pointed over to Freddy and Hans, waiting silently behind him at a respectful distance — and they had broken their skis. They needed to get down the mountain as quickly as they could so that they could rejoin his unit. Could they borrow some extra skis, or perhaps a sled of some sort?

The Ortsbauernführer was more than happy to help. Franz was struck by just how friendly he was under the odd circumstances; he seemed willing to do anything he could to assist a fellow Nazi. He led Franz to a long toboggan that he owned; he used it for transporting farm supplies and workers, and it was usually drawn by a horse. But Leutnant Schmitzer was certainly free to take it; he only asked that he return it to a friend at the base of the mountain when they were done with it.

The Gulliver team had gotten lucky again. Franz thanked the farmer, and the three of them packed into the toboggan: Franz in the front, tasked with steering; Hans jammed in the middle; and Freddy in the back as a brakeman, using his wooden ski poles to slow them down as needed. Stuffed between them on their seats were their rucksacks filled with radio equipment, codebooks, gold, cash, and the rest of their supplies.

The huge sled, with animal horns for handles, looked to Freddy like it could be one of Santa's sleighs — but with two Jews and a Nazi defector delivering surprises through the snow. They pushed off down the icy, snow-covered outlines of a dirt path — slowly at first, then building up speed with each steep incline. Franz didn't hold back, flying around turns with abandon. He was in his natural element now. This was just another sledding trip down the Alps for him, like so many he had taken as a boy, but with a different mission. His two passengers, however, were increasingly unnerved. Hans gripped the sled, fearing he would fly off at any second. OSS hadn't trained him in tobogganing either. He tried to calculate their speed: sixty miles an hour at their frightful peak, he guessed; his slog from the glacier now seemed uneventful in comparison. And the bottom of the mountainside was still nowhere in sight.

Normally so unflappable, Freddy grew wide-eyed with alarm when he saw sparks flying from the tips of the ski poles due to friction. As brakes, he realized, the poles were practically useless. He would later recall the sleigh ride as the most hair-raising trip of his life.

More than three hours after they started, Franz and his white-knuckled passengers made it to the base of the mountain. And still in one piece, Hans thought with relief. As promised, they returned the sled in town to a friendly woman who offered them supper and a place to stay for the night. There, Freddy plotted their next move — on the fly, like most everything he did these days. They were still more than thirty miles from Franz's hometown, and they were now four days into their mission with no radio signal; Hans knew that OSS in Bari must be getting anxious.

There was a railway station nearby where they could get a train for the hour-long ride to Oberperfuss. Franz affixed to his face some large bandages — hoping to evade recognition as they moved closer to his hometown. That was the extent of his disguise. When they got to the train station, it was swarming with armed Nazi guards and transportation police. Too risky, Freddy decided. Franz's cover as Leutnant Schmitzer had served them well so far, but he didn't want to test their luck in a station teeming with Nazis. Franz remembered a smaller, less well-traveled station a few miles away. They walked there, and exchanged their reichsmarks for tickets at the ticket window.

Waiting for their train, Freddy heard a woman on the platform cursing the Americans for bombing her home and leaving her with no place to live. They would stay away from her. On board, they noticed a few passengers eyeing their snow capes. A Nazi security officer approached them and asked for their papers. Franz produced his *Soldbuch,* and the officer glanced at it before motioning to Franz's two companions, signaling for their papers. Freddy and Hans waited silently. Franz spoke for them; they didn't speak German, he told the officer. "These two are foreigners who work for us, and we are now en route to Salzburg to our unit," he said. They had lost their papers on the mountain in a ski mishap, he explained. "This can happen," the officer acknowledged, as he moved on down the carriage.

Barely ten minutes later, another officer — this one Gestapo — approached them, looking less amenable than the first. Freddy gripped the .38 pistol hidden inside his coat. It was the first time he had thought about using it since they landed. This was the "scare pistol" he had told Lieutenant Billings about when they were stranded at the air base in Italy. *If I have to use it,* he had said to Billings then, *I'm finished.*

The Gestapo officer asked to see their papers. Franz gestured to his traveling companions and explained that they had already produced them for another officer. "We've just been checked," he said. Hans struggled to maintain his composure. If the Gestapo officer pressed them, Hans thought to himself, the mission would be over before it had even started. He didn't want to think about what would happen to them at that point. But after regarding the three men for a moment, the Gestapo officer nodded at Franz and kept walking.

After making it undetected past two Nazi officers, the trio relaxed a bit as the train rumbled east toward Innsbruck. A few small children traveling with their parents were playing in the aisle nearby. Hans played with them for a few minutes, trying to look like he fit in. Austrian laborers on their way to work talked among themselves. Freddy watched as a group of schoolchildren boarded the train, schoolbooks in hand. One girl, who looked to be about thirteen or fourteen, stared in his direction through a glass partition in the carriage before walking toward them, a look of curiosity on her face.

"Franz?" the girl asked as she drew nearer. "Is that you?"

7

"Franz Weber Sent Me"

The war was exacting a heavy toll on Franz's small hometown by the time he set out to return there. Fathers and sons from Oberperfuss had gone off to fight for the Nazis, and fifty-seven had not made it back. While Allied ground troops were still hundreds of miles away, fighter planes regularly screamed over the small farming town, on their way to cascade bombs down on the Tyrolean capital of Innsbruck, less than ten miles away. The schools that many local children had attended in Innsbruck had been bombed to bits, forcing them to commute to new schools twenty miles away.

So it was that fourteen-year-old Elsa Weber and her classmates were taking the train from their new school back home to Oberperfuss that bone-chilling March day. Their commute was a long one now, almost an hour. Across the train, Elsa thought she recognized a face from the past. She noticed a young officer in a Wehrmacht uniform standing on the train's outer platform with two men in big hooded ski capes. Beneath the bandages obscuring his face, he looked just like an older boy she knew named Franz, whose family lived down the road. She was startled. She knew Franz had become a Nazi officer, but he had been missing now for many months, and no one in town seemed to know for certain what had happened to him — not even his family or his fiancée, Annie. Was he killed in action, captured, maybe even a deserter? Wartime rumors swept through the small community of fewer than a thousand people.

Elsa summoned her courage and approached the young man, with her classmate behind her. Franz's eyes held a look of alarm as he stared down at the brown-eyed girl who had called him by name. He seemed to recognize his old neighbor almost immediately, and he began speaking to her in hushed, forceful tones. "You must promise not to tell anyone," he said. That meant no one on the train, no one at home in Oberperfuss, no one anywhere, he said. Elsa nodded fearfully, and she and her classmate took their seats again. Franz was a decade older than the girl, and she had always looked up to him; shaken, she didn't know what to make of it all. Franz was alive, here on a train heading back to Oberperfuss. And the two men accompanying him: who were they? She had noticed the heavy boots peeking out of the bottom of their huge snow capes. The boots seemed odd, out of place, but she couldn't quite say why.

Elsa sat anxiously with her classmate, Marianne, for the rest of the train ride. She kept her word and said nothing to her father or mother when she got home. It was just another day at school, she told them; nothing out of the ordinary. But her friend Marianne was disturbed by what she had seen, and unable to remain quiet. She did what she had been taught to do in such a situation: she went to the Catholic church in the center of town, Saint Margareta, and confessed what she had seen to Father Mayr. "Imagine who we met," the girl told the priest. She feared it would be wrong to keep a secret that perhaps should not be kept.

Father Mayr now had a dilemma of his own. A confession from a congregant was sacrosanct, of course, but the Nazis didn't much care about religious vows. The Gestapo would surely want to know about a missing soldier who had mysteriously returned to Tyrol and had been spotted on a train. Many priests throughout Austria had developed strong alliances with the Nazis, and in similar circumstances might have run to the Gestapo with such news of a possible security threat. Fortunately for Franz, Father Mayr was not one of them.

The Gestapo, in fact, had begun to question the priest's loyalty to the Reich recently, forcing him to transfer from a church in a neighboring town after he made an imprudent political comment about the Nazi movement during a sermon. The Nazis' control of all aspects of life in this staunchly Catholic region had left him disillusioned. The mandatory Hitler Youth activities on Sunday morning were causing the children to miss mass. The parades for Hitler's birthday and other Nazi events had replaced the popular church processionals in town. Life had changed, and not for the better. So instead of running to the Gestapo to report the news of Franz's sighting, Father Mayr absolved Marianne of her guilt and rushed to Elsa's home to speak privately with her father, giving him an urgent warning. Marianne already knew to stay quiet, but Elsa and her family also needed to stay silent about what the girls had seen on the train, the priest warned. "You keep quiet, otherwise you will all end up in the KZ" — the Nazi concentration camps — he said. "And then it will be very bad for you."

On the outskirts of town, a long-missing resident of Oberperfuss and two strangers hid out in a farming shed crammed with hay and waited for nightfall to come.

Freddy, Franz, and Hans had made it to town hours earlier. They had gotten off the train a few stops before Oberperfuss to avoid the prospect of anyone else recognizing Franz; one neighbor was enough of a jolt for the day. Then they hiked the last five miles through backwoods trails, their rucksacks on their backs. A hard snow pelted them along the way, their latest Alpine storm. They stopped at a cluster of tree stumps to sit and rest, smoking German cigarettes that Franz had packed away.

Franz could have taken that moment to slip away from his two partners and leave them in the woods. Or he could have bolted from the train, or disappeared on the mountain before that, or fled at a dozen points in between. Freddy and Hans could fend for themselves; they had the maps and money and food rations in their rucksacks, and Franz had gotten them this far already. He could simply disappear, just as a number of the ex-Nazis working for OSS had done before him, their missions still unfinished. Franz had deserted an army once already, after all. But something

made him keep going—perhaps the *Gewissen,* the pangs of conscience that impelled him to stick with the mission, stick with the
Americans. And so he and his two partners took a few last drags
from their cigarettes for warmth and kept on walking in tandem.

Their most urgent task, now that they had survived the descent from the glacier, was to find allies in Tyrol. Freddy was fear-
less, but he wasn't stupid; he knew his team would need locals
willing to assist them—even though making such contacts could
put them in clear peril. Without help on the ground, Freddy said,
they might as well turn themselves in to the Gestapo right now.
This wasn't France, where throngs of anti-Nazi resisters would be
waiting to join forces with OSS agents parachuting down. Freddy
remembered what Lieutenant Ulmer and the other OSS officers
at Bari had told him about Austria: *You can expect ninety percent
of the Tyroleans to be pro-Nazi.* Their first mission now—Franz's
mission, really, as their point person on the ground—was to
somehow find the other ten percent.

Franz knew from his own conflicted experience with the Nazis that many of the townspeople, like Austrians in cities big and
small, had cheered the arrival of Hitler's troops seven years earlier in the Anschluss, the annexation of the country. Hitler, with
his Austrian roots and personal flamboyance, had promised jobs
to his brethren and pledged to reverse the "economic deteriora-
tion" that he contrasted so starkly with the "flourishing new life
in Germany." It was all part of Hitler's long-held vision of re-cre-
ating a Greater German Reich. The message held wide appeal in
Oberperfuss, where many people were hurting financially. Franz's
own father, a widower trying to feed eight children, struggled to
find odd jobs to supplement his small farming income. Their life
had always been *einfach und bescheiden*—"simple and modest," as

Franz put it — and now came the Nazis, promising him and the Austrians "all sorts of grandiose things for the future," he recalled. It had all seemed so hopeful to a boy of seventeen.

Almost overnight, it seemed to Franz, the past had disappeared. Nazi flags flew from the windows. Soldiers from the Gestapo began roaming the town and countryside. In Innsbruck, uniformed Nazi Party officials took over many of the institutions in the capital of Tyrol, including Franz's own school, under the iron hand of Franz Hofer, a Hitler acolyte who became the Gauleiter for the region. It was a dramatic shift, but few people questioned it. Many Tyroleans were happy with the new regime, and even among the skeptics, there was a long tradition in Austria of abiding by orders from the government and the military, no matter what. *Befehl ist Befehl,* as the saying went. An order is an order.

As for the Nazis' terror campaign against the Jews, that was irrelevant to most people in town, if not welcomed outright. There were no Jewish residents within miles even before the war, and decades of anti-Semitic tropes across Austria had the intended effect of dehumanizing the Jews. The country's largest Jewish settlement, tragically, was now more than two hundred miles away in Upper Austria at the Mauthausen concentration camp, where tens of thousands of Jews from across Europe, along with political opponents, foreign soldiers, homosexuals, Roma gypsies, and other "undesirables," were imprisoned in horrific conditions. Nearly 120,000 people would die there.

The closest that many people in Oberperfuss would come to the Nazis' brutal mistreatment of its undesirables was when the Germans trucked in crews of forced laborers to build a water line running through town to a Nazi military factory nearby; the workers appeared half-starved, but when a few sympathetic locals went to the construction site to bring them some food, a Gestapo officer warned them off. "Do that again," he said, "and you'll end up in the camps."

The barbarism extended to some residents personally. When a three-year-old boy named Anton began suffering seizures after a fall down the stairs, the Gestapo came for him with an order signed by Gauleiter Hofer himself. The Nazis first took the boy to a nearby facility for disabled children, then to an infamous castle known as Hartheim, near the Mauthausen camp, where he was killed with other children in the "T4" euthanasia program, the family learned. For thirty reichsmarks, the Nazis offered to return his ashes to the family.

No one would dare say so publicly, but by the time of Franz's return in early 1945, the allure of the Nazis had begun to fade for some of the townspeople in Oberperfuss. Franz's challenge was to figure out which ones might be willing, as he put it bluntly, to consider "playing with life and death" by helping them. He didn't want to risk going directly to his own family in town, or to Annie, his fiancée — not yet, anyway: the Gestapo might well have them under surveillance, given his desertion. Besides, there was no certainty that even his family members would risk helping the Americans. In an OSS mission that started weeks earlier on the opposite side of Austria, another Nazi deserter, who had become an American agent like Franz, snuck back into his hometown but was turned in to the Gestapo by his own father, a die-hard Nazi supporter; he escaped capture only by jumping out a window. Trust was a commodity in short supply in the Reich.

Once the Gulliver team had reached the farmlands at the edge of Oberperfuss, Franz found an unlocked shed where the three of them could hide out and plot their next steps. It wasn't a random location; Franz had chosen it because of its proximity to a farm-house belonging to an older man who he hoped might be willing to help them.

The man's name was Alois Abenthung, and he had been the Bürgermeister in Oberperfuss — the mayor — before the An-schluss; the Nazis quickly removed him from office for not be-ing "loyal enough" to the new order. Before Franz left for the war, he and Alois had become friendly and would occasionally share a few drinks at the pub. The Nazis were a bitter topic of conversa-tion; Alois had no great affection for Hitler, Franz knew.

What Franz didn't know was that his friend's views had only hardened since the two men last saw each other. Alois had tried, covertly to start a political opposition group in Oberperfuss in-spired by Otto von Habsburg, a staunch Nazi opponent who was the last ruling member of Austria's royal Habsburg family. Eleven months earlier, after the Gestapo learned of his political stirrings, he was convicted by a sham Nazi court in Innsbruck of violat-ing an edict "prohibiting the formation of new political parties" — other than the Nazi Party. The court sentenced him to four months in jail, but, surprisingly, allowed him to remain free at his farm for now. The unexplained showing of leniency would prove pivotal to the OSS.

The three American spies waited in the shed until nightfall, then went over their plan one more time. Alois's farmhouse was just a short walk: up the dirt road, the first house on the left, with a big wooden barn and a large silo behind it, a majestic view of the Alps in the distance. Freddy would make the first approach, since Franz ran the risk of being spotted again.

Freddy headed up the dirt road, knocked on the door, and waited. After a short interlude, the door opened a crack, and an older man peered from behind it cautiously. He was a short man with stern gray eyes and a tiny, toothbrush mustache — the same style made fashionable by the Führer himself. Dressed in his pajamas, the man was obviously unsettled by the unexpected visitor. "Franz Weber sent me," Freddy said quietly in German, hoping to reassure the man. But the farmer revealed no hint of recognition. "Franz Weber? I never heard of him."

The man was clearly agitated now, Freddy saw. Perhaps he thought the late-night call had been ordered by the Gestapo, to test whether he was mingling with subversives. Perhaps Franz had misread the ex-mayor's allegiances altogether. Or maybe Freddy just had the wrong house. With Freddy standing in the dark on a stranger's doorstep in the middle of Nazi Austria, no explanation seemed any more implausible than the next.

"You are Alois Abenthung?" Freddy asked. "Ja," the man said, nodding. Freddy repeated his script, telling him again that Franz Weber had sent him, merely to talk; he was not there to make any trouble. But again, the man said he did not know any Franz Weber, and finally shut the door. Freddy returned to the shed in frustration, telling his two shivering compatriots what had happened. The old farmer had insisted that he didn't know any Franz Weber, and Freddy thought he was telling the truth.

Franz was flummoxed. He thought for a moment, then realized his error. "Oh, my God," Franz said, angry with himself. The old-timers in Oberperfuss had an odd local custom of using the name of their *property* as a first name to identify one another. Franz had been away so long, he had practically forgotten the practice.

"Go back and tell him *Tomassen* Franz sent you," he said.

Freddy walked back to the farmhouse, where the farmer answered the knock on the door with even greater agitation than before. Freddy tried to assuage him, apologizing for getting the name wrong. *"Tomassen* Franz sent me." This time there was a glimmer of recognition in the farmer's face. Yes, he knew Tomassen Franz, he said. He was still clearly nervous, still suspicious of Freddy, but his demeanor had now changed. He was pensive, yet curious. Tomassen Franz, the missing Nazi officer from town, had sent this young man with the unusual German accent? What could that possibly mean?

Franz was nearby, Freddy explained. And he was hoping to speak with Alois. The farmer mulled over the request. Come back in a few minutes, he said finally. Alois went upstairs and changed out of his pajamas. By the time he had come back downstairs, all three OSS agents were there at his door, with Franz leading the way.

Franz dispensed with the pleasantries and explained his sudden reappearance. He was working with the Americans now, and he needed help: help to find safe houses where the three of them could stay, help to make contacts among anti-Nazi resisters, help to gather intelligence. In short, he wanted Alois, the kindly elder statesman in town, to help the Americans take down the Nazis. It was a leap of faith, but he told Alois that he knew his politics and that he hoped he might be amenable.

It was a lot for Alois to take in. The presence of the three agents terrified him; the Gestapo would surely kill him if they found out about any of this, he told Franz. He was already an enemy in their eyes. But at the same time, he wanted nothing more than to rid his town and his country of the Nazis. This was not the Austria he had once known. The enormity of the decision showed on his face. Yes, he would help, he declared finally; he would give Tomassen Franz and his friends "all possible assistance," he said.

Franz could take satisfaction in knowing that his hunch about Alois had proven right. Freddy, in fact, would come to call Alois "my first and most reliable contact on my secret intelligence mission in Austria." Franz, with a single introduction in a darkened doorway, had earned the trust that Freddy and OSS had placed in him.

Alois hurriedly summoned his visitors inside the farmhouse and found them places to sack out for the night. The next morning, as discreetly as he could, he went into the village to look for longer-term accommodations. He went to the Gausthaus Krone — not to look for a room, but to speak with the owner's daughter, Annie, a young woman with long brown hair, an easy smile, and a round, cherubic face. He found her working in the back of the hotel and divulged the news: her missing fiancé, Franz, was back in town. "He came with two Americans," Alois whispered.

Annie's mind raced: Franz was alive — in Oberperfuss, with two Americans. She knew instantly what that must mean, as improbable as it sounded: Franz, the rising young Nazi officer, was somehow working with the Allies. She wrestled with a flood of emotions — relief, fear, anger — as she tried to process what Alois was telling her.

Annie and Franz had grown up in the same small town, but they had little to do with one another for years. They came from different backgrounds, with Franz the son of a struggling farmer, and Annie the daughter of the only hotel owner in town. She and Franz would see each other occasionally at school or church; she always thought he was fit and good-looking, with his dark, slicked-back hair, but nothing more than that.

It wasn't until Franz went away to war with the Nazis and returned home on furlough that the two ever really talked. Annie was taking the bus to Innsbruck for an unofficial dance class —the Nazis had banned public dancing in the city—and Franz was on the bus with her. "Where are you going?" he asked. Franz didn't dance much, but before she knew it, he had arranged to be there, too. A wartime courtship ensued—the Nazi officer and the hotel owner's daughter—and on another furlough home, Franz proposed.

Then came Franz's disappearance months later. Annie had no warning. With all the speculation stirring in town about what had happened to him, she feared that the worst of the reports—that the Nazis had captured him as a deserter and sentenced him to death—might be true. For months, the uncertainty gnawed at her. And now here was Alois, showing up at the hotel with the unexpected news of his return. He took her to a house outside town where he had arranged for Franz and Freddy to hide for the night. It all seemed so surreal to her. Incredulous, she walked into the darkened room to see her missing fiancé alongside a stranger —a short, squat man wearing a snow cape, smiling. One of the Americans, she guessed. Freddy excused himself to give the two of them some time alone for their impromptu reunion.

As she gazed over at Franz in his well-worn Wehrmacht uniform, Annie didn't know whether to hug him or slap him. He had done such a foolish, stupid thing in coming back, she thought. The Gestapo would hang him in the center of the church square if they found out. Annie glared at Franz. "This is not a good idea," she told him, mustering her sternest tone. The risk he was taking —to himself, to his family, to *her*. Then she rushed into his arms and kissed him, over and over again, before bursting into tears.

Hans, meanwhile, was alone—holed up in a cold, musty attic. Alois had hidden him for the time being in the home of his next-door neighbor, Herr Schatz. A gamble, to be sure, but Alois figured his neighbor would be willing to help without asking too many questions. In a town where everyone once knew everyone else, Oberperfuss had seen an influx of new residents lately: forced laborers, prisoners of war, soldiers, families bombed out of their homes, and more. The Nazis had forced Alois himself to find housing for a handful of the new arrivals — a German family, and a couple of laborers from eastern Europe — and he thought all the new faces about town might help Franz's friends escape notice. Freddy and Hans hoped he was right.

Hans knew his most urgent task at the moment. It had now been more than a week since the team had landed on the glacier, more than a week with no radio contact to Bari. He knew that OSS must be frantic. They might have even stopped monitoring the line by now. Settling himself in the sparse attic, he fiddled with the balky radio transmitter once again and tried jiggering the glass vacuum tubes. Still no signal. He had another idea. He unspooled a thin copper antenna nearly twenty-five feet long from his cache of supplies, and he made a tiny hole in the attic roof; he hoped Herr Schatz would understand. OSS had assured him that the antenna line would work just fine indoors — the technicians had even made a "how to" film for him and other radio operators, with a hidden antenna running along an inside wall — but he thought that hanging the line outdoors could only boost his chances of getting a signal.

A long clothesline was hanging between Herr Schatz's house and Alois's home next door, with wet linens and overalls set out to dry. That night, when Alois crept up to the attic to bring him some dinner, Hans decided to ask him for another favor. *What-*

ever I can do to help, Alois had said. Hans handed him the antenna, and with no one in sight, Alois ran it along the clothesline between the houses, as taut as he could get it. In the daylight the next morning, lost among the laundry, Hans's antenna was practically invisible from the ground.

Hans tried the radio again. This time, he was able to reach the covert radio channel that OSS had instructed him to use, a victory in itself, but he still couldn't send a transmission through on it. He had a message all ready to go, with their status translated into a secret code built around random five-letter sequences. But Hans was still powerless to actually get the message to Italy. He imagined the radio signal bouncing vainly from one mountain wall of the Alps to another without ever leaving Austria. His frustration was mounting. This was why he was here, and he was failing.

Lieutenant Ulmer and the other OSS officers in Bari had all but given up hope of ever hearing from Freddy and his men again. Each day of silence seemed to confirm that Ulmer's Austrian section had lost another team of men — and another opportunity to gather critical intelligence that General Eisenhower and the troops could use to win the war. On the other side of Italy, OSS commanders in Caserta were so concerned by the string of blown missions from the Austrian section that they sent two colonels to Bari in early March, just as the Gulliver team was making its descent, to find out why things were going so badly in their Mediterranean outpost. Ulmer had inherited the "circus" at Bari just months earlier, but he knew its success or failure now rested on him. The visiting commanders went over all the recent failures with him before finally zeroing in on the still-missing Gulliver team.

"You've had no message from them since they dropped?" one colonel asked. Lieutenant Ulmer nodded glumly. "Don't you think that if this team is safe, it would send a message so stating?" the colonel asked.

Ulmer bluffed. "Not necessarily, sir," he said. Freddy and Hans might just be waiting for something of importance to send rather than risk the Gestapo intercepting a routine cable, Ulmer said, knowing that they were supposed to cable when they landed, regardless. "Within four days," Ulmer predicted with false confidence, "we will probably get a message."

The next night, after the visiting colonels had left Bari, a dejected Ulmer went to see a forgettable movie at the base, hoping to take his mind off the latest disaster in his spy shop. Halfway through the film, one of his officers tapped him on the shoulder and told him he was needed in the message room. A newly arrived cable was waiting for him. Ulmer rushed to the message room in anticipation and picked up a terse, seven-word cable.

ALL WELL. PATIENCE UNTIL MARCH 13. HANS.

Cheers of raw relief erupted in the room. Ulmer went looking for Walter Haass, the jump master on the plane who had given the men the "go" signal eleven days earlier; he wanted to tell him the news himself. He grabbed an expensive bottle of Scotch that he had been saving for just such an occasion. Ulmer finally had something to celebrate: the Gulliver team was still alive.

8

The Führer's Bunker

INNSBRUCK, AUSTRIA
Late March 1945

His head wrapped in a large bandage, Freddy marched up to
the barracks for wounded Nazi officers with all the swagger of a
man who belonged there. A gray Nazi lieutenant's uniform hung
smartly from his five-foot-seven-inch frame; Freddy had lifted it
from a dead Nazi with the help of Alois's budding network of allies in Oberperfuss. His military papers, stamped with two offi-
cial-looking Nazi seals, were folded in his pocket; he had obtained

the papers after convincing a helpful young woman in Innsbruck that his identification had been stolen in Italy. OSS hadn't wanted him to pose as a Nazi soldier, but Freddy, not for the first time, had his own plans.

A Nazi guard stood watch at the door of the VIP barracks as Freddy approached from the street. Inside were scores of injured Nazi officers recuperating from their wounds — and passing the time over drinks at the officers' club. Freddy had heard stories about this place, and now, two weeks after parachuting into Austria, he was determined to try to talk his way inside. It was a brazen play, nothing that OSS in Bari had sanctioned beforehand, but Freddy figured he had the element of surprise in his favor: he told himself that no one would ever expect to find an American spy inside a Nazi officers' club.

"I need temporary quarters," Freddy explained to the guard at the door. "I have to report in to the hospital daily." He clutched the papers in his pocket, waiting for the sentry to ask for them. Instead, the guard simply waved him toward the officers' quarters. It all seemed too easy, Freddy thought. At least the Nazi officer on the train had inspected Franz's fraudulent papers for a few moments. This time, not even a look. So much for the Nazis' meticulous efficiency. The only explanation Freddy could muster was that a low-level enlisted man knew better than to question a wounded Nazi officer in uniform.

Soon enough, Freddy was assigned not only a room in the officers' quarters, but an orderly to press his uniform, shine his boots, and provide whatever other assistance he might need. He had practically free run of the place, coming and going as he pleased. He discovered that the hub of activity was indeed inside the officers' club at the barracks, where the Nazis would watch movies, play cards, smoke, and have a beer or a glass of schnapps at the bar — sometimes with other officers, sometimes in the company of young fräuleins from the city. Many of the recuperating Nazis did not seem to be in any hurry to get back to the front line.

Freddy made full use of the club, sitting for hours alone in the beer hall–style bar in hopes of overhearing something of interest. No one seemed in the slightest bit suspicious of him, and no one asked to see his papers. Sometimes he introduced himself — "Leutnant Frederic Mayer" — with a smile and a "Heil Hitler!" He had decided to use his real name, even on his fake papers, because it was a common one in Germany, for Christians or Jews. It sounded authentic. He had his cover story ready if anyone asked: a Nazi officer born in Germany, he was recuperating from a head wound suffered in the fierce fighting in northern Italy, and he was being treated at the military hospital just down the main road in the center of Innsbruck.

A handful of combat medals and ribbons, pinned neatly to his chest, spoke for themselves. One was an Iron Cross — the same renowned German medal that his father had earned when he fought for the Kaiser three decades earlier. To the Nazis who saw it on him at the club, the ribbon was an affirmation that this young wounded officer had fought bravely for the Führer. But for Freddy, the ribbons and the uniform — the whole image he presented — held a much more complicated meaning. He had finally transformed himself into a German officer, just as he had dreamed of doing as a boy in Freiburg, when he would listen to his father's war stories and strut around the house in his military belt. He had never envisioned doing it this way, as an enemy incognito hoping to assist his new country in defeating his old one.

One night in the bar, Freddy sat by himself, as usual, while a small group of older officers sat together at a table nearby. One of the officers, a captain in his midthirties, seemed to be dominating the conversation. He was drinking wine, lots of it, and the more he drank, the more he talked. Another officer noticed Freddy and beckoned him over; Freddy gladly pulled up a chair. He figured that they must have felt sorry for him — a young officer, newly arrived at the club and sitting by himself.

He soon picked up enough of the conversation to tell that the garrulous, drunk captain was an Austrian who served in the Nazi engineering corps; he had returned to Innsbruck from Berlin just days earlier. The nature of his injuries was unclear, but the engineer seemed determined to impress his drinking mates with everything he had done in Berlin. He told them how he had been stationed at Nazi headquarters in Berlin, and that he had worked on fortifying the Führerhauptquartier — Hitler's underground bunker.

Now Freddy's interest was piqued, but he tried not to appear too interested. He signaled to the bartender for some more wine for his new friend. The captain kept talking, tossing out one striking detail after another about the underground complex: the precise location, the dimensions and thickness of the walls, the layout of the rooms, even where Hitler usually slept. The man clearly had a memory for numbers. He was throwing out so many details, in fact, that Freddy worried he wouldn't be able to remember them all.

The Nazi engineer kept talking, describing one particularly notable scene during his time at headquarters. Just a few weeks earlier, he said, a haggard Hitler had watched with apparent fatalism from his balcony at the Berlin compound as the Allies launched their latest bombing raid on the city. "Hitler is tired of living," the engineer declared to his listeners. Then, as if suddenly remembering the sensitivity of what he was revealing, the officer motioned to Freddy and made an oblique remark to the group suggesting that the young stranger sharing drinks with them might be a spy. Freddy sat frozen for a moment — until the smirks and smiles around the table made him realize he was the punchline for the joke.

Around midnight, the group dispersed. Once alone, Freddy hurried to record the engineer's revelations. So many details; he hoped he could commit them all to writing. He finally turned his scribblings into a lengthy message for Hans to transmit to OSS. It began:

Fuehrer HQ is 1½ km southeast of the Zossen Lager rail station.

The next day, a young woman with a plain face and unkempt blonde hair stood alone on a historic stone bridge in Innsbruck, leaning against the railing that separated her from the icy river below. Bundled in her winter clothes, Maria Hortnagl gazed down at the water, looking forlorn. Military jeeps rumbled over the bridge, and Nazi soldiers roamed the city's cobblestone streets in every direction. A stranger in civilian clothes approached her, a look of concern on his face. "Are you all right?" the stranger asked. "I'm tired of life," Maria answered.

That was the cue. The stranger took Maria by the arm, and together the pair walked toward the old section of Innsbruck — across the river from Gestapo headquarters on the other side of the bridge. They reached a dark, secluded alley, where the stranger slipped Maria a sealed envelope and walked away. Maria tucked it away without opening it. She didn't need to know what it said; she just had to get it back to Oberperfuss.

In the span of just a few weeks, Maria — "the first link in the cutout system," as OSS would call her — had already become a key player in the network of intermediaries and accomplices working for Freddy on the ground in Austria. She was among more than a dozen townspeople in Oberperfuss whom Alois ultimately trusted enough to help the Americans. They served as couriers, cooks, decoys, and drivers, bonded by both a shared hatred of the Nazis and, often, by personal ties to Alois or Franz. That most of them were women only helped to make them less noticeable in the male-dominated Reich. These "cutouts" knew little about the purpose or the details of the American operation itself, or about the two mysterious Americans hiding with Franz somewhere in town. Even Alois, the organizer, knew only what Freddy or Franz decided he needed to know. But on one central point, there was little confusion: Maria and her cohorts knew enough to realize that they were helping the enemy — and that they were putting themselves and their families at enormous risk if the Gestapo were to find out.

Franz soon found a command post for himself in Oberperfuss with the help of Annie's mother, a commanding presence who was known around town as Mama Niederkircher. A widow, she owned the only hotel in town, Gausthaus Krone, along with a farm and a food business. But she had a hidden agenda as well. She was a devout Catholic — stern and quiet, but strong-willed — and she vowed privately to Annie that if Hitler won the war, "I no longer believe in a God."

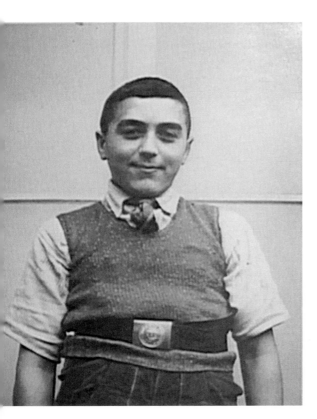

Freddy "Fritz" Mayer in Freiburg, Germany, around age eleven, wearing his father's World War I military belt.

Freddy and his family before leaving Germany in 1938. *From left:* his sister Ruth; his mother, Hilda; Freddy; his father, Heinrich; and his youngest sister, Ellen. His older brother, Julius, is not pictured.

Hans Wynberg (*left*) and twin brother Luke in a photo they sent back to their parent in the Netherlands, months after fleeing to the United States in May 1939.

William "Wild Bill" Donovan (*above left*), head of the Office of Strategic Services, inspects wartime training exercises at "Area F," a converted country club in Bethesda, Maryland. Freddy (*above right*) at an OSS training facility in Europe.

ans (*left*) and Freddy during OSS training in Italy.

he Amberger Hütte in the Austrian Alps, where Freddy Mayer, Hans Wynberg, and ranz Weber hid out after parachuting onto a glacier in February 1945.

The Nazi flag flies near the Churc of Saint Margareta in the center of Oberperfuss, outside Innsbruck, Austria.

Nazi workers' barracks atop an underground military airplane factory in Kemater Austria, as seen today. Freddy Mayer posed as a French electrician at the factory.

reddy in the Nazi uniform he wore in nnsbruck while posing as a wounded officer.

Franz Weber in his Wehrmacht officer's uniform, before his defection in 1944.

Franz Hofer (*right*), the top Nazi official who served as the Gauleiter for Austria's Tyrol region, shakes hands with Adolf Hitler in Berlin in 1940.

I than returned to Mayer and informed the SS- men. The ques
began anew, but MAIER remained by his former statements. I as we.
SS-men gave him several slaps in the face. Than Kriminalinspect
PRAUTZSCH joined us and also beat MAIER . BERINGER has hit MAIER
face several times, and quite strongly. PRAUTZSCH and BERINGER
that MAIER was a Jew, but I denied this with "Ach Quwatsch" (Oh
since I did not have this impression under any conditions. BEF
undressed MAIER completely naked, since he was of the opinion

An excerpt from an American military report on the interrogation of Gestapo officer Walter Güttner, who admitted after his capture that he was involved in the beating of Freddy Mayer (misspelled "Maier") in Innsbruck.

Franz Weber (*left*), Hans Wynberg (*kneeling*), and Freddy Mayer pose for a victory photo on May 8, 1945, a day after Germany's surrender, in the Oberperfuss backyard of their Austrian accomplice Alois Abenthung.

"Mama Niederkircher" (*above left*) and Maria Hortnagl, two other key associates in Oberperfuss.

Occupying American soldiers from the 103rd Division in the Alps outside Innsbruck, shortly after the division took control of the Tyrol region.

Freddy Mayer with a display of some of his war medals at his home in West Virginia. He died two months later, in 2016, at the age of ninety-four.

Wehrmacht soldiers stationed in Tyrol had taken over an entire wing of the hotel, but Mama Niederkircher reserved an out-of-the-way room in the back for use by Franz and Freddy. There were now so many new faces roaming the area that the agents' nighttime maneuverings attracted little notice.

Once Franz's three sisters learned that their brother was still alive, they were anxious to help as well. Gretl, the eldest, let Freddy use a loft in her row house apartment, where he stashed some of his gold, papers, and supplies. Alouisa, a nurse at the hospital, managed to smuggle out the uniform of a fatally wounded Nazi lieutenant, the medals still affixed, for Freddy to wear. After trying it on, Freddy declared it "a perfect fit." Eva, meanwhile, was a government clerk and introduced Leutnant Mayer, in his new uniform, to a woman she knew in Nazi document control. Freddy always had a smile for the ladies, and he convinced Eva's friend that his military papers had been stolen in Italy; "I lost everything, I lost my papers down there," Freddy told her. Back in Bari, OSS had denied Freddy's request for counterfeit Nazi papers — too risky, the officers said — but in Austria, Freddy was now carrying his new German identification book with the official Nazi seal of Tyrol on it.

Then there was Maria, a versatile accomplice who would shuttle secret messages, act as a decoy, locate safe houses, or simply lend Freddy her bicycle to get down the mountain to Innsbruck and back on a backwoods path, avoiding the Gestapo. She cleaned rooms at Mama Niederkircher's hotel, and she, too, had grown to loathe the Reich; a "genuine anti-Nazi," Franz called her. But her eagerness to help was driven as much by personal motivations: she had become smitten with the handsome American spy. Her father had agreed to let Freddy and Franz sleep on a bench next to the woodburning stove in his home for their first few nights, and Maria, whose bedroom was nearby, quickly took a liking to the flirtatious young man with the infectious smile. Maria was still single at twenty-eight, unusual for the era in Oberperfuss, but her parents were not happy about her obvious infatuation. They didn't want her becoming too friendly with an American soldier-spy — and that was before they came to learn he was Jewish. They soon decided that Alois would have to find another safe haven for his new friends. Freddy and Franz were no longer welcome there.

The pair moved to another hideout in town, but Maria continued for months as Freddy's Mata Hari any way she could. She was not the prettiest woman in town, he would later remark, but "an absolutely wonderful" operative and "a hell of a good girl." Maria might have lost Freddy as a houseguest because of her parents' protests, but he could still count on her help.

Hans, meanwhile, whiled away the late-winter days in an attic in Oberperfuss, waiting for news from Freddy to relay to OSS, now that his transmitter was finally working. Alois had arranged for Hans to move from his original hideout to the attic of another helpful ally, Herr Kirchebner — not because of any romantic entanglements this time, but for safety concerns. The longer the Americans stayed in one place, the greater the risk that a nosy neighbor might notice something peculiar and alert the Gestapo.

With Alois's help, Hans once again rigged a hidden radio antenna to a clothesline outside his hideout. A few written messages had begun to trickle in from Freddy, with Hans dutifully encoding them and radioing them on to Italy. Still, days and weeks would go by with nothing but silence from his fellow agent. He and Freddy had been side by side for nearly a year, brothers in arms wandering together in exile from Maryland, to Africa, to Italy, and now Austria, but lately his only contact with him was limited to cryptic messages on scraps of carefully folded paper.

Boredom was Hans's main adversary between transmissions — that and the physical demands of waiting until the middle of the night to tiptoe downstairs to use the bathroom; daylight trips were too risky. Impatient by nature, Hans was going a bit stir-crazy in the house. At least he had his chemistry books to distract him; he spent hours at a time copying and rewriting complicated chemical structures that mapped out the composition of molecules. Like the OSS coding he had learned, this was his own secret language that almost no one he knew was able to understand. He thought he might have the makings of a college thesis in mind.

Eventually even his chemistry studies became monotonous, though. Looking for a new diversion, Hans began carving a chess set out of some old wood scraps in the attic. Waiting for news from Freddy on the real war, Hans gamed out the battle in miniature in a stranger's attic, with the white knight he had carved trying to pierce the defenses of the dark king. Kirchebner's teenage daughter, Frannie, felt sorry for the foreigner hiding upstairs, so under a vow of silence to her father, she tried to find amusements to occupy Hans. She taught him how to play Mühle, a popular board game exported from Germany; it became one of Hans's favorites.

Then, in late March, came the handwritten note marked "Führer HQ," passed from courier to courier, one hand to the next, from Maria back to the Krone hotel, until it ultimately reached Hans in the Kirchebners' attic. Hans had already relayed some intriguing tidbits from Freddy to OSS in Bari, but nothing like this.

He realized the significance of the message as soon as he began reading it. The length of the note alone—a weighty 146 words—was unusual: compared to the terse messages of a line or two that he had received before now from Freddy, this was a virtual *War and Peace.* Hans took out his OSS codebook and began translating Freddy's words into a cipher, one letter at a time, using OSS's elaborate five-digit system. He had to destroy each page of original coding after using it just once, then start with a fresh page of new codes from his pad book. It was a tedious, hours-long process, but he wanted to make sure to send the cable exactly as Freddy had written it; he couldn't risk misconstruing information this important.

Once the encryption was complete, Hans began tapping out the transmission to Bari in Morse code. "Fuehrer HQ is 1½ km southeast of the Zossen Lager rail station," he wrote. "Pay attention to group of 5 houses ... Roofs very steep and camouflaged black, white, green." The houses were built of "reinforced concrete; all walls one meter thick;" thirteen meters underground—beneath four separate levels of flooring that were each one meter thick—lay a whole additional complex of secret rooms, the cable said. "First house in southwest end is Adolf," it continued. Two trains, each with twenty-four cars, were in constant service around the compound, with an "air warning tower in center of house group."

Hans continued tapping away, almost done now. A recent Allied bombing raid in mid-March had hit an officers' club near Hitler's bunker, the cable continued; Hitler himself had watched the bombs hit. "Adolf tired of living—watched last attack from balcony. Alternate HQ at Ohrdruf..." Freddy's dispatch closed by noting the source of the intelligence scoop, but not his drunkenness: "Austrian staff officer [who] left HQ March 21."

The cable landed like a live grenade at OSS's transmission center in Bari; it was almost as jolting as the one Hans had sent nineteen days earlier announcing that the Gulliver team was still alive. Freddy had given American intelligence a dramatic peek inside Hitler's bunker, complete with precise locations and fortifications. Ulmer and his team in Bari pored over every word. This was "a ten-strike," declared Ulmer, a bowling fan: a piece of raw intelligence so potentially important that he rushed it up the chain to intelligence officials outside the usual distribution group, across western Europe in London, Paris, and Florence, and to Washington. The subject line on the OSS memo detailing Freddy's intelligence read simply "Hitler's Headquarters."

The detailed information gave Allied commanders the ability to fine-tune their targets during bombing runs over Berlin, although they still remained unable to penetrate the well-fortified bunker. Freddy was beginning to make a name for itself, albeit anonymously. Military intelligence officers, not just at OSS but in the army, the air force, and beyond, were learning that Bill Donovan's cloak-and-dagger brigade, long derided as a minor-league outfit, had managed to plant an unnamed operative inside Tyrol who was generating valuable intelligence. The other branches wanted a piece of the operation as well, asking OSS what their Austrian operative could find out for them about imminent threats from the Nazis in Europe.

Leutnant Mayer had become a man in high demand.

9

The Birth of a Frenchman

INNSBRUCK, AUSTRIA
Early April 1945

From his barstool at the Nazi officers' club, Freddy had proven he could pry loose even the most sensitive information from the Third Reich. American military officials were scrambling to put to use what they now knew of the Führer's fortified underground bunker. But a string of other startling discoveries — including the one that Freddy would call "my biggest coup" — still lay ahead. And he would pull off most of them not in the crisply ironed uniform of a dead Nazi, but in the bedraggled garb of a French factory worker.

For three weeks in all, Leutnant Mayer wore the Nazi officer's uniform as he recuperated from his "injuries" and culled bits of information from every corner of Innsbruck. His sheer confidence seemed to open doors for him. He walked the streets of the Tyrolean capital — from the officers' barracks, to the military hospital, to the train station, and all points in between — as if he had lived there all his life. He watched and he listened. He would talk to anyone, but trusted almost no one. Out of uniform, late at night, he would sneak over to Gretl's apartment on Anichstrasse, in the heart of Innsbruck, to exchange covert messages or, sometimes, meet another ally that Alois had found for him.

Tyrol was tilting toward chaos, even as Gauleiter Hofer and the Nazis were bringing in more troops and stockpiling more weapons to brace for a violent last stand against the Allies. In his travels under the guise of Leutnant Mayer, Freddy burrowed into the widening cracks in the Nazi machine, coming face-to-face with a motley cast of characters worthy of Gulliver himself: Nazi fanatics who pledged to fight the Reich's enemies with their last breath; disaffected Wehrmacht soldiers who had grown tired of the cause; grifters and black-market scam artists devoid of ideology, who could be persuaded to work for either side if the deal was enticing enough. Freddy met with a one-eared ex-Nazi officer with the Schupo police force who was anxious to save himself if the Germans lost. He spoke with a grizzled Austrian con man who claimed to have hundreds of anti-Nazi resistance fighters at the ready, for the right price. He even heard talk of a notorious one-legged woman named Diane, who the Nazis suspected might be an American spy roaming the hinterlands. Every new contact he made offered the promise of information — and the threat of exposure. As an OSS official said with a sense of wonderment in one memo, "Each individual contacted could have turned Mayer over to the Gestapo had he been so inclined."

Almost every day, Freddy put to paper the most useful information he had garnered and passed it on through his network of anonymous hands — on to Maria, he hoped, and on to Oberperfuss, then on to Hans, and then, if all went well, on to OSS in Italy. The radio cables were racing now. Only a few weeks earlier, as the three agents were struggling to make it down from the glacier, the haunting radio silence had led Bari to fear they were dead. Even when Hans had finally succeeded in sending his first cable, he had urged "patience" from OSS to give them time to get settled. Now, Freddy was determined to make up for the lag, firing off a blizzard of cables to the agency beginning in late March. Their network of cutouts had become so polished that Freddy could pass a message through to Hans and get it to Bari in a few hours. In just two frenzied weeks, Freddy and Hans relayed two dozen messages in all, reporting to OSS and the military on everything from troop movements to bomb-making factories and train schedules.

There was good news: an OSS agent code-named George Mitchell, thought to have been executed in Austria, was "alive and working" elsewhere in the country, Freddy wrote excitedly, and he was hopeful of making contact with the missing operative.

And bad news, too: The Nazis were "making grenades and small explosives" at a camouflaged underground facility, he relayed in another cable, and the Volkssturm, the militia-style group set up by Hitler as a last-stand "People's Army," was rebuilding a vacant school to serve as its new command base. Then there were the sightings of important figures, friend and foe, that Freddy passed on to Bari. Three French allies, including the sister of Resistance leader Charles de Gaulle, were imprisoned but safe at a VIP prison the Nazis set up at Schloss Itter, a castle east of Innsbruck, he reported in a discovery that elated the French. Meanwhile, the Italian dictator and Hitler ally Benito Mussolini was purportedly in hiding at a hotel seventy miles in the other direction, he wrote in a separate cable. And SS leader Heinrich Himmler himself had supposedly arrived with some of his Nazi aides just days before at a hotel outside Innsbruck, Freddy reported — in one of the few cables that turned out to be erroneous. Some of the notorious SS leader's top staff had indeed traveled to Tyrol for a possible "last stand," but Himmler himself had stayed behind with Hitler in Berlin.

Freddy was careful to describe the sources of his information in most of his cables: a "trusted worker" at a Nazi assembly plant, a carpenter, even a local teacher he had met. This was raw intelligence he was passing on, intriguing but unconfirmed, and he wanted officials in Bari to assess the reliability for themselves. On its own, OSS was able to confirm many of the leads that Freddy passed on, and the military's official grading of his team's usefulness quickly jumped from "untested" — the bottom rung — to "usually reliable," near the top.

The adrenaline rush he felt from picking up a useful nugget of information kept Freddy going at a frenetic pace into the early hours of the mornings. The hunt became a thrilling game: outwitting the Nazis, chasing military information, passing it on to Hans. The bombs dropping regularly from Allied airplanes above Innsbruck were a loud reminder of the game's mortal consequences, but they were little deterrent to Freddy. When the

Nazis' air-raid sirens went off in Innsbruck, signaling another in-coming strike, Freddy would simply head for a bunker or a safe space with everyone else. He never really worried — except for the time that he bicycled outside the city for an arranged meet-ing with a small group of supposed resisters-in-waiting. The re-sisters were all no-shows. Heading back to Innsbruck, Freddy missed the air-raid warnings and was practically thrown off his bike by a thunderous incendiary bomb that detonated behind him, shaking the ground under his wheels. The force at his back was so great, it sent Freddy hurtling down the path, clinging furi-ously to the handlebars.

After that scare, Freddy and Hans contacted Bari with a per-sonal plea: For the safety of their own man in Tyrol, could the air force give him a heads-up in the future as to where and when they would be dropping their bombs? OSS dutifully forwarded the re-quest and sent back a terse response:

AIR FORCE WILL NOT GIVE ADVANCE INFO ON BOMB-INGS. HEADQUARTERS DIRECTS YOU TO USE CUTOUTS AND STAY OUT OF TOWN.

Hans was relaying more cables than ever to Italy, but he re-mained restless up in the Kirchebners' attic, with hours of down-time still left to fill. Between cables, he played chess against him-self on his newly carved board, and Frannie still came upstairs for the occasional game of Mühle. Looking for new diversions, he tried to pick up the spotty radio signals bouncing around the Alps from the BBC or American Forces Network. With the vol-ume turned down to a whisper to avoid notice, Hans would listen for the jazz notes of the American bandleader Ray McKinley, his favorite, and he became enamored of the popular tune "On the

Sunny Side of the Street." It appealed to his optimistic side. Except for a few terrifying moments sledding down the Alps with Franz, he had always convinced himself that things would turn out all right for him — in an attic hideaway in Austria now surrounded by Gestapo; in his sudden relocation to Brooklyn six years earlier; even in the unknown plight of his parents and his little brother in the Netherlands. The song's refrain, and its message of putting aside your fears, resonated: *Life can be so sweet / On the sunny side of the street.*

What was there to be afraid of, anyway? Hans told himself that he wasn't really in harm's way there in his attic: that he was only playing a passive role in the war, and that what he was doing took no real courage — not like Freddy, out roaming among the Nazis; or his twin brother, sent to Normandy with the US army. Sitting alone in an attic did not constitute, in his mind, what he had always thought of as "the realities of a world war." He could almost hear his father, wherever he was, telling him the story about the heroic Dutch naval commander who blew up his own ship rather than let the foreign marauders aboard. *I'd rather light the fuse in the dynamite!* Yet there was Hans hiding out in an attic, tapping out codes on a radio transmitter and playing board games with an Austrian teenager. What real courage did that take?

He wanted to do more. In late March, soon after he had sent out Freddy's bombshell dispatch on the Führer's bunker, Hans seized on an idea: he would start an underground newspaper. Goebbels and the Nazis had mastered the art of propaganda to devastating effect, spewing vile messages on radio and in print about the evils of Jews and the Reich's other "enemies." Hans wanted to counter the Nazis' lies — by letting people in Tyrol know the truth about what was actually happening in the war. He even had a name in mind for his paper: *Freies Österreich* — Free Austria. His radio brought him a wave of news in those first days and weeks of April, much of it foretelling advances for the Allies, but he had no way to get it out. So he passed word downstairs to the Kirchebners, requesting supplies for a new project. A typewriter and a small stack of carbon paper soon appeared in the attic. Who brought them, how they were acquired — Hans never knew. He didn't care. He just started typing, with one ear to the radio receiver. The news alerts would come in from the BBC about the latest shocking Nazi atrocity discovered by the Allies, or the latest troop surge, and Hans, who had always dabbled in writing, would translate it into German and turn it into news stories: *Eastern Front Collapsing... Vienna Liberated from the Nazis... Roosevelt Dies; Truman Is President... Soviets Launch Offensive on Berlin.* For some editions, he would draw a makeshift map of Europe showing the advance of Allied troops, along with a section he wrote called "Do You Know?" — with facts about what life in America was really like.

He would deliver his fledgling newspaper downstairs — a few dozen sheets off the carbon paper at a time — and Alois and his cohorts would distribute the copies, as discreetly as they could, to sympathizers throughout the valley. It was a small-time operation, reaching perhaps a hundred or so people that April. OSS had never envisioned its radio operator in the Alps taking on the role of a modern-day Thomas Paine, but Hans's bosses in Bari were thrilled when they learned how he had been using his spare time. "His little paper," OSS reported, "made a terrific impression on the people who were very eager to learn more about America and to understand the nature of Nazism."

Freddy, meanwhile, was now generating intelligence leads from all parts of Nazi-controlled Tyrol, but the one target that became a near-obsession for him was the Nazis' massive railway system. The mechanic in Freddy had always gravitated to engines and locomotives, and he knew how badly OSS wanted intelligence that would allow them to cut off the Brenner Pass — the Nazis' gateway between southern Austria and northern Italy in one of their last remaining strongholds in all of Europe.

It was Franz's youngest sister, Eva, who first helped Freddy maneuver his way inside the railway system. Only twenty-one years old, Eva was a petite woman with an unassuming manner who faded into the Nazi bureaucracy in her government job filing paperwork in Innsbruck. Freddy soon discovered that beneath her guileless facade was a determined woman passionately opposed to the Nazis — and she knew other people in the city's underbelly who might help him. She had already steered Freddy to the woman who supplied him with his vital Nazi identification. Just a few weeks later she set up another meeting to introduce Freddy to a gritty black-market operator named Leo, who made a living by paying off railway workers to move his underground wares. Leo told Freddy he could get him information on the Nazi trains: where they were running, what they carried, who was working on them. Leo had no obvious political loyalties, except to the gold marks in Freddy's pocket. He showed little concern over what Eva's new friend planned to do with the information, or even which side he was on. For $10 or $20 per transaction, Leo was willing to pass on whatever information Freddy wanted. The two men soon had an arrangement, and $150 later, OSS had a whole new stream of intelligence reports coming in from Leo's underground network on the Nazi rail system.

The payoff was immediate. When Bari informed Freddy that a large cluster of Nazi soldiers had inexplicably disappeared from the fighting lines in northern Italy, he soon located the enemy soldiers — at a train station near Innsbruck. "Three trains of paratroops arrived at Innsbruck from Brenner night of march 30," he wrote in a cable back to Bari. "They carried no heavy weapons."

At a rail yard near Innsbruck, meanwhile, laborers were working around the clock to repair 150 broken locomotives, and dozens of trains were ready to go back into operation, Freddy reported in another cable, citing a "railway engineer" as the source. At another yard, he wrote, the Nazi trains — their cargo unknown — were loaded each night like clockwork between ten thirty and midnight.

Then there was the lingering mystery that OSS had laid out for Freddy before he had even left for Austria: how did the Nazis manage to rebuild their railway bridges in Tyrol so quickly, time after time, after being destroyed by Allied fighter planes? "The trouble," an exasperated Ulmer complained to one air force officer, "was that the Krauts had devised so many ways to repair the line as fast as it was cut." The answer, Freddy discovered on the ground, was that the Nazis hadn't really repaired the bridges at all, because they weren't damaged in the first place. Instead, as he learned with the help of Leo's underground network, the Germans had built massive *movable* bridges to pass over the ravines in the valleys; they kept the bridges out of sight, inside tunnels, and then painstakingly rolled them into position before the trains passed over them. By the time the allied planes dropped their bombs, the bridges had been rolled back out of their path, with nothing left to hit. Even as he forwarded the startling discovery, Freddy had to give the Nazi engineers grudging credit for their ingenuity.

Armed with Freddy's new intelligence, the air force soon began changing the time and patterns for its bombing missions
in Italy and Austria to target them more precisely. Still, Freddy
was anxious to follow up more aggressively on Leo's leads himself—but in person. The Nazis had used their intricate Reichs-
bahn train system with brutal efficiency to move soldiers, weapons, and millions of human prisoners across Europe, and Freddy
was beginning to learn all the routes and switchbacks practically
as well as any train conductor. He figured he could put his newfound knowledge to use, so he took a trip on the bicycle Maria
had loaned him to one of the region's main railway junctions, in
the town of Hall, about seven miles east of Innsbruck. There were
throngs of people coming and going: railway workers, soldiers,
Nazi bureaucrats. One more Wehrmacht lieutenant milling about
the yard for a few hours would attract little notice, Freddy figured.
If anyone asked, he would claim he was an Alpine patrol officer recently wounded in the fighting in Italy, just over the Brenner Pass.

He watched and he listened, his placid expression masking his
disdain for the Nazis filing past him at the station. No one seemed
to pay him any mind. He took more trips out to the rail yard, and
he began to ask questions: nothing too pointed, just a dutiful Nazi
lieutenant checking on train operations for security purposes. He
even met the head yardmaster, a friendly fellow in overalls, and
very chatty. From the man's body language, Freddy suspected he
was no Nazi loyalist, maybe even an old-time Social Democrat
who had deemed it in his best interests to get in line with the Nazis, just like everyone else. It was only a hunch, but Freddy engaged the man in conversation. In the yard, Freddy had noticed
row after row of Nazi train cars, some freestanding, hundreds of

cars in all. He hadn't expected to see such a large operation. He asked the yardmaster about them.

"These twenty-six trains are going to go out in two days," the yardmaster answered.

The trains were headed for Italy through the Brenner Pass, he told Freddy. And it appeared that they were being loaded with enough military equipment and supplies to last the Nazi soldiers fighting in northern Italy for weeks, even longer.

Leaving the yard, Freddy hurried back to the city. He suspected that this might be his most important find yet: a massive Nazi caravan of military supplies heading for the front line in Italy in a few days' time. He jotted down the salient details and passed the message on to Hans through a courier line that was well-tested by now. At the rail yard outside Innsbruck, the cable to OSS read, the Nazis had assembled "26 trains . . . 30 to 40 cars each . . . loaded with ammo, tractors, ack-ack [antiaircraft] guns, gasoline, light equipment. Leaving for Italy via Brenner April third after twenty-one hundred GMT. Source loadmaster of Hall."

Bari rushed the dispatch into the hands of the 15th Air Force in southern Italy, which quickly sent out a reconnaissance plane high above Innsbruck to verify the sighting. Six weeks earlier, one of these same "recon" planes had been flying high over the Alps not far away, looking for a possible drop point for Freddy and his team. Now, thanks to Freddy's intelligence, the reconnaissance plane was looking instead for the ominous outline of a massive caravan of Nazi trains outside Innsbruck.

The flight crew found it — parked in the rail yard in Tyrol, just where Freddy said it would be. Bari sent him back the news: the 15th Air Force was "delighted" to report that it had "verified by photos" Freddy's intel on the presence of trains outside Innsbruck. Not only that, but fighter planes from the 15th were planning a heavy-bomber operation against the trains as they left Austria for the Brenner Pass. More bad weather in the Alps had scuttled the bombing mission for the moment, but the air force was hoping it would get another shot once the trains passed slowly through the other end of the winding pass.

Freddy had rarely been as excited to get a cable from the bureaucrats in Bari, and he decided he would try to see for himself the results of his spy work. Like many of his unorthodox decisions, this one was not in the OSS training manual. At the Nazi officers' club, Freddy hitched a ride with a military transport heading south toward the Brenner Pass. It was an unusual request: the pass was more than seventy miles away through dangerous, snow-covered mountain terrain, with American fighter planes not far off. But Leutnant Mayer explained to the driver that, after spending the last few weeks recuperating in Innsbruck, he needed to get back to his old platoon in northern Italy to retrieve his belongings and personal papers. The driver took him at his word.

When the truck finally stopped at a Nazi outpost near the Italian side of the pass, Freddy stared down the Alpine mountain ridge. Off in the distance, there it was, the reason he had made the long trek — not only the one that day from Innsbruck, but the one before that, from southern Italy, and before that, from northern Africa, and before that, from Maryland and from Arizona and from Brooklyn. He had spent nearly two and a half years with the army and OSS, often in limbo, frustrated by inaction, but now he could see that the waiting had paid off. Down the mountainside were the smoldering remains of the Nazi supply trains, loaded

The Birth of a Frenchman | 163

with guns, ammunition, gasoline, and equipment, derailed on their path to the frontline Nazi troops in Italy.

Freddy hadn't made it in time to see the bombing itself, but he was there for its aftermath. While bad weather had prevented the bombing run in Austria, B-17 fighter planes from the 15th Air Force had gotten a second look at the train line in Italy and met it with a hail of fire that, as Ulmer said, "destroyed virtually the entire lot." Freddy stared at the wreckage in solitary satisfaction. *They bombed the hell out of them,* he thought to himself.

They did indeed. As OSS would later attest, Freddy's intelligence had enabled US bombers to "destroy completely heavy shipments of critically needed German ammunition and materiel for the Italian front." American bomber planes had made scores of runs over the Brenner Pass in the past five months, but few were deemed as critical as this one. The Nazi troops in Italy were in dire need of gasoline and equipment, and the cache of supplies on the train line could have extended the fighting by months, officials believed.

Freddy rarely gave any thought to dying, or even to the threat of being captured. But at that moment, staring down at the destruction he had set in motion, it occurred to him that even if his true identity were revealed and the Nazis executed him on the spot, it would all have been worth it. Because he had made this happen.

Freddy took off his Nazi uniform for good just days later; he had a new disguise in mind. This latest idea had come to him in the same roundabout way that produced many of his best leads: he heard something from someone who knew someone else, who had been somewhere and might know something. An ally of Alois's had connected Freddy with another black-market operator in Innsbruck, named Fritz Moser, who claimed to have soured on the Nazis. His uncle was an electrical contractor for Nazi factories all around Austria, Fritz said, and some of the foreign-labor electricians working for him at a Nazi plant in eastern Austria, near Vienna, were fleeing west to Innsbruck to stay ahead of the advancing Russian military. They were coming without any papers or identification, Fritz said, and getting jobs at an airplane factory outside Innsbruck where his uncle handled all the electrical work.

The Nazis were so desperate for more skilled workers at their factories that they put the foreign laborers to work — with pay and food rations, no less — alongside Jews, POWs, and other prisoners being used as slave laborers.

Freddy soaked in everything he was hearing. He knew that his bosses in Bari were keen to get information on German aircraft production; the air force had been sending OSS queries on that very topic for their man inside Innsbruck to investigate. The outlines of a new undercover role began to come into focus in Freddy's mind. He assumed he could handle whatever "skilled labor" job the Nazis might throw at him. He was a diesel mechanic by trade, not an electrician, but when it came to building and fixing things, he was confident he could make a go of most anything.

In early April, five weeks after their glacier landing, Freddy set out in search of a new job. Dressed in workman's apparel, with a French beret on his head to top it off, Freddy showed up at the *Arbeitsamt*, the Nazi foreign-labor office in Innsbruck that Fritz had told him about. He hadn't known that such a place even existed. There was a long line of men ahead of him — French, Italian, Dutch, eastern European; all apparently waiting

for jobs. Freddy had run through his new cover story: a Frenchman, he had been working at a Nazi electrical plant in eastern
Austria — the Boehler Werke, the one that Fritz's uncle serviced
— but the incoming Russians had run him and other foreign
workers out of town.

The language wasn't a problem. As a boy growing up in Germany close to the western border, Freddy had learned to speak
French; it was one of the few subjects he excelled at in school.
He decided, again, to keep his real name for his newest identity,
simply adding a French accent: *Freh-deh-REEK May-YEHR*. He
sounded like a true Parisian as he practiced the pronunciation.
That was about as much rehearsal as Freddy ever did. He never
considered himself much of an actor; he simply went with his in-
stincts and improvised instead.

Freddy's turn in line came, and he walked to the desk. The
clerk was a young woman; that always seemed to help Freddy's
prospects. He smiled as she asked for his name, birthplace, and
work skills.

"Frédéric Mayér," he stated in French. "Born 19 February, 1920,
in Marseille, France. Electrician." "Papers?" she asked. Freddy
shook his head. "They're gone. I was in Vienna fleeing the Russians."

The clerk nodded; she seemed to have heard the same explanation from many of the workers of late. She waved him on with
a form authorizing him to get new work papers and a meal ticket
for three days of food rations, a prized commodity at a time when
food in Innsbruck was so scarce.

Hours later, Frédéric Mayér, French electrician, had his new
Nazi papers in hand, allowing him to stay in Innsbruck as a duly
registered foreign worker. He couldn't get over how official the

papers looked, even more impressive than his previous papers as a Nazi lieutenant. Better still, the labor office soon gave him his first assignment: a job at a Nazi airplane factory seven miles outside Innsbruck in the town of Kematen — the very same factory that Fritz had mentioned.

Freddy had been hearing about the airplane factory for weeks, in fact. Eva, in another one of her helpful introductions, had set Freddy up with an Austrian friend who worked there. Her friend liked to drink and talk — two things that served Freddy well — and he mentioned over a few beers that the plant was having problems getting enough parts and metals to build its planes. Freddy had promptly reported to Bari that "production [is] zero" at the factory because of supply problems. The cable, citing a "trustworthy worker," immediately caught the attention not only of OSS's analysts, but of air force and army officers across Europe looking to determine how many of the newly remodeled aircraft they would be facing in the skies.

The Nazis, in their frenzy to find more workers, had now handed Freddy the opportunity to go down into the factory in Kematen himself and witness firsthand what was happening. He realized from his very first shift that Kematen was not just an ordinary airplane factory. For one, the sprawling plant — run by the giant German manufacturer Messerschmitt — was built beneath an Alpine ridge with a labyrinth of underground tunnels that were still being dug by slave laborers as Freddy descended for the first time. And the airplane he was supposed to help build was not just any airplane. This was the first jet-propelled fighter plane ever put in operation, the Nazis' Me 262; nicknamed "Schwalbe," for the fast-flying swallow, it could outrace any Allied plane by 120 miles an hour. The Schwalbe was one of the "secret weapons" that

Hitler was desperate to throw at the Allies en masse. The Führer clung to the hope that the jet fighters, like the V-2 missiles that famed Nazi scientist Wernher von Braun was building for him at another mountainside factory, in Germany, called Mittelwerk, might change the tide of war in his favor. The Luftwaffe had managed to get only a few hundred of the Me 262s out of production and into the air beginning the year before, but American military leaders worried about the potential for the Nazis to ramp up production. Hitler was trying to do just that at factories run by Messerschmitt, like the one outside Innsbruck, which had doubled the number of workers to four hundred just a few months earlier.

For the next three weeks, in his new role as Frédéric Mayér, Freddy worked in electrical maintenance at the jet factory; he was assigned to a housing barracks at a compound where throngs of voluntary laborers bunked. The forced laborers — military POWs, Jews, and others from camps like Mauthausen, some two hundred miles away — were kept apart, normally in horrid, subhuman conditions. Freddy was to show up promptly each morning at eight o'clock and proceed through the dark, dank tunnels to his section. His main job was fixing fuses and other blown electrical parts on the massive pieces of machinery used to assemble the jet planes. He quickly overcame his limited training in electrical work, but he couldn't stomach the idea that his labors might, in some small way, help get one of the Nazis' new jets off the ground. So when the plant supervisors weren't looking in his direction, he would tinker with the circuitry and electronics in an effort to disable them. "I blew more fuses than I fixed," he later boasted. On a good day, he spent "one hour building and three hours destroying." At the Nazis' military factories, acts of sabotage like this usually ended with the offending worker being put to death by the SS, hung from a giant crane while the other workers were made to watch. Freddy, however, always managed to avoid getting caught.

The truth, he learned, was that there wasn't all that much work to sabotage at the jet-plane plant. The pace was slow and sporadic. Freddy could see that the plant worker's earlier assessment of the production problems here was spot on. With the Allies blocking supply routes, and raw materials becoming more and more scarce for the Germans, the plant operators in Kematen waited in frustration for shipments of supplies that never seemed to come. A decade earlier, the Nazis had starved Freddy's father of the metals he needed to run his hardware business in Germany. Now, in a bit of golden karma, he was witness to a supply crisis of the Nazis' own on a much bigger scale.

Freddy saw only a handful of airplane assemblies that looked close to completion. Otherwise, the assembly lines were all but stalled. If this first-of-its-kind fighter jet was truly designed as one of Hitler's secret weapons, the Führer would be waiting a long time indeed.

Freddy recognized just how welcome this news would be to OSS and the rest of the American military, as the Allies sought to ground the Luftwaffe's once-dominant air fleet. This was one of those moments, Freddy realized, when knowing what the Nazis *couldn't* do was almost as valuable as knowing what they could do. That news alone, he realized, would be an enormous relief to American military planners.

The foreign workers housed at the plant weren't supposed to leave the compound, but Freddy would routinely slip out of the barracks unnoticed after dark and ride Maria's bicycle to meet up with his contacts from his growing network of allies scattered around Innsbruck. The treks uphill on the rugged mountain paths were exhausting, even as fit as Freddy was. To ease the strain, he gave one of his black-market contacts a few gold coins in exchange for a small motorcycle that he was promised. Freddy never saw the man or his money again.

Some nights on his journeys, he would hide out with Fritz at his apartment, or at the row house apartment that Gretl shared with her two small children and with Eva, then be back at the factory by daybreak for his morning shift. Once a week or so, he would bike at night uphill to Oberperfuss. There, he met with Alois and Franz under cloak of darkness at one of their designated hideouts, usually at Mama Niederkircher's hotel, to quietly plot out their next steps. Freddy was growing more ambitious, emboldened by his success. He had heard talk of Austrian resisters who might be willing to actually take up arms against the Nazis — real resistance fighters, not con men looking for a payoff — and he was anxious to find out if the talk was true.

On his trips back to Oberperfuss, Freddy always found a few minutes for a clandestine visit with Hans as well. After spending so many months side by side, the two men had been separated for nearly six weeks, their only contact the scraps of paper relayed by courier. Freddy still felt protective of the man he had come to think of as a little brother, and it was calming to confirm that Hans was still safe and healthy, if a bit bored, in his attic home.

Freddy never stayed long in Oberperfuss, just a few hours or so. But Mama Niederkircher would never let him leave without eating first. The farming town had no food shortages, not like in the city, and she and Annie, or sometimes Maria, would bring Freddy dairy products galore: whipped cream, eggs, real butter with his bread, and as much milk as he could drink. Freddy felt a perverse satisfaction, a schadenfreude, in knowing that "I got whipped cream while the Germans were starving." He always biked back to the jet-plane factory on a full stomach.

There was one issue still gnawing at Freddy, however. He had worn a Nazi lieutenant's uniform all those weeks, and before that, the uniform of an American officer as he parachuted down onto the glacier. Pretend stuff, all of it. In real life, he was a lowly enlisted man, a "tech corporal," or T/5, in the United States army, and he had been stuck at that rank since he had shipped off almost a year earlier. He wanted to be made an officer, or at least earn a promotion. He knew that OSS was thrilled by what he had accomplished so far in Austria, but he didn't think his rank, or his pay, reflected it.

When he was still in Italy, he had angled for promotions for himself and for Hans, but that had gone nowhere. As a mechanic in Brooklyn in his teens, he had quit any job he didn't think was paying him properly, leaving to find a better-paying job at another garage. He couldn't very well do that here, not as an undercover agent in the middle of a war zone. But the inequity still grated on him, and it simmered over as he was scribbling down another message for OSS about the Nazis' railway lines. At the close of the cable, Freddy veered off topic and wrote bluntly: "What are arrangements for our commissions . . . Fred." There was no question mark.

A week later, after sending off more cables about the Nazi operations in Innsbruck, a frustrated Freddy had still not heard anything back from OSS on that question. He fired off another message, referring back to his earlier query. This one was even blunter than the last. "Reread 14. Definite answer expected," he wrote in a tone verging on insubordination.

Ulmer and his men in Bari were now becoming almost as frustrated with their brash young agent as he was with them. They spit back a response that same day, telling Freddy that the ranking officers above them in Europe had "cabled Washington for promotions. Hold your horses."

OSS could not risk having a disgruntled spy deep inside the Reich, especially not with all the valuable secrets that Freddy had collected. After a rushed review, a decision came back from Washington just a week later. OSS passed on the good news not only to Freddy and Hans, but to family in Brooklyn as well. In a letter to Freddy's parents, Ulmer wrote that while he was not free to disclose their son's whereabouts, he wanted them to know that "he is alive and well . . . [and] is continuing to do an outstanding job for his country . . . To express in some small way this organization's appreciation for Freddie's work, he has just been promoted to Tech Sergeant." It wasn't the rank of an officer yet, but Freddy, in absentia, had gotten a promotion.

10

"Take Innsbruck"

Hans was growing anxious — anxious about Freddy and all his "grandiose ideas" for defeating the Nazis. Freddy wanted to start his own army. Drop weapons into Tyrol. Arm Austrian resisters. Meet force with force. Just thinking about the scattered schemes made Hans nervous, as he waited in his attic hideaway for more cables to relay to Bari. Their main job, he had tried to persuade his zealous partner, was to gather intelligence for OSS — and by all accounts they had been doing a damn good job of it. Let General Eisenhower and the military men — the ones with the bombs and the guns and the platoons of soldiers — figure out what to do with all the information Freddy was supplying them.

As the radio man, Hans had been willing to stretch his own job description, becoming a journalist provocateur and typing up his *Free Austria* newspaper on carbon paper to counter the Nazis' propaganda. But that was about as far as his ambitions reached. What Freddy's team was already doing, he felt, was "good enough." From all the BBC bulletins that Hans was typing up early that April, it seemed as if the Germans were well on their way to defeat anyway: General Patton's troops had crossed the Rhine weeks earlier, and American soldiers were pushing toward Innsbruck from both Germany to the west and Italy to the south in order to head off Hitler's feared last stand. The Nazis, he believed, seemed on the way to being vanquished with or without Freddy's heroics.

Franz shared his partner's nervousness. The Nazi defector, still hidden in the back of Mama Niederkircher's hotel, also worried that Freddy was becoming too reckless, wanting to single-handedly "play war." He could get them all killed. When he huddled with Freddy in secret at the hotel every week or so to plot their next steps, Franz found himself trying to talk Freddy into scaling back his ambitious plans. Franz knew Austria far better than his American friend, he pointed out gently, and he knew the Nazis better, too; he had been one of them until six months ago.

But Freddy — well, Franz and Hans both realized that their team leader viewed danger differently than most people they knew. As successful and as risky as his weeks of sleuthing had been, Freddy felt that merely gathering up intelligence — "just sitting there and sending a telegraph every now and then," as he put it — was *not* enough, not with the Nazis now on their heels and facing defeat. He wanted to help deliver the final blow, and Hans and Franz weren't going to dissuade him. So when Freddy relayed one of his more unnerving messages that April, all that Hans could do as the team's radio operator was to encode it and tap it out, just as written, for OSS.

IF DESIRED CAN TAKE INNSBRUCK AND AREA AHEAD OF AIRBORNE LANDINGS. POLITICAL PRISONERS WOULD NEED 500 M-3 PISTOLS. DETAILS AWAIT ANSWER.

This wasn't the first time such an audacious plan of action had occurred to Freddy, of course. Hans was there in Bari at OSS training months before, watching with wide-eyed alarm when his fellow agent pitched the idea of parachuting into the concentration camp at Dachau with guns and explosives to free the Jewish prisoners. Impossible, their instructor, Dyno, had told him then; Freddy might as well go jump out the window.

Since Freddy's very first days in Innsbruck, he had been tempted by the idea of building a band of resisters. Tyrol as a whole remained staunchly in Hitler's camp, with "the highest proportion of Nazi supporters of anywhere in Austria," as one scholar would note. But beginning in late 1943, even before the D-day invasion, Wehrmacht deserters began to show up in small numbers at a wooden cottage on a picturesque seaside cliff less than twenty miles east of Innsbruck. Their main aim was to hide out from roaming Nazi manhunts, not to resist them. As the Reich's fortunes continued to decline in late 1944, however, scattered pockets of deserters and Nazi opponents in Tyrol and elsewhere in Austria began plotting acts of sabotage, and one loosely formed resistance group managed to make contact with OSS headquarters in Switzerland a few months earlier in hopes of forming an alliance.

The resisters had little impact in Tyrol for the most part, except to risk getting themselves jailed and executed. Yet by the time Freddy began talking about an armed resistance, Austrians quietly claiming to be "anti-Nazi" suddenly seemed to be popping up everywhere in his underground travels. Many of the so-called resisters, Freddy found, were poseurs looking to make money off him in bribes, or get on the winning side of the war if the Nazis went down to defeat. In Oberperfuss, Freddy's allies, like Alois and Mama Niederkircher, were motivated mainly by their hatred for the Nazis, asking him for little other than a few cigarettes now and then. But in the city, in Innsbruck, almost everyone seemed to be on the take, looking for a few gold coins for their help.

Early on, Freddy met with a Wehrmacht deserter named Karl Niederwanger—another introduction set up, indirectly, through Eva—who claimed to lead a covert resistance group of five hundred men, holed up somewhere in the Alps and ready to fight. Freddy was skeptical. Something about the self-styled Nazi opponent didn't ring true to him. Freddy decided to test the man's mettle. He tasked Niederwanger with blowing up a generator outside town. If the test run succeeded, Freddy would talk about a real mission—and about money. When the day of the test came and went with the generator still untouched, Freddy dismissed him as a pretender.

But as Freddy's web of underground contacts grew, his hopes for an armed band of real resisters and saboteurs grew with them. To the amazement of Ulmer and his OSS men in Bari, "more than one hundred natives of Innsbruck" now knew that an undercover American agent was somewhere in the area, yet no one had turned him in to the Gestapo. A prospective ally in Innsbruck — a legitimate one this time, Freddy decided — was a Nazi police officer named Alois Kuen, a former SS agent who now worked for the Kripo, the criminal branch of the Nazi police forces. With word circulating about a mysterious agent in Innsbruck, Kuen — using the alias of "Karl Kern" — decided that he wanted to meet the man. He and Freddy arranged a clandestine meeting in mid-March. As the two men — one a Nazi, the other a Jew recently disguised as one — sized each other up, Kuen said he had become disillusioned with the Reich, despite his senior position with the Kripo. So had a number of Nazi officers under him, he said. Kuen and some of his supporters had been secretly printing anti-Nazi "propaganda sheets," not unlike the ones Hans had circulated, and they had also destroyed the internal Kripo files of anti-Nazi officers in the area to protect them from arrest by the Gestapo. He said they were willing to do more to bring down the Nazis — with the Americans' help.

Freddy realized that the Kripo officer speaking in hushed tones across from him could be laying a trap. Kuen might simply be trying to get more information from him about the American operations in Austria before tipping off the Gestapo about Freddy's true identity. Yet for reasons that Freddy could never fully explain, he believed Kuen; the Nazi police officer seemed genuine, even impressive, Freddy thought, and an alliance was born.

Kuen claimed to have a large band of Kripo officers already on his side, ready to join with Freddy, and he said he knew where he could find still more. The Gestapo had imprisoned five hundred political opponents—all of them ardent anti-Nazis—at a barracks in Kematen, the same town where Freddy, or Frédéric Mayér, was still working at the airplane factory. Kuen proposed a prison break: he could arrange to free all the political prisoners, team them with the other resisters, then take up arms against the Nazis. But first, Kuen said, they would need a cache of guns —thus the five hundred military-grade pistols that Freddy requisitioned in his earlier cable to "take Innsbruck."

Freddy loved the idea. His bosses did not. Like Hans and Franz, some OSS officers were also becoming concerned about an agent who, as William Casey, a senior OSS official in Europe, put it, had to be reminded "that he was on an intelligence mission, and not acting in an Errol Flynn movie." Colonel Chapin, the OSS officer who had sent Freddy and Hans to Bari months earlier, fumed when he learned the pair had asked for a heads-up about Austrian bombing missions, so that Freddy could stay out of their path. Chapin took that as a clear sign that Freddy was spending too much time inside dangerous bomb zones himself —and failing to find Austrian cutouts to do the risky groundwork for him. The colonel sent off a dispatch to Ulmer's OSS crew on the other side of Italy. They needed to let Freddy know "in strongest terms," Chapin wrote, that "his personal security [is] highest importance . . . If as leader he gets burned, whole setup is finito." Chapin stressed that "nothing he could do in person, however courageous," would justify getting caught and exposing the operation.

The idea of dropping five hundred guns into Austria struck Ulmer and his aides in Bari as half-cocked. Freddy's latest proposal didn't seem well thought out, and it was a distraction from more important intelligence-gathering work, Ulmer concluded. "If you have top-notch plan," he wrote back to Freddy, "give complete outline and will resubmit" for consideration. "Otherwise continue your intelligence program which G-2 [the intelligence section] likes."

OSS's reluctance was clear to Freddy, even behind the veil of bureaucratese, and he took it as a personal rebuke: *Stick to your first assignment and don't be in a hurry to get killed.* He didn't bother to come up with a "top-notch plan" that might pass muster with Bari. But nor did he give up completely on his hopes of arming the Nazi opponents. Instead, he simply devised a new plan that was even more eye-popping than the last. He met again with Kuen, this time alongside a Wehrmacht major named Hein who claimed his people were ready to dynamite local bridges in the Alps to deter the Nazis. More confident than ever after the meeting, Freddy penned a new cable declaring that he now had "one thousand partisans . . . under my command. A full plane load of explosives for bridges sabotage and a quantity of propaganda material should be sent to me at once."

OSS had never done anything quite like what Freddy was proposing, and Ulmer had every reason to quash Freddy's latest brash pitch. Under his watch, the Bari section was continuing to lose agents in bungled operations. In a particularly gruesome episode that same month during a parachute mission into northern Italy, the tether on an OSS agent's parachute failed to release on the drop. He was slammed repeatedly against the bottom of the plane and killed. Only a month before, OSS headquarters had sent the two colonels to Bari to diagnose all the problems in the field operations. With the recent failures so glaring, Ulmer didn't need to risk losing Freddy, one of his best field agents, just as an Allied victory seemed in sight. His agent in Innsbruck was already generating valuable intelligence without organizing any armed revolts.

Still, Ulmer found it difficult to say no to Freddy. He considered many of his OSS agents wildly overmatched for their missions, but Freddy's agile spy work and his judgment had earned Ulmer's unflinching trust. "He was magnificent at bluffing and lying," Ulmer would remark, "and everything you needed to survive."

If Freddy believed he had the manpower to "take Innsbruck," Ulmer decided he was not going to be the one to stand in his way. He gave the tentative go-ahead for the improbable plan to drop the cache of weapons and supplies. But the decision was twisted into a Gordian knot that left Freddy's own role open to wide interpretation. Freddy could work to organize the resisters, Ulmer decided, but "under no circumstances" should he become involved "too closely with any sabotage missions." He wanted him to "keep aloof" from the resisters and their actual operations, "to continue the priceless flow of information." That delicate balance would require Freddy to rein himself in — something he had never found easy to do.

Freddy continued bringing in all sorts of valuable intelligence on the Nazis, even as he planned his armed resistance. "Fifty fighter planes expected at New Innsbruck Airport. This shipment by rail," he reported in one cable on April 14. His source: "a bragging major with the air force." The very next day, he sent another cable, about a sighting of "67 four-ton trucks with trailers loaded with coast artillery." Then came some frustrating news he had picked up from a worker on a Nazi bomb-defusing crew in the city: In two recent Allied air raids, Freddy cabled, six hundred bombs that American fighter planes dropped over Innsbruck included "one hundred duds. Repeat: duds."

Freddy continued to ply new avenues for information. At Kripo, Kuen had obtained for him a thick stack of internal Gestapo documents that revealed, among other things, the names of many Nazi *Spitzel,* or insiders suspected of opposing the Reich. The documents promised to be an invaluable spy tool against the Nazis, and OSS officers were keen to get their hands on them. But they were so voluminous that Hans couldn't send them all back to OSS by cable, so Bari was scrambling to arrange for Freddy to hand the originals off, through his cutouts, to an OSS operative in Switzerland.

The supply team in Bari, meanwhile, was busy loading a B-24 fighter plane with all the supplies that Freddy wanted OSS to parachute down for his resisters: eight containers filled with explosives, pistols, submachine guns, hundreds of rounds of 9 mm ammunition, and enough other weaponry to arm a large band of disaffected Nazis. There were electronics parts, a new receiver, and batteries for Hans, along with cartons of cigarettes, coffee, more gold coins, and another $1,500 in cash; more than fourteen hundred pounds of supplies in all, "plus special stuff Freddy wanted," as Ulmer noted. That included one particularly hard-to-come-by item: insulin for Freddy to bribe a diabetic Gestapo official who ran security at the Kematen labor plant and who was running out of medicine; ten tubes of insulin were packed away.

Perhaps most important of all, Freddy wanted OSS to forward all the personal mail that he and Hans had received while they were gone, no doubt stacked up somewhere in a mail room in Italy. After seven weeks spent incommunicado in Austria, Hans was anxious to hear how Elly was liking her studies at Cornell University, and Freddy was desperate for any news from his parents and his little sisters in Brooklyn. He knew his mother, in particular, must be fretting over him after the long silence. The mail from home was so eagerly anticipated that the supply people tied a red sash around the container for easy identification amid all the guns, ammunition, and explosives.

The sash was an inspiring touch of sentiment in the midst of a brutal war. But in a mission that Ulmer declared had been "phenomenally successful," things soon began to go phenomenally badly for the Gulliver team, setting off three weeks of bedlam.

On a moonless Saturday night in April, Freddy finished his shift at the airplane factory and snuck out of the labor camp to meet up with a handful of Kuen's men. They drove out to a secluded area in the mountains far outside Innsbruck, hidden from passersby, and gathered for the weapons dropoff at the designated "pinpoint" location—which, on OSS's vegetable-coded maps, was marked inside the grid for "peas."

"Awaiting drop tonight," Freddy had cabled. This was a moment of such expectation—the start of an armed rebellion, he believed—that Hans and Franz put aside their misgivings and came out of hiding in Oberperfuss to meet up with Freddy and help gather the supplies. Maria, always willing to assist Freddy, tagged along as well. A driver with a two-and-a-half-ton German truck was waiting at the site to haul it all to a hiding spot.

Before midnight, Freddy began flashing a white signal light into the night sky. He watched, and he waited. Someone thought they heard an engine rumbling in the distance, but nothing ap-

peared. Kuen's men, armed with rifles, kept an eye out for any
Nazi patrols in the area. Freddy continued flashing his signal in
vain. An hour passed, then another. Finally, Freddy sent everyone
home. It didn't look like their supplies were coming after all.

The next night, Freddy came back to the field alone, still ran-
kled over OSS's no-show. Hans had heard nothing more from
Bari in the meantime. Freddy began flashing his white signal
again. This time, he saw a plane approaching in the distance. He
thought it looked like a British, not an American, aircraft. Stranger
still, the plane was shooting bright flares toward the ground — so
bright that Freddy thought the Nazis must surely be able to see
them from halfway across the valley. What the hell was going on?
No one had said anything about using flares; that was practically
inviting the Nazis to locate him and his people.

Freddy's frustration only mounted the next day, when he
made his way back into Oberperfuss. A new dispatch from Bari
explained the missed dropoff that first night: Freddy's team had
the wrong day. The drop wasn't scheduled until the *next* night,
Hans said. Freddy hadn't factored in the two days of lead time
that the air force would need once they received the go-ahead for
the drop, OSS said. Freddy had gotten sloppy.

That night, Freddy went back out to the drop site for a third
time, bringing along his full complement of assistants. Again, he
flashed his blinking signal into the sky — white and green, this
time, on Bari's orders. He thought he heard a faint crackle over a
special "Eureka" shortwave radio designed to communicate with
an overhead plane, but the signal was too far away to pick up. De-
moralized, he left empty-handed again, the truck still empty. He
had an army of resisters ready to fight the Nazis, and the banality
of aerial logistics was getting in the way.

Only days later did Freddy get the cable that explained the latest foul-up: the B-24 had made it into Austria, almost reaching the drop site, when one of its engines blew out. To lighten the plane's load, the pilot made the decision — much to OSS's chagrin — to jettison all eight containers of cargo. "A great screw-up," Ulmer called the episode.

All the supplies — the weapons, the explosives, the gold coins, even the insulin and the red-sashed package of letters from Brooklyn — were now scattered somewhere high up in the Alpine Mountains. And Freddy was left to fume.

The commotion in the mountains was not lost on the Gestapo. The flares from the mystery plane had gotten its attention, just as Freddy had feared. By the next day, the Gestapo agents in Innsbruck were on high alert in a now-urgent hunt for spies and saboteurs believed to be hiding in their midst. "The whole area was alerted," OSS said. The Nazis had grown accustomed to Allied bombing raids over Innsbruck, but this was clearly something different.

During Freddy's time in Innsbruck, the Gestapo had always been a menacing presence, but recently, he had sensed a growing complacency in its ranks, as if the Nazis sensed imminent defeat. It had been almost too easy to evade them all these weeks. Now, in the wake of the botched airdrop, the atmosphere had become ominous almost overnight. Teams of Gestapo agents, hundreds in all, were suddenly swarming the Inn Valley to try to determine what had happened in the mountains — and who was behind it. They searched homes, interrogated townspeople, imprisoned enemies and innocents. Everyone, it seemed, was a suspect.

All hell has broken loose, Freddy thought. From Italy, Ulmer realized it, too. They would have to hold off for now in trying to drop down any more weapons or supplies. "Area became too hot," he cabled Freddy. With the Gestapo banging on doors throughout the city, Innsbruck had become too dangerous for him to maintain his cover, so Freddy did something he rarely did: he hid. For two nights, he stayed alone in the woods, up in the mountains toward Oberperfuss, waiting until it was safe enough to return. He was cold and hungry, living off berries, mushrooms, and roots. He would have gladly settled for a slice of the Spam that he used to give away. The waiting — not knowing what was happening in Innsbruck, in Oberperfuss, or in Bari — was excruciating. He felt useless, left to ponder what had gone wrong in the dropoff. The flares shooting from the plane that night were the most confounding part. From a British plane, no less. Weren't the Brits and the Americans on the same side?

After three days hidden in the woods, Freddy finally decided to venture back into Innsbruck, unsure what he would find there. It was April 20 — Hitler's birthday; a bad omen, perhaps. He soon learned from one of his contacts that the Gestapo's hunt for possible saboteurs had only intensified while he was in hiding. The Nazis had jailed Fritz Moser, the informant who had told him about his uncle's foreign electrical workers. Leo, the black marketeer who sold him information on the rail lines, had been arrested, too. Whether the Gestapo had connected him to either man, Freddy didn't know. Even now, he imagined he was safe. The idea that the Nazis would discover him, after he had eluded them for so long, seemed inconceivable to him.

He went to Gretl and Eva's apartment for the night. He had never had any problems at the sisters' flat, and the small loft upstairs where he usually hid seemed like the safest spot for now. Some of his belongings were still hidden in the crevices there — his gun, his money belt, and, most important, the Gestapo papers that Kuen had given him. If he was forced to flee the area for good, he would need them all.

In his hideaway upstairs, Freddy took off his shoes to rest his feet. A stove was burning nearby, keeping him warm, and he began flipping through the large stacks of Gestapo documents. He needed to put the prized papers in order so he could arrange the planned handoff. Despite all the tumult in the last few days, OSS wanted to move ahead with the transfer they had planned to get the documents into American hands in Switzerland. In fact, Bari had already cabled Hans with the details, with the handoff scheduled for the very next day. Somehow Freddy was supposed to use his cutouts to relay the documents to an American agent waiting more than a hundred miles to the west, in Lichtenstein, who would be holding a copy of the newspaper *Der Bund*, OSS informed him in a cable. "Your man should follow him to quiet spot and use password '*Welche Zeitung lessen Sie?*'" the cable advised. "What newspaper are you reading?" This would be a challenging bit of spycraft in the current climate, even for Freddy. With Gestapo agents now roaming the city, Freddy wasn't certain how he was going to arrange his end of the handoff.

As he continued assembling the documents, a pounding at the front door downstairs interrupted his work. It was eleven o'clock at night. He hadn't scheduled any meetings with his local allies, not with the heightened state of alert, and his contacts knew better than to use the front door anyway. He listened in silence as Eva went to open the door. Freddy heard voices that he didn't recognize, loud and insistent, and then a name that he did recognize: *Frederic Mayer*, its lyrical French pronunciation not evident in the German utterance. The Nazis were here.

Still, he downplayed the threat. Freddy's first thought was that the late-night callers were looking for him because he was a foreign laborer who had left the barracks after dark, violating the camp rules. It was probably nothing more than that, he convinced himself. He wasn't worried; he still figured he could talk his way out of the situation. *What can they do to me?* he asked himself. Maybe a few days of hard labor in a Gestapo prison for his transgression.

The conversation seemed to be getting more heated downstairs. The men were asking Eva questions, and Freddy could hear her explaining that she had met a Frenchman in Innsbruck earlier that night. She seemed to be trying to stall for time. Looking around, Freddy realized that if the Nazis searched the apartment, the intelligence documents alone would make clear that he was much more than simply a French electrician. His confidence faded. He wouldn't be able to talk his way out of that. Hurriedly, he threw the Gestapo papers into the fire in the stove. Then he grabbed his gun and his money belt, filled with his cash and the gold coins, stuffed them all in his rucksack, and shoved the bag as far beneath the sofa as he could reach.

He tried opening a window so he could flee out a back fire escape, but it was frozen shut. He couldn't budge it. That was when he heard the thundering sounds of footsteps coming up the stairs, and the door slamming open. He turned to see what looked like a half-dozen Nazi officers rushing into the room with pistols drawn. He thought for a moment about reaching for the gun under the couch, but he realized he stood no chance against a swarm of armed Nazis.

"Frederic Mayer?" one of the officers asked.

"Oui," he answered.

"You're under arrest."

11

The Water Treatment

GESTAPO HEADQUARTERS
INNSBRUCK, AUSTRIA
April 21, 1945

"Je suis un électricien," Freddy kept telling the Nazi officers. *I am an electrician.*

Yet no matter how many times he said it, or how calmly, his three interrogators clearly didn't believe him. They thought he was a spy. They did think enough of his French to find him an interpreter in the building, once he had convinced them he didn't speak German. The rest of his story, though, they dismissed as *eine Lüge* — simply a lie.

The main interrogator sitting across from Freddy in a dank basement office at Gestapo headquarters was a blond-haired, pasty-faced man named Walter Güttner, who looked to be in his midthirties. Güttner, an Obersturmführer — a midlevel Nazi officer — was a diminutive man: shorter than Freddy at about five foot four, with a skinny frame and a nervous demeanor: not at all like the hulking presence Freddy had come to expect from the Nazis in Austria. Güttner's slight physique and his eyes — small and beady, darting constantly — put Freddy in mind of a "little rat." Or perhaps one of the tiny, treacherous Lilliputians who terrorized Gulliver in his travels.

Güttner, flanked by two senior SS officers, had started the conversation civilly enough as guards nearby stood watch over the unshackled prisoner. He spoke in a cordial, almost fatherly tone. Freddy would not be mistreated if he answered all their questions truthfully, Güttner promised him. The Gestapo just needed to know some basic things: where was he from; how had he gotten into Austria; who else came with him; what local contacts he had among the loose association of Austrian resisters.

Freddy sat stoically and listened. He wasn't worried. Even now, hours after the Nazis had taken him from Eva's apartment with his hands tied behind his back, even after they brought him to Gestapo headquarters and started questioning him, he told himself that he could still somehow talk his way out of his latest predicament. He always had. They had "nothing concrete" on him, he told himself with calming reassurance.

Piece by piece, he gave Güttner his well-honed cover story: His name was Frédéric Mayér. He was a French electrician who worked at a Nazi plant in eastern Austria until Russian troops forced him to flee with other foreign laborers. Weeks earlier, he had come to Innsbruck and begun working at the Nazi aircraft facility in Kematen. He had his labor papers. He worked in the maintenance section. He didn't know anything else, he insisted.

He was determined to stick to his answers no matter how the questions were posed, and his French cover gave him a few extra seconds to mull over each question thrown at him while the interpreter translated it from German. But he could see that Güttner was growing frustrated. The Gestapo investigator didn't want to be there either. It was the middle of the night, and the interrogation seemed to be going nowhere. He was a bit drunk after a few glasses of schnapps at the office earlier; he had assumed he would be home long ago, with his wife and four children. Plans changed when his boss, Friedrich Busch, who was the second-ranking Gestapo officer out of roughly a hundred employees at headquarters, directed him to interrogate a new prisoner. Güttner had hoped it could wait until morning, but Busch had insisted.

With Freddy showing no signs of wavering from his story after more than an hour, Güttner wanted to quit for the night. Busch directed him to keep at it — and to get answers this time. Out of earshot of Freddy, Güttner asked Busch whether that meant using "extreme, severe" measures. "Naturally," Busch said.

The Nazis had begun employing the tools of torture almost immediately after Hitler's rise to power, in 1933, in an effort to extract information from the regime's "enemies." The early victims included political opponents jailed in the first concentration camps, as well as suspect foreigners, like an American doctor in Berlin who had been whipped until his skin was a "mass of raw flesh." Knives, sticks, whips, nooses, chemicals, and human excrement all became the means of torture to bring to heel those prisoners who were not executed outright. Twelve years later, torture had become so routine that a Gestapo chief like Busch was surprised that his underling would even question whether or not to use it against a prisoner.

Güttner and the two SS men who were with him moved Freddy to a barren room next door. This was the place reserved for "severe" interrogations. Down the hall, locked in cells, were another thirty or forty prisoners the Nazis had rounded up in the past few days as suspected resisters. Güttner and the SS men began the litany of questions all over again; while Freddy's answers never changed, his interrogators grew ever more insistent. They were determined to break him, and Güttner was acting as though Freddy knew more than he was letting on.

Abandoning the charade of civility after another of the prisoner's scripted responses, Güttner abruptly slapped Freddy across the face. "Are you a spy?" he shouted. "Are you a spy?" Freddy shook his head. "Je suis un électricien," he repeated. Now one of the SS men slapped him, harder this time, and soon all three Nazis were taking turns slapping and punching him in the head.

"Where is the radio operator!" Güttner demanded. "Where is the radio operator!" Güttner seemed intent on getting an answer to this question more than any other, but it was the last thing Freddy would be willing to disclose. "Je ne sais pas," he said again and again. *I don't know.* Another question, another denial, then another blow to the head, and another, and another. When one of the SS men boxed both of his ears at once, puncturing Freddy's eardrum, the pain rifled through his body. Blood from his mouth and face began to drip onto the concrete floor.

"Je ne sais rien!" *I know nothing,* Freddy kept insisting. The

Gestapo would keep him alive, he believed, only if they thought there was information they could extract from him. *If.* Otherwise they might as well kill him right then. He was becoming woozy, and every blow made it more difficult to speak, even if he had wanted to say something of consequence.

He thought for a moment about the suicide pill that OSS had given him for an occasion like this. And he thought about Hans and Franz in Oberperfuss, but especially Hans. He wondered if his Dutch comrade was still safely in hiding. He was determined the Nazis not find out about his fellow traveler.

Staring at the bloodied prisoner, one of the SS men remarked, apropos of nothing, that he suspected Freddy was a Jew. Güttner scoffed at the notion. "Ach Quatsch," he said. *Nonsense.* No lowly Jew could withstand such punishment. Freddy, half-conscious, took silent satisfaction in the exchange. *They underestimated me,* he told himself.

The Nazis began stripping off his clothes, looking for valuables or documents that might have been missed during an initial search at Eva's apartment. Freddy recoiled as they grabbed at his clothes, punching and kicking at his captors to keep them at bay. He knew that the Nazis routinely stripped male prisoners to see if they were circumcised Jews. Freddy wasn't going to let that happen without a fight. That boy in grade school, the one in Freiburg who had called him a "stinking Jude," had learned his lesson when Freddy decked him. Now he managed to fight off all three Nazis as they converged on him. In a fair fight, Freddy thought, he could take down Güttner with one hand. He swung and squirmed so effectively that a few wild swings from the SS men missed him and struck Güttner instead, causing the Gestapo officer to complain later that "my arms were sore."

The prisoner's strength took Güttner by surprise. Once they finally had Freddy pinned down and finished stripping him, Güttner ordered Freddy handcuffed. Freddy continued to struggle, and when his hands were finally restrained, Güttner brought out a long, cowhide whip and began lashing at his bare back with the practiced strokes of a man who had used it many times before. Ten lashes, twenty lashes, thirty lashes, and still the blows kept coming. "He hit him wherever he could," said one Austrian woman who worked at the Gestapo headquarters and witnessed part of the beating.

Putting down the whip, Güttner took out his pistol and stuck the barrel in Freddy's mouth. "Go ahead and shoot," Freddy said in French, taunting him. "We don't do it that easy," Güttner replied with a smirk. He pulled the barrel of the gun out of Freddy's mouth and jammed it back in — sideways this time, with the cold metal stretching out the inside of Freddy's cheeks. With the gun lodged inside Freddy's mouth, Güttner then delivered a looping uppercut, a haymaker, to his chin. Freddy could feel his back teeth snapping out, and he tasted blood as Güttner ripped the pistol out of his mouth. He spat out the blood, and a mouthful of teeth along with it. Blood oozed from wounds across his entire body: his back was ripped raw, his face was battered, and his genitals were bloodied.

Güttner told the prisoner that he had *proof* he was a spy. He was determined to break him, Jew or not. His boss, Busch, and several other top Nazis had now assembled in the interrogation room to watch the spectacle. Dazed, Freddy could make out the glint of gold threads gleaming from the formal brown Nazi uniform of one of the men, who looked to be the most senior among them. His beating was attracting quite an audience.

A guard led another man into the room — another shackled prisoner this time. Freddy recognized him immediately: It was Fritz Moser, the black marketeer who had fed him information about his uncle's foreign laborers. Freddy might never have become Frédéric Mayér without Fritz. He had come to rely heavily on him, using his apartment as one of his hideouts, and he had learned from Fritz's girlfriend a day earlier that he, too, had been arrested in the roundup. Still, seeing his ally standing in the prison just a few feet away from him was a jolt for Freddy, lying naked and battered on the floor.

He pretended not to recognize his former source. Fritz looked as if he had been roughed up himself, and he had an apologetic expression on his bruised face. It struck Freddy as a look of betrayal. "It's no use, Fred," Fritz said in German, the interrogators looking on. "Tell them the truth." The pieces fell into place immediately for Freddy, even in his beaten haze: *Fritz had talked.* Fritz knew where Eva lived; he must have told the Gestapo where to find him. Not only that, but he could have told them that Freddy was an American, and a spy. He tried to remember what else Fritz knew from their many conversations in the past month: his work at the airplane factory, information about the train lines, the identities of his other cutouts. He didn't know anything about Hans, thankfully, or about Oberperfuss; Freddy had been careful about that. But he knew enough. Freddy was furious. Why couldn't Fritz have just kept quiet? He might never have been captured if he had. Freddy had the urge to spit in his eye, but he couldn't muster the energy.

"I don't even know this man," Freddy said finally. His interrogators looked incredulous. Even as he said it, Freddy realized that he was going to have to change his story. The Gestapo knew far more than he had thought, and it seemed futile to stick with his Frenchman's farce at this point. He decided to tell the truth, or at least a small part of it.

"Ich bin Amerikaner," he said in perfect German. *I am an American.* It was a rare moment when Freddy was confronted with his own tortured identity. What *was* he really? He was an American, no doubt; not just an American "immigrant" with second-tier status, but an American citizen who had completed his citizenship papers a year earlier on break from the army. But he was a German, too, and a proud one; or at least he had been for most of his childhood before Hitler robbed him of that. Then he became defined as a German *Jew,* a deadly distinction; then a German refugee on a boat to Ellis Island; then an American soldier; and now an American spy with so many cover stories that his own parents didn't know his true identity.

He was able to be whatever he needed to be, John Billings, the B-24 pilot who had mistaken him for a fellow aviator, would later marvel. After nearly four hours of brutal beatings at the hands of the Gestapo, Freddy was finally admitting he was an American — but his Nazi interrogators still didn't believe him. Güttner was convinced he was lying; Freddy's German was too perfect for him to be an American. Güttner detected the Swabian accent of a man from Germany's southern region; he was convinced Freddy had come to Austria to foment resistance.

No, Freddy said; he was an American, and he had come to Austria by way of Switzerland. He had come alone. Exactly why, though, he wouldn't say. "I refuse to answer any further questions," Freddy said, "and I'm willing to take the consequences."

The consequences were swift. Güttner sent for "the sticks," and a Gestapo messenger returned with two long poles. "Where is the radio operator!" Güttner demanded again. Freddy said nothing. With his hands cuffed behind his back, he tried to resist once again as the three Nazis forced him down into a crouch, doubled him over, and jammed the poles beneath his arms and knees. They then threw him onto a table and hoisted the poles to the ceiling. Freddy dangled from the poles above the table, head down and naked, as Güttner and the SS men sent for a jug of water and a bucket. They dunked his head in the water and, cupping his mouth, took turns pouring the water up his nose and into his ears. This was what Güttner and his men benignly called the "water treatment." Freddy felt as if he were drowning. Choking and spitting up water, he was unable to breathe, and the pain caused by the water gushing through his burst eardrum was excruciating. He was barely conscious. He tried to force himself to pass out, hoping to ease the pain, but he couldn't do it.

The water finally stopped. Someone teased him with a piece of food, holding it in front of his face, then snatching it away when he tried to take it. Were they laughing at him now? The Nazis and their psychological tricks — he wouldn't be so gullible again.

Güttner left him hanging from the ceiling for hours, letting him ponder his plight. How long exactly, Freddy couldn't say; time seemed an abstraction as he hung there, motionless. Eventually his torturers returned and began another round of the water treatment, but Freddy's answers, barely audible in his current state, didn't change. He was an American. He had come into the country from Switzerland. Alone. He didn't know a radio operator.

Finally, after he had been suspended from the poles for a gruesome six hours, Güttner and the SS men took him down and dropped him on the bone-cold floor, his teeth chattering, only to begin kicking and punching him all over again. Freddy lay motionless, pretending to be unconscious; he had no strength left to resist.

"Better stop. He's unconscious," Freddy heard someone say; it was a voice he didn't recognize. The pummeling ended on command. This man was the same senior Nazi he had seen in the interrogation room earlier, the one with the gold threads on his uniform. His name, Freddy would learn, was Max Primbs. He was a doctor, but much more important in Innsbruck was his title as the Nazi Kreisleiter for the entire region, the second-ranking position under Franz Hofer. Primbs was a powerful figure in Tyrol; he didn't spend a lot of time at Gestapo headquarters, but he had taken a personal interest in the new prisoner. The man needed to be kept alive, Primbs told Güttner. If he really was an American, he said, then Hofer would need to know about it immediately.

Güttner had been at this all night now, and morning had come. He needed to update Busch on what he had found out — which wasn't nearly as much as he had hoped. Even if the prisoner was an American, which Güttner continued to doubt, he did not know why he had come to Innsbruck or who had accompanied him. But Güttner had an idea that he thought might break the impasse. He ordered his men to find a cell for Freddy. There was another man Güttner wanted to find.

Months earlier, when Freddy and Hans were still training in Italy for the Alpine jump, OSS had given strict orders to them and all the other would-be spies at the base in Bari: they were not allowed to talk about their missions with anyone, or try to learn about the other operations in the works. The OSS officers were loose about many military rules, but violating that one could get a man sent home. The agents weren't even supposed to know the identities of the other agents at the base. The secrecy was for their own protection, Lieutenant Ulmer said. "If you are captured, you may be sure that every effort will be made to force you to tell all you know," he warned. The less they knew about other operations, the less they could reveal under pressure. The problem with many of the OSS agents roaming around the Italian base, Ulmer grumbled, was that "the guys just weren't smart enough to keep their mouths shut."

Freddy didn't need any warnings; he was determined to stay quiet, even after the Gestapo had beaten him bloody and dumped him, naked and cuffed, on a flea-ridden straw mat in an ice-cold cell. Now that Fritz had told the Gestapo what he knew, Freddy figured the Nazis had already found out all that they could about him. What he didn't know, however, was that there was another OSS spy in Innsbruck at that same moment who knew all about Freddy's true history — and he was willing to tell the Gestapo men anything they wanted to know.

His name was Hermann Matull; the Gestapo knew him as Max. He was a German-born huckster who had worked as a Nazi radio operator in the war, until he deserted. OSS's Dyno Lowenstein, in his hunt for "deserter volunteers" to bring back to Bari, had spotted Matull in a POW camp in northern Italy six months earlier and thought he would make a good spy. Others at OSS weren't so impressed. With his slicked-back hair, checkered history, and scattershot banter, Matull seemed slippery even by Nazi standards. "A Mississippi steamboat gambler," Ulmer called him. "A real guttersnipe," said Walter Haass, who helped train Matull in Bari.

In Bari, Matull trained for an unusual solo mission into Germany at the same time the Gulliver agents were at the base preparing for their own jump. Freddy didn't remember hearing anything about Matull during his time at the base, and he knew nothing of his parachuting operation. But Matull—ignoring OSS's demands for strict secrecy—had managed to learn all about Freddy and many other commando agents while he was in Bari.

Matull's mission, code-named Deadwood with unintended irony, had begun just three weeks before Freddy's capture, at the beginning of April. Haass was the jump master for the flight from Italy, just as he had been for the Gulliver team, but he and Matull had a frosty relationship. As their plane whizzed over Austria toward Munich, just as Haass prepared to give Matull the "go" signal to jump through the Joe hole, the Nazi defector turned to him. "I know you bastards don't trust me, but I'm going to prove you wrong," he vowed.

He didn't. Matull was supposed to be gathering military intelligence inside Germany, but soon after getting to Munich, he got on a train and headed back toward Italy with the thousands of dollars in cash and gold that OSS had given him for the mission; he wanted to see a girlfriend in Milan. The Nazis picked him up on the train after he was spotted smoking American cigarettes, a sure giveaway; it almost seemed as if he wanted to get caught.

Matull soon agreed to cooperate with his Gestapo captors—as a double agent working, once again, for the Nazis against the Americans. Under the direction of his new Nazi handlers, he radioed a series of muddled messages back to OSS with supposed updates on his "mission," and the Gestapo sent him to Innsbruck to help root out resisters and spies in Tyrol. He arrived there on the very same day as Freddy's capture, but instead of getting a cell at the jail, he was housed, under guard, at a comfortable Nazi guesthouse nearby.

The Gestapo had assigned Güttner to debrief Matull, aka Max. Between the all-night torture of Freddy and the roundup of the Innsbruck resisters, Güttner had practically forgotten about Max and the assignment. But as Freddy's brutal interrogation wore on, Güttner realized that Max might know something of relevance. He knew that the new arrival was a German defector and an American spy who, after his capture, had "already declared himself willing to work for the Gestapo." He regretted that it hadn't occurred to him to go talk to Max earlier, as he headed for the Gestapo guesthouse just a few blocks away.

He asked Matull almost immediately whether he knew a man named Fred Mayer. He might be an American spy, he said; dark brown hair; short and stocky, very strong. Matull said the name sounded like someone he remembered from his training at OSS in Italy. If it was him, Matull said, he was a "big catch"; he might know for certain, he said, if he could see a photo.

Güttner returned to headquarters to tell his Gestapo supervisors what he had found, then headed to the basement to Freddy's jail cell. It had been a brutal day for Freddy, with the straw in his makeshift bed cutting into the open wounds on his naked body, and the handcuffs behind his back making it almost impossible to sleep. The soup and bread that the jailers gave him were putrid, but one guard, with a surprising sense of sympathy, slipped him part of his sandwich, along with a handkerchief to wipe away the dried blood on his body. It was the closest he would come to medical attention.

Güttner arrived with an oversized pair of old pants and a jacket, both far too big for Freddy, and directed him to get dressed. Then he led him out of the cell and threw a raincoat over his head so none of the jailed resisters would see his face as he walked past the cell block. Freddy was going to have his photo taken. His whole face was swollen and badly bruised, with his eyes glassy and bloodshot. Even so, when Güttner returned to the guest-house with the black-and-white photograph in hand, Matull recognized the face immediately. That was the man he had known as "Lieutenant Fred" at the OSS base in Italy, he said; he was an important man there. Matull went on to tell Güttner all about Freddy and the OSS spy-training operation in Bari: where exactly it was located, who ran it, how the men trained, where they went for R&R in town. He got some of the details wrong, but it was far more than Güttner had hoped to get from him.

Güttner returned to Freddy's cell. Ever resilient, Freddy smiled at him disarmingly, despite his injuries — "a happy and friendly face," Güttner reported later. He didn't see that very often from the men he tortured.

"Lieutenant Fred!" Güttner said. Excited to show off the store of information he had received, he mentioned OSS and Bari by name and proceeded to toss out for Freddy all sorts of details about life in training: names of agents and instructors; oddball stories from the mess hall; the name of the theater in town, the Teatro Piccinni, where the men would see shows; and even Villa Suppa, the name of the grassy quarters at the base where Freddy had been sequestered with Hans and Franz.

Freddy remained quiet, though the level of detail his Nazi interrogator had displayed was stunning. It was clear the Gestapo had an inside source — deep inside the American spy operation.

"We also have our agents," Güttner told him by way of explanation. "We have another man from OSS."

Freddy did not doubt it, and he had every reason to expect that Güttner would haul him down to the interrogation room again for another round of "severe" questioning. Yet he didn't. Güttner left him in his cell, on his uncomfortable straw mat. Freddy wasn't going to ask why. There was no point in trying to read the motives of a Nazi torturer in going easy on him. Psychological strategy, exhaustion, a rare bit of mercy—his reasons didn't matter.

Or maybe it was the air-raid warning. Not long after Güttner left, the sirens blared, and the guards hustled him down to an underground bunker ahead of an oncoming Allied bombing raid over Innsbruck; it seemed the Nazis really did want to keep him alive. But the wailing of the air-raid sirens through his injured ear made him feel as if his head were going to explode.

Güttner had not wanted the other prisoners to see Freddy, his "big catch." But the air raid left the jailers little choice but to put him inside a small room in the bunker with a handful of other prisoners. Freddy was surprised to see his new neighbor. Right next to him was his friend and ally, Kuen; the Gestapo had picked up the Kripo police officer three days earlier, a major blow to the resistance fighters. The roundup had reached even further than Freddy had thought.

Freddy had managed to evade the Gestapo with seeming ease for nearly two months on the ground in Innsbruck, becoming ever more aggressive in his tactics. But the Gestapo's officers, ruthless as they were, were still intent on crushing their enemies. They had worn down his onetime ally Fritz Moser, forcing him to identify Freddy. They had turned OSS spy Hermann Matull into a double agent. And unknown to either Freddy or Kuen, they had a mole within the clan of Innsbruck resisters.

Freddy, in fact, had met unwittingly with the mole weeks earlier. The informant, Karl Niederwanger, was the same man who told Freddy he could produce five hundred resistance fighters for him, before failing the test run they had arranged. Freddy had never trusted him — with good reason, as it turned out. Niederwanger, a Wehrmacht deserter, was working for the Gestapo. He had gone to the Nazis with information about Tyrolean resisters — including ranking officers in the Kripo police force. The Gestapo promptly dispatched him to join the resistance forces. The information that he had collected in his undercover role as a self-proclaimed "resister" had triggered the roundup days earlier of Kuen, along with a number of his men in the Kripo — and ultimately of Freddy himself.

Less than a week earlier, Freddy and Kuen were exchanging internal Nazi records and waiting together in a darkened field in the mountains for a supply of OSS weapons to start an insurrection. Since then, all their plans had turned helter-skelter, and the two of them were now sitting side by side in a Nazi bunker, waiting to see whether an Allied bombing raid or a Gestapo beating killed them first.

Talking in hushed voices to avoid the guards' notice, the two men compared notes about their harrowing experiences in the past few days. Kuen told Freddy that after his own arrest, he had escaped by jumping out of a second-floor window at the jail, but he badly injured his arm in the fall, and the Gestapo soon chased him down. He had not told the interrogators anything, despite the harsh questioning that inevitably followed, he said.

As badly as Freddy and Kuen were beaten, other prisoners clustered among them in the bunker had fared even worse. One of those arrested in the roundups was Fritz Moser's uncle, Robert Moser, the electrical contractor for the Nazi factories. The Gestapo whipped and beat him mercilessly for hours. His offense: interrogators accused him of landing Freddy his job as an undercover spy at the factory in Kematen. Freddy would later say that Robert Moser had known nothing about the operation, but no matter: the Gestapo beat the Austrian businessman so badly — "in the most animal-like manner," said his wife, Margot, who was arrested with him — that he died of his wounds soon afterward at the jail.

The next morning, his second day in jail, Freddy awoke to find Güttner back at his cell door, along with three Nazi guards with machine guns. It was five thirty in the morning. The "little rat" had become his personal tormentor, his Inspector Javert, seeming to stalk his every step. Güttner was taking him on another trip, though he would not say where.

It was still dark outside when the Gestapo men shoved Freddy, in shackles, into the back of a green military transport truck. Güttner rode in the front, and the driver headed west in the valley, up toward the mountains. Freddy knew the route well; it was the same direction he traveled, with the same scenic backdrop, when he biked from Innsbruck along the back trails to the airplane factory in Kematen. An April storm had left a blanket of snow in their path, as the Gestapo truck passed patrols of heavily armed Wehrmacht soldiers roaming outside the city.

Six or seven miles later, they approached the turn for the airplane factory and kept going. Freddy thought he knew where they were headed now; or at least he feared he did. In just another few miles they would be in Oberperfuss. But how? How had the Gestapo heard anything about Oberperfuss? The thought confounded him. Fritz had told the Gestapo what he knew, unfortunately, but he had known nothing about Oberperfuss; Freddy had been careful never to mention the town to him — or to any of the resisters, for that matter — for fear of exposing Hans. Freddy knew that he himself could have been followed biking back to town, or Maria or one of her couriers, but he didn't think so. He would have heard that by now. Perhaps Güttner had made the link through Eva and the arrest at her apartment, realizing that her brother was Franz, a Nazi deserter missing in Italy, and they were from Oberperfuss. Freddy had to acknowledge that Güttner was cunning, after all — for a little rat. It was possible.

He hoped he was wrong. Then the truck arrived — back in Oberperfuss once again, almost two months after he had first knocked on Alois's door to report that Franz Weber had sent him. Many nights since then, Freddy had returned to the town — but never like this, with a truckload of Gestapo agents, and himself shackled in the backseat. It was a crushing turnabout for Freddy; the townspeople had leveraged everything to help him, and now he was bringing the Gestapo back to their doors, with no way to protect them.

It was a Sunday morning, and Annie, Franz's fiancée, was leaving for early mass at church at six o'clock, as she usually did, when she saw the Nazi truck and a flank of Gestapo agents standing in front of her mother's hotel. They were yelling, demanding to search the place. All around Oberperfuss, from farmhouse to farmhouse, the agents were banging on doors, rousing people from their Sunday-morning slumber or stopping them on their way to church.

Freddy stared blankly as Güttner and the agents went from one farmhouse to the next and brought the scared occupants outside to look at his face, bruised and swollen. Did they know this man? No, no one recognized him, or so they said. No one knew anything about a "radio man" in town either. Then the agents drove up to the Kirchebners' farm, where Hans had been hiding in the attic for a month. Frannie, the teenager who had been teaching Hans to play Mühle, was still asleep, but her older brother was out by the stables tending to the horses. The boy seemed nervous when Güttner began questioning him. Güttner slapped him across the face. He quickly "lost his nerve," as OSS related the scene, and admitted that he knew the Dutch radio operator and the Austrian deserter. They had fled the night before, he said. The boy said a woman in town named Maria was with them.

The agents quickly stormed the farmhouse. Güttner waited with Freddy downstairs as the agents went through the house room by room, looking for the radio operator. They made their way to the attic, ransacking the place. They did not find anyone there, but strewed around the attic, they did find a store-bought radio, spare electronics parts, some gold coins, and a chemistry book written in English. It looked as if someone had left very quickly.

Hans himself was now three miles away, hiding with Franz in a farmer's hayloft in the neighboring town of Ranggen. They had gotten a two-day head start on the Gestapo thanks again to the tag-team operation of Franz's sisters in Innsbruck. After the Gestapo captured Freddy at her apartment, Gretl alerted her sister Alouisa, the hospital nurse who helped him get his Nazi uniform, and she set out for Oberperfuss by bicycle to warn her brother. Freddy had been arrested, she reported; Franz needed to flee. Franz grabbed his rifle and roused Hans from his attic hideout nearby. The two of them packed whatever they could fit into their rucksacks, trudged down a snow-covered hill toward the train tracks, and kept running.

They found a temporary refuge up in the hayloft on a farm owned by another resister, hiding alongside two Russians also running from the Nazis. They were safe for now, but Hans was terrified for his friend. *Freddy had been arrested.* As many risks as Freddy had taken, the news still came as a shock to Hans. "We have to do something to rescue Fred," he told Franz. There was nothing they could do, Franz said. "If anybody could help Fred," he said, "he himself could do it."

In Oberperfuss, Güttner was bristling once he realized that the radio operator and the Nazi deserter were nowhere to be found. With the Gestapo threatening to torture Maria if she did not tell them what she knew, Maria admitted that she had seen the pair fleeing, and she agreed to show Güttner's men where they had gone — leading them up the mountains in the opposite direction in a fruitless, hours-long search. Güttner felt duped. He was convinced that, somehow, Freddy "was able to warn his comrades and make it possible for them to escape." He thought about arresting the whole lot of possible accomplices in town on the spot, but decided to wait on the arrests "to save expenses."

But he still had Freddy. Güttner had his men put the shackled prisoner back in the truck and head back to Innsbruck to lock him up once again.

Hours later, after the Gestapo had left town, Mama Niederkircher decided to organize an unscheduled mass at the Church of Saint Margareta. The church bells rang for an hour that night, and she and a few dozen other townspeople whom she trusted gathered to pray — not for peace or salvation, but for the safety of an American named Fred.

12

A White Flag

GESTAPO HEADQUARTERS

INNSBRUCK, AUSTRIA

April 24, 1945

Güttner was back.

It had been two days since the trip to Oberperfuss, and Freddy had seen mercifully little of him since their venture into the mountains. But now the tiny Gestapo investigator had returned, and he was standing at his cell door with another Nazi, this one dressed in a regal brown uniform with gold threads. Freddy recognized him. It was the man who had brought a halt to the vicious beating administered by Güttner and his thugs.

"This is Kreisleiter Dr. Primbs," Güttner told Freddy. "You're going with him. The Gauleiter wishes to see you."

Another surprise trip — this time to see the most powerful Nazi in Tyrol: Gauleiter Franz Hofer. Primbs was Hofer's top deputy, a close friend of the Gauleiter's as well, and the two men would hold court together at parades and public events in Tyrol to extol the Führer and the new order of the Reich. Freddy could only guess at the purpose of this latest trip, as Güttner led him in handcuffs to Primbs's black BMW convertible, with his personal chauffeur waiting.

All three men climbed in for the ride, but Güttner was largely invisible. The prisoner was the one who held Primbs's rapt attention. The Kreisleiter brought up the brutal beating he had witnessed a few days earlier. Primbs found it astonishing, he told Freddy, that someone could withstand such punishment — all without answering their questions. Primbs had already told Hofer all about the interrogation, he said, and the Gauleiter was anxious to meet the stalwart young American. They would be having lunch today at Hofer's home.

Primbs had a charm and civility that Freddy found striking in a Nazi; he seemed like one of the decent ones. Freddy thought that the Kreisleiter might well have saved his life in the interrogation room, after all. Perhaps the rescue was all just a ruse — with Primbs pretending to be the "good cop" to win his trust — but Freddy didn't think so. Primbs was a critical cog in the Nazis' brutal machinery, but his one apparent act of valor had eclipsed, in Freddy's mind at least, whatever horrific things he might have done in enforcing the Nazis' rule in Tyrol for years.

Güttner noticed the unusual way that the Nazi leader spoke to Freddy. Primbs talked to the prisoner in both English and German, as if they were old friends. Freddy was "a fine boy," Primbs told Güttner, the man who had beaten him bloody just days earlier. Güttner didn't know what to make of the odd dynamic between the two men.

Primbs's chauffeur drove east toward the mountains and on to the town of Hall, about six miles from Innsbruck. Just weeks earlier, dressed in his Nazi uniform, Freddy had visited the sprawling rail yard in the town, spotting the huge Nazi caravan headed to the Brenner Pass with weapons and supplies. Now he was on his way to the Gauleiter's stately home nearby in the paradoxical role of both prisoner and guest — a turn of events that even Freddy found dizzying.

Güttner uncuffed Freddy when they arrived at the house, but he himself was told to wait outside — another reminder of the Gestapo man's subordinate role in the new scheme of things. Hofer greeted Primbs and Freddy at the door, smiling gregariously. He was a big, portly bear of a man, with fleshy cheeks and a baby face that belied his reputation as a Nazi tyrant. The husky build and Nazi uniform made Freddy think of Hermann Göring. He didn't look evil, not exactly, but Freddy knew his reputation: a hard-core Nazi, "100% pro-Hitler," a personal friend and devotee of the Führer's since Hitler first seized power.

Hofer, in fact, had been an early Nazi leader in Austria even before the Anschluss, when party membership was still illegal. Imprisoned in 1933 for his work on behalf of the Nazi Party, Hofer made a dramatic escape from jail that left him wounded by gunfire, only to give a speech from a stretcher at a Nazi rally in Nuremberg soon after. His dramatic appearance at the rally "is remembered by all," read the text beneath his portrait in an official Nazi calendar that featured Hofer for the month of November in 1939. He even had a part in *Triumph of the Will*, the infamous Nazi propaganda film made by Leni Riefenstahl.

Hofer, born the son of a hotel manager in central Austria, had run Tyrol as his private fiefdom for years — "my territory," he called it. Early in his brutal reign, he declared his perverse dream of making it the Reich's "first Jew-free region," and he was accused of ordering the roundups of tens of thousands of Jews, Communists, Catholics, mentally ill, and other "enemies" in the area — many of whom were sent to concentration camps and ultimately killed. He was the main architect of Hitler's "Alpine fortress," a project still more an aspiration than a reality, and like Hitler himself, whom he had met with weeks earlier at the Berlin bunker, Hofer had vowed there would be "no surrender" on his watch. Just two months earlier, he ordered thousands of maltreated Nazi slave laborers to build still more fortifications outside the city, and he urged Tyroleans to brace for a final battle and earn "the German victory in which we all fanatically believe."

Hofer invited Freddy to sit down in his living room, along with his wife and several other Nazi dignitaries, while they waited for lunch to be served. Freddy — unshaven, badly bruised, wearing the same soiled, oversized clothes for days now — was not exactly dressed for the occasion. After all his weeks spent in cramped, grimy hideouts, this was a discomforting place to find himself — in the well-appointed den of a Nazi lion. Hofer was enjoying the life of a bon vivant — with a beautiful home, a beautiful blond wife, a beautiful lunch buffet awaiting — while the Reich was burning, Freddy thought.

"Well," Hofer surprised him by asking, "what do you think about the war?"

Guest or not, Freddy didn't mince words. "I think it's about over," he said. The Russians had entered Berlin the day before, and American forces were coming at Austria from all sides, with General Patton's Third Army Division leading the way from the east. Freddy had only a vague glimpse of the Allies' recent advances, but he was ready to predict the outcome nonetheless. Hitler "can about throw in the towel. It will be over very shortly," he told his Nazi host with a brashness outstripping his new rank of sergeant.

It was time for lunch.

After a steady diet of inedible soup and rock-hard bread in the Gestapo jail, Freddy feasted on a four-course meal of potatoes, fresh breads, jams, and Wiener schnitzel, and other Austrian delicacies. It still hurt to chew, but he wasn't going to pass up a real meal. When Hofer offered him some wine, however, he demurred. Sensing his discomfort, Hofer laughed and switched glasses with him, as if to demonstrate that the wine had not been poisoned.

Freddy struggled to understand Hofer's aims. He looked like a half-dead hobo in his clownish garb, yet here Hofer was, treating him like Nazi royalty. He might be trying to lull Freddy into giving up more information — the location of the elusive "radio operator," for one. Or he might be trying to ingratiate himself with the Americans in the event the war was truly lost. The Gauleiter might be employing a carrot-and-stick strategy, Freddy thought: Güttner had beaten him senseless with the sticks, and now Hofer was feeding him the carrots.

Hofer steered the conversation back to the war. He seemed conflicted, and he was looking to his mysterious guest — an American, Hofer seemed to assume, although he still did not know Freddy's true identity — for a possible way out. The Bolsheviks in Moscow were the world's real enemy, Hofer told Freddy, not the Germans. He proposed an alliance. "Why don't the Yanks and Brits join forces with the Germans against the Russians?" he asked plaintively. Out of the question, said Freddy, suddenly cast in the role of international diplomat. Hitler had never lived up to his agreements before now, Freddy pointed out. What made anyone think he would start now?

Hofer seemed desperate, and defeated.

American military leaders were still vexed by the question of how much fight the Nazis had left in Tyrol and the Alpine region. Eisenhower and his top generals were hotly debating that April whether the Alpine fortress was a "phantom" or a massive threat that could marshal two hundred thousand Nazi SS men and extend the war by months, or longer, as one media report weeks earlier had suggested. OSS itself fed the fears, saying in a report in March that "it is believed that eventually the Redoubt will hold 15–25 divisions composed chiefly of SS storm troopers."

History would show most of the predictions to be wildly exaggerated, but the threat was considered grave enough that General Eisenhower decided to send troops toward the Alpine region to head off any troop surge. "Operations in Berlin will have to take second place," Eisenhower said, leaving the city to the Russian forces in a strategic decision that would help shape the Cold War for years in a divided, postwar Germany.

The truth was that even Hofer was uncertain how many garrisons of Nazi soldiers were available — and willing — to defend "my territory." Thousands of heavily armed Wehrmacht soldiers were still patrolling the region, but they were hindered by low morale, depleted numbers, and a dearth of fuel and supplies. Hofer himself clashed with Field Marshal Kesselring, the top military commander for the region. The Nazi field marshal wrote later that, in those critical weeks in April, "Gauleiter Hofer's behavior was hard to understand, and he interfered so alarmingly in the conduct of operations that I actually had to transmit an order that the Innsbruck Gauleiter's instructions on military matters were not to be followed."

Freddy now found himself face-to-face with Hofer's erraticism, as the Gauleiter veered from a defense of Nazi supremacy and might one moment to regrets about the war the next. He startled Freddy with an olive branch: he might be willing to negotiate with the Americans to end the fighting in Tyrol, Hofer said. And he might want to use his lunch guest, Freddy, as his liaison with the Americans to do it.

It was an unpredictable moment. Hofer's words didn't sound to Freddy like those of the man who had vowed to fight until the end for the Thousand-Year Reich. If he was sincere — an obvious question with any Nazi leader — Hofer appeared ready to end the fighting, and Freddy was eager to push him down that path. "I suggest you surrender," he said, "without damaging any more [of Tyrol] than you have to."

Freddy, in his newfound role as unofficial peace negotiator, asked for a show of good faith from Hofer: he wanted to get a message to OSS to let them know that he was okay. It had been four days since his arrest, and because Hans and Franz had fled Oberperfuss, he knew that Bari would be anxiously waiting to find out what had happened to the team. Hofer quickly assented, and Freddy scribbled out a message — with his usual brevity and aplomb.

Am at present in hands of Gestapo, but will get out one way or another shortly. Don't worry.

Hans, wherever he was, couldn't radio this one to Italy. But Hofer promised to get the written note to OSS headquarters on neutral ground in Switzerland, and he sent Freddy off from the house with some bread, salami, and chocolate to bring back to the jail. He was still a prisoner, although no ordinary one. After the day's strange events, Güttner fully understood that new reality. Back at the jail, the Gestapo man made a point of unlocking Freddy's handcuffs once he was inside his cell, and he went to find a newspaper for him to read while he munched on his treats.

Freddy's message made it from Hofer into the hands of OSS agents in Switzerland, as promised. But the carefree guidance — "will get out one way or another shortly. Don't worry" — met with as much skepticism as relief from his handlers. The OSS man in Switzerland who received the message knew Freddy from the base in Bari, and he knew his wry nonchalance. Still, it was difficult to feel confident when one of your best agents was in the custody of the Gestapo. And OSS had no faith in the Nazi diplomat who delivered the message, after an unpleasant exchange with him just weeks earlier over a possible cease-fire offer. OSS let the diplomat know that if the Gestapo were to harm Freddy, he would be held "personally responsible with his life."

Meanwhile, Freddy's status as a VIP prisoner now seemed strangely in doubt. For days after his lunch with Hofer, Freddy stayed in his cell and heard nothing more from the Gauleiter about his interest in a surrender. The news that Freddy did receive, though, was not good: Güttner was transferring him and the rest of the prisoners at the Gestapo jail to a different location — for reasons unknown.

Their destination: a concentration camp a few miles outside Innsbruck called Reichenau. Güttner assured Freddy that there was no reason for alarm, nothing to fear. The Nazis wouldn't hurt any of the prisoners, he said pleasantly. It was just a concentration camp. Freddy said nothing. The name "Reichenau" meant little to him; it was just another stop on his journey. But the wild extremes of his wartime life were now taking another unthinkable pivot: seven years after Freddy had fled Hitler's Germany, the Nazis were sending him to a concentration camp.

Reichenau was an obscure place in the grim collection of Nazi camps throughout Europe. It wasn't nearly as large, or as notorious, as other camps like Dachau, in southern Germany, or Mauthausen, in Upper Austria. But the stories of death and savagery within its walls since its founding in 1941 were almost as graphic for the foreign laborers, political opponents, Jews, Roma gypsies, and others imprisoned there.

In just the last few weeks, Reichenau had become more critical to the Nazis' desperate plans. With American troops advancing toward them, Nazi jailers at Dachau, outside Munich, abandoned the camp and began relocating their most "valuable" prisoners there by bus to the Reichenau camp about 120 miles to the south. More than 140 of these *Prominenten*, with credentials from across Europe, were hauled to Reichenau: captured enemy officers from Britain, France, Norway, and Yugoslavia; high-ranking German defectors and saboteurs; prominent politicians from Greece and Hungary; even the former French prime minister and a distant relative of Winston Churchill. They were too important to leave behind at Dachau. The Nazis saw them, like Freddy, as possible bargaining chips.

The Nazi guards moved a stoic Freddy and other prisoners from the Gestapo jail to Reichenau in late April, a week after his arrest. Güttner went along with them. POLICE EDUCATION CAMP — REICHENAU announced a metal sign at the barbed-wire gate in the shadow of the Alps. Freddy was shoved into a decrepit barracks along with a pack of other prisoners. His first impression was of chaos and commotion: there were lots of people huddled together, but it wasn't clear who they were or which of the Nazis, if any, were actually in charge. There was a sense of dread among the prisoners. Just a few days earlier, the guards at Reichenau had hanged three Austrian resisters at the camp for unspecified offenses; the other prisoners held a silent vigil in their memory.

Freddy's ever-present confidence was waning. He could see the unmarked graves of prisoners killed at the camp. He thought of himself, for the first time, as a dead man walking, just waiting for one of his Nazi jailers to shoot him on the spot there at the concentration camp. He had been so defiantly optimistic just days before in the message that Hofer relayed to OSS for him. *Will get out one way or another shortly. Don't worry.* He wasn't so certain anymore.

Hours after he arrived at Reichenau, a jailer called his name and led him from the prisoners' barracks. More unexpected news: Freddy was being relocated yet again. In fact, a BMW and a driver were waiting for him outside the gates. It was the chauffeur of Dr. Primbs, his new ally. Primbs had learned that Freddy was at the concentration camp and quickly arranged to have him released into his personal custody. Primbs's driver had the official papers with him. Güttner, frustrated again by Freddy, protested the order briefly before giving up the fight; he wasn't prepared to butt heads with the second-ranking Nazi in all of Tyrol over the fate of a single prisoner. He let Freddy walk out the metal door. Many prisoners would never leave those gates at all; leaving in a chauffeured BMW was a rarity indeed.

The war was unraveling quickly for Hitler and the Reich in those last days of April. American troops marched into Dachau on April 29 and discovered the unimaginable atrocities that it hid. Nazi troops in Italy surrendered that same day in the secret deal engineered by the OSS's Allen Dulles with a notorious war criminal, Nazi general Karl Wolff. Hitler, facing the inevitable, married his longtime companion Eva Braun in his Führerbunker in Berlin — the same bunker that a drunk Nazi engineer had revealed to Leutnant Mayer. Hitler and his newlywed wife killed themselves in the bunker the very next day, with a Nazi admiral, Karl Dönitz, taking his place as Germany's head of state.

But in Innsbruck, Hofer remained strangely silent about the future of Tyrol, even as American troops had moved less than twenty miles west of the city by the start of May, fighting off sporadic attacks from Wehrmacht units and bands of civilian resisters. An all-out assault by the Americans seemed imminent. No one was clear on what Hofer planned to do.

Primbs thought the outcome appeared all but final; it was time to end the war. He was alarmed to learn, however, that Hofer, the only Nazi in Tyrol who outranked him, was planning to deliver a major radio address rallying the Tyrolean people to fight on. The remarks that Hofer had prepared ahead of time for the speech were an exhortation to the people to make "a last-ditch stand."

Primbs had no success in convincing Hofer that his stance was futile, but he thought that hearing it from an American — from Freddy — might change his mind. Together, he and Freddy went to see Hofer on May 2 — marching unannounced into the Gauleiter's office, not far from Primbs's own. Hofer was at his desk, getting ready for the radio address, which was now scheduled to begin in less than half an hour.

"Mr. Hofer, you're making the mistake of your life," Freddy told him. "Surrender the territory and I'll make you a POW instead of a Nazi," he said.

Hofer, a cornered animal, began rambling on about the need to defend Tyrol. He would not agree to an unconditional surrender, he told Freddy. He planned to follow the lead of Admiral Dönitz, the new leader of Germany, who had pledged the day before to continue waging war against the Russians — in order "to save German men and women from destruction by the advancing Bolshevist enemy." He was willing to lay down German arms against the Americans and the British, Dönitz claimed, but only if they would accept his terms. Hofer aimed to take that same tack in Tyrol.

"That proposal will never be accepted," Freddy declared, without knowing what American officials high above his new pay grade might or might not accept. "The only course for you is to surrender unconditionally." Otherwise, he said, the American army would surely invade Innsbruck. Once they made it over the mountains, there would be a bloodbath in Tyrol. And, Freddy said, he had no trouble predicting which side would win.

Hofer was terrified for his own safety — not only from an oncoming attack by the Americans, but also from Austrian resisters now roaming some parts of Tyrol with greater abandon in the past few days, as the Reich was collapsing. Hofer knew what had happened in northern Italy to Mussolini, just on the other side of the Brenner Pass: Italian partisans had captured and executed him, hanging his disfigured corpse from a meat hook in a town square. Hofer worried that he could face a similar fate after his own dictatorial reign over Tyrol.

Freddy, raising his bluff, vowed to protect Hofer and his family. He could put him under "house arrest" and make sure that the Americans kept him safe once Tyrol surrendered; Hofer would be better off as a POW than a Nazi dictator who refused to relinquish power. But none of that was going to happen, Freddy said, if he went on the radio and told his people to continue fighting. It would be crazy, Freddy added, to keep fighting a war that was already lost.

Hofer mulled over the dire situation in which he now found himself. He was supposed to begin his radio broadcast in less than ten minutes. He told Freddy that he wanted a firm assurance that the Americans would protect him. Freddy said he would give him his word "as an officer" — not mentioning that, for now, he was still an enlisted man, or that he had no authority, regardless, to give Hofer any such assurance.

With his Nazi fiefdom crumbling, Hofer agreed. He would make his radio address — but instead of rallying for the last-ditch battle that the Americans had feared for months, he would tell Tyroleans that the war was over. He would order his people to stand down, declare Innsbruck an "open city," and agree to an unconditional surrender.

Freddy did not wait to hear Hofer's address. He wanted to get to the front line as quickly as he could to relay the Gauleiter's intentions. Hofer agreed to have his men drive Freddy to the Americans' advance guard, now positioned less than fifteen miles to the north of Innsbruck, to notify them that Hofer was surrendering.

But first, Freddy insisted on making another stop — to find Hans. He didn't trust the Germans to radio OSS with the dramatic developments, and his knowledge of Morse code was too rudimentary to do it himself. He wanted Hans, the radio operator, to make the transmission himself — and just as important, he wanted to find out if his "little brother" was still safe after his harried flight from Oberperfuss.

Primbs and his driver took Freddy back to Franz's hometown. Hans and Franz had returned to Oberperfuss after their escape, and Hans excitedly came out of hiding when he was told that Freddy was looking for him. They hadn't seen each other for weeks. When Freddy told his fellow agent that he had negotiated a surrender with Hofer and needed Hans to cable the news, Hans stared back in astonishment. He didn't know what surprised him more: that the Nazis might surrender, or that Freddy, last seen in town in Gestapo custody, was alive and free — and being driven by a Nazi chauffeur.

Primbs's chauffeur drove Freddy the next day, on May 3, from Hofer's home, past scores of Wehrmacht patrols outside Innsbruck, and toward the oncoming American troops perched over the mountains to the west. Near the town of Zirl, eleven miles outside Innsbruck, he saw in the distance a Sherman tank and about fifty infantrymen that the 103rd Division had set up as its advance guard. Freddy pulled out a white flag he had brought — a bedsheet tied to a pole — and began waving it furiously. The American infantrymen eyed the car warily as it pulled forward.

Freddy approached the tank, saluted smartly, and told a stunned officer that he was an American and needed to speak with someone from the "G-2," the army's intelligence division. The call went back to the command post, and a senior officer,

Major Bland West, made his way to the advance line. There, he faced the baffling sight of a German civilian vehicle and, standing next to it, a badly bruised but smiling young man in mismatched clothes, with a white makeshift flag in his hand.

Freddy saluted again and introduced himself: Sergeant Frederick Mayer from OSS, he said in a German accent with a Brooklyn flourish. He had negotiated a surrender with the Gauleiter of Tyrol, he told the flummoxed officer matter-of-factly. He went on to inform him that the Gauleiter was under arrest at his home in Hall, he had ordered the Nazis under him to stand down, and he was awaiting the arrival of the Americans.

The rest, in Freddy's mind at least, was practically a formality. Not so for Major West. He and the 103rd had no idea that the Americans and OSS had any spies inside Tyrol, much less that one of them might be negotiating a surrender. But once he was convinced that Freddy's dramatic appearance was not some sort of bizarre Nazi setup, West and a small platoon warily followed Freddy back into Innsbruck in their vehicles, through open roads, to Hofer's home to formalize what Freddy had started. Hofer, anxious to secure favorable treatment, told the major everything he wanted to know about the Nazi defenses in the area and agreed to make another radio broadcast directing Tyroleans to lay down their arms. As the Americans led Hofer out of his house and took him into custody, he gave one final Nazi salute and yelled: "Heil Hitler!"

The bloodless surrender of Tyrol became official at quarter past ten in the morning the next day, and American tanks rolled into Innsbruck to take control of the city and the entire Nazi stronghold. Not a single shot was fired. People in Innsbruck, many of them now claiming they had long opposed the Nazis, flooded the streets, with red and white banners — the colors of Austria's flag before the Anschluss — replacing the onerous Nazi swastikas.

Germany agreed to a full and unconditional surrender three days later, on May 7. Freddy and Hans went back to Oberperfuss the day after that for what amounted to a victory lap. Hans got drunk on a bottle of champagne he had swiped — "liberated," he joked — from the Nazis; it was the first taste of alcohol he had ever had, and undoubtedly the best. He and Freddy, reuniting with Franz, thanked Alois, Maria, and all the other townspeople who had helped them, and Mama Niederkircher told Freddy about the mass they held to pray for his safety.

The three American agents then returned to Alois's farmhouse, two months after Freddy first knocked on the door to ask for his help against the Nazis. Alois's son was quite ill, and Alois wanted to get him to a hospital. So Freddy wrote a letter vouching for him — "my first and most reliable contact on my secret intelligence mission in Austria," he called him in the letter — to get them through the American lines for medical care.

The three members of the Gulliver team posed for a triumphant photo in Alois's backyard, with Freddy and Hans wearing their American uniforms once again, and Franz — flashing a rare smile — dressed in a natty suit and tie. The majestic peaks of the Austrian Alps, the starting point for their long journey, shone in the distance behind them. "Das verwegene Trio," Alois wrote on the back of the photo. *Three swashbuckling guys.*

Weeks later, after the American military had taken control of the region, the army captured Güttner and jailed him. Searching him, an officer found inside Güttner's wallet the photo he had taken of Freddy at Gestapo headquarters, with his face swollen and bloodied.

OSS let Freddy know that Güttner was in custody, and Freddy went to see him at the POW jail. Freddy thought about giving the "little rat" a whack or two himself in retribution. He decided against it. Güttner, once so smug, with his whip, his gun, and the power of the Third Reich in his hands, now looked pitiful in his prison garb. He begged for mercy. He was just following orders from his bosses at the Gestapo, he insisted. He pleaded with Freddy not to hurt his wife and four children, no matter what else he did to him.

Freddy just smiled down at him. "What do you think we are — Nazis?" he said. Then he walked away.

EPILOGUE:
AFTER THE FALL

Known officially as Greenup, the Gulliver mission proved to be one of the most successful American spy operations of World War II. The men of the mission earned recognition not only for providing vital intelligence needed to bomb Nazi supply trains, track German troop movements, and pinpoint Hitler's bunker, but also for managing "to arrange the surrender of Innsbruck to American troops" in the critical Nazi battleground of Tyrol.

The operation was "by far the most successful" mounted against the Nazis in central Europe from the secret American base in Bari, Italy, according to William Casey, a senior OSS officer who went on to lead the CIA. He marveled that the operation allowed the American army to take over Innsbruck "without a drop of blood being shed." OSS's official war report, meanwhile, described the mission as "the most productive" of all its spy operations in Nazi-occupied Austria.

The Innsbruck mission brought an abrupt end to the war in the Nazis' greatest remaining stronghold in Austria, four days before Germany itself surrendered. One of the mission's chief intelligence targets — the grand Alpine fortress that American military leaders had so feared — turned out to be more myth than menace, a defense that was porous and half-finished. Even so, the surrender that Freddy negotiated with Nazi Gauleiter Franz Hofer avoided an imminent American invasion that military officials said could have lasted weeks, perhaps even months, with untold numbers of casualties.

Likewise, the fighting in northern Italy on the other side of the Brenner Pass might have extended far longer, without the critical intelligence that Freddy and the team generated in the weeks before the surrender. Most notable of all was his "ten-strike" discovery of the massive caravan of Nazi supply trains heading for Italy from the rail yard outside Innsbruck, which allowed American bombers to "destroy completely heavy shipments of critically needed German ammunition and materiel for the Italian front." The bleeding of supplies destined for the German troops was one critical factor in Nazi general Karl Wolff's decision to negotiate a surrender of his own troops in Italy. As Wolff himself acknowledged after the war, "The front died of slow starvation."

OSS itself died just a month after the end of World War II, despite "Wild Bill" Donovan's best efforts to keep intact his band of "glorious amateurs." President Truman, who was never as high on the agency as Roosevelt had been, signed the executive order abolishing OSS. In 1947 Truman created its successor, the Central Intelligence Agency, built partly from the remnants.

Eleven days after the fall of Innsbruck, Fred Mayer went for his first medical treatment after the beating he endured at the hands of the Nazis weeks earlier. Among his injuries, an American army doctor reported, were "severe" cuts to his backside and a "moderately severe" contusion in his left ear, suffered "in action when an enemy Gestapo agent struck him with a club in Innsbruck," which would create lifelong hearing problems. He had lost six teeth as well.

A few weeks later, Freddy appeared before an officers' review board in Italy for his chance at a second promotion in less than two months. OSS, citing his "outstanding performance" in Innsbruck, rushed to make Freddy a second lieutenant in postwar Europe.

Still wearing his dirt-crusted military boots, he noticed that everyone else in the room had on their best shined shoes. The cuts and bruises on his face were still visible as he stood before the board. "You look as though you've had a little trouble with the Nazis," one of the army reviewers said to him. "Obviously, sir," Freddy said with a smirk, his characteristic brashness on display. He got the promotion.

Officials at OSS thought that Freddy's wartime heroics deserved still more recognition. He did earn several medals, including a Legion of Merit awarded by Donovan himself. But Colonel Chapin at OSS — the man Freddy had lobbied so strenuously in Italy for an assignment — pushed for months for him to receive the military's highest distinction, the Congressional Medal of Honor. The military turned Chapin down. That honor was normally reserved for combat troops, not spies, and as hazardous as Freddy's service in Austria was, it did not demonstrate "actual conflict or direct physical contact with an armed enemy," one general wrote.

The army would reconsider sixty-seven years later, in 2013, with the backing of Freddy's home-state senator in West Virginia, Jay Rockefeller, who considered him "one of the great unsung heroes of World War II." The result was the same. The army once again denied Freddy the honor, based on the same rationale, stating that "the fact the applicant was not directly involved in armed conflict during the cited period supports the original decision."

After the war ended, Freddy — now newly commissioned as Lieutenant Mayer — spent a few months in Germany investigating Nazi war crimes as part of the military's "de-Nazification" of Europe. While in Germany, he walked the grounds of the concentration camp at Dachau. He had pushed OSS to let him parachute into Dachau with an arsenal of weapons, and now he was finally there. He saw firsthand the enormity of the Nazis' atrocities — "the residue of human misery," as he called it. The brutal executions were over now, but he wondered whether some of the misery he witnessed could have been prevented if OSS had not "wasted so much time" sending him from one training assignment to another all those months before the jump.

From Dachau, Freddy went back to his birthplace — in Freiburg, in Germany's Black Forest. The vestiges of Nazi barbarism were gone, replaced by an occupying army and a city in rubble. Allied bombers had destroyed most of the houses in his old tree-lined neighborhood, but there, standing untouched between two craters, was his boyhood home, as if the bombs had simply passed over it. He went next to the Jewish cemetery, where the gravestones of his father's parents sat undamaged as well. He took a photo of the gravestones to send to his father in Brooklyn; he would like to see that, Freddy knew.

OSS thought Freddy had a bright future as a spy — but out in the field, not at a desk, considering his penchant for mischief. "Has great postwar possibilities as an agent . . . but is *not* suitable for staff or office work," OSS wrote. Freddy wasn't interested. He wanted to go back to his adopted home in the United States. One improbable spy mission was enough for him.

He left the military with an honorable discharge and returned home to his family in Brooklyn in late 1945 in time for Thanksgiving — after three years in the army, seventeen months overseas, and seven days in Gestapo custody in Innsbruck. He came home a celebrity of sorts, at least in his local neighborhood; a story about his exploits had run just the month before in the *New York Times* under the headline "Torture Endured by Brooklynite Made Innsbruck Entry Bloodless." His father, the decorated German soldier from the First World War, was now beaming with pride for his son, the American war hero; Hilda was just happy he was alive. On one of his first shopping trips in New York, Freddy bought a pair of silk stockings and sent them by international mail to Oberperfuss — to Maria. She had always wanted a pair.

Freddy worked for General Motors in New York for a few years, troubleshooting diesel locomotives. Then he got a call from one of his old OSS supervisors asking him if he was interested in working for Voice of America, the global radio network that the US government started during the war. Freddy went to work as a plant supervisor for the radio network in the Philippines, spending the rest of his career working at different plants around the world. He rarely missed the spy work. He had had his moment as a secret agent, and he had relished it. But those days were done.

Like Freddy, Hans Wynberg revisited his homeland soon after the war. His journey was a much more emotionally wrenching one. He and his twin brother, Luke, had not heard anything from his parents and Robbie in nearly three years. Hans, promoted to lieutenant along with Freddy, asked for leave from his post in Austria and drove more than six hundred miles to his hometown of Overveen, outside Amsterdam. (Freddy had taught him how to drive after the war.)

Hans had no clear sense of what he might find in the Netherlands now that the Nazis were defeated, but he held on to hope. He walked up to the door of his family home, six years after the farewell party there for him and his twin, only to find the house empty and abandoned. He found a neighbor who told him the news he had dreaded: his parents and Robbie had fled the Netherlands, and the Nazis had caught them in France. They were thought to be dead; killed in a concentration camp. The neighbor had salvaged two paintings — winter scenes — and some family photos from the home to give to Hans; the Nazis had seized the family bike-tire factory, and the paintings and photos were all that was left now.

A letter that Hans received from the Red Cross in Holland years later filled in the sobering details of his family's fate:

Your parents and their son Robert fled the Netherlands . . . and were arrested at the end of August 1942 in Paris and imprisoned in Drancy [a Nazi internment camp]. On the 19th of October 1943 they were sent from France to Auschwitz together, where your mother and brother shortly died after their arrival. From Auschwitz, your father was put to work in the working camp Tsjechowitz, 50 km East from Auschwitz, where he, according to the statement of a witness, died of exhaustion at the end of October 1944. More information is not available.

Hans was determined to suppress the memories of his parents and Robbie, pushing them as deep into the recesses of his mind as he could. "Okay, this part of your life has ended," he told himself after he learned of their murders. "The Netherlands is gone, family is gone."

Work and chemistry helped fill the void. For months after the war, Hans worked in military intelligence in Europe — spying on America's new Cold War enemy, the Russians — then left the army in early 1946 to return to the United States. He focused on chemistry, putting his studies on chemical structures, conducted for weeks in an Austrian attic, to good use, earning an undergraduate degree and a PhD. He became a chemistry professor in the United States before being offered a Fulbright fellowship in the Netherlands in 1959. His twin brother, also a science professor, was never willing to move back to Holland — a country that he saw as complicit in allowing the murders of his parents, his brother, and more than one hundred thousand other Jews. Hans, however, accepted the prestigious position, returning to his homeland with his wife, Elly, and their children. "Never forget, always forgive," he wrote of the Holocaust.

He placed a gravestone in the backyard of his new home for his parents and his brother. Still, he was rarely willing to discuss the Nazis or the war. He tried to teach his children Morse code — they weren't interested — but if they asked him about the Holocaust or details of the war, he would simply send them to one of the many books on the subject in his well-stocked library. "Too much about that past and the misery is not healthy," he said. If he talked to his children at all about the war and the Gulliver mission, it was usually to extol Freddy and downplay his own contribution. "I just tagged along. The only thing I knew was Morse code," Hans told one of his sons.

Franz Weber stayed in Tyrol and, months later, married Annie, his dance partner before the war and his accomplice during it. Fabrics were in short supply, so Annie made her wedding dress partly from the parachutes the team had buried near the glacier; Franz went back up the mountain soon after the war to retrieve them.

He did not seek to publicize his involvement with the Americans until many years later. He became a lawyer and a politician, winning seats in the state and federal legislatures in Austria in the 1950s and 1960s, yet his role in the mission against the Nazis was not even listed on his official résumé. Austria was wrestling with its own conflicted — and complicit — relationship with the Nazis, and Franz realized that some of his Tyrolean neighbors, even many years after the war, did not look favorably on a man who had deserted the Nazis and joined with the Americans. In their view, he had dared to break with the deeply held tradition that "Befehl ist Befehl." *An order is an order.* "This was a great problem for me," Franz said. While many Austrians did support what he had done, "some [were] negative," and they would let him know it, he acknowledged.

Only decades later did Franz begin to come to terms publicly with his involvement in the mission. In 1969 his role was recognized with a prestigious national award "for service to the Republic of Austria," and in 1988 — in the midst of a heated national debate over then-president Kurt Waldheim's long-hidden role with the Nazis — Franz wrote in support of honoring three of the women in Tyrol who helped in the operation: Maria, Frannie, and his own sister, Gretl. (Both of his other sisters involved in the mission, Eva and Alouisa, had since died.) The operation "would have never achieved its success without the support of local Tiroleans," he wrote. "I believe that the decision to honor the 3 named Persons and many others (most of them deceased by now) who had risked their lives to liberate Austria is the right one."

Franz Hofer, the powerful Nazi Gauleiter for Tyrol, was arrested three days after the surrender and jailed in an internment camp to await possible prosecution for war crimes. Freddy's half-hearted promises to protect him if he surrendered would do Hofer little good in the face of possible charges over the roundup and killings of many thousands of prisoners in Tyrol under his brutal reign. OSS was willing to overlook the questionable assurances that Freddy, after his beating, had given Hofer — with "his word as an officer" — in an effort to negotiate the peace. The promises, which Freddy did not have the authority to offer anyway, were made "under duress, so we ignored that," OSS's Lieutenant Ulmer said.

Any ethical questions surrounding the negotiations proved moot, however, because Hofer — like dozens of other senior Nazi war criminals — would never be brought to justice. He managed to escape from American custody three years after his arrest and fled to Germany, where he worked as a salesman and lived freely under his real name for decades with his wife and children. A year after his escape, he was tried in absentia by a court in Austria, which sentenced him to death for war crimes. Yet he remained free, even after reports in 1965 in Jewish and Catholic publications that he was living openly as a "respected businessman" in West Germany. He died of natural causes in 1975.

Walter Güttner, the Gestapo agent who led the torture of Freddy, was released from American custody without explanation after the war. In 1955 he was belatedly put on trial in Austria for war crimes, including the beating of Fred Mayer. But the charges were dropped after the American government was unable to locate Freddy or other key witnesses, even though Freddy was working for the American government in Europe at the time for Voice of America.

Max Primbs, the Nazi Kreisleiter in Tyrol under Franz Hofer, was also jailed in an American internment camp for a short time after the war before returning to Germany, to practice medicine. Freddy met with him several times in Germany after the war and came to consider the onetime Nazi leader a "good friend," crediting him with saving his life.

In 1993, a half-century after Freddy and Hans joined OSS's band of "glorious amateurs," they traveled back to Austria to reunite with Franz, as well as with pilot John Billings and other members of the B-24 flight crew that dropped them into the Alps. Freddy and Hans stayed once again at the Gausthaus Krone hotel in Oberperfuss, not as agents-in-hiding this time, but as honored guests. Mama Niederkircher had passed away years earlier, but Freddy and Hans reminisced with Annie, Maria, and many of the other accomplices still in town about the remarkable adventure that had brought them together to help defeat the Nazis.

While the three ex-agents were not as spry as they once were, Freddy, Hans, and Franz hiked part of the way up the Alps toward the Sultztaler Glacier — not nearly to the top, but far enough to bring back the images of that wartime winter all those years before.

Four years later, in 1997, Freddy sat down for an interview at his home in West Virginia for a historical project initiated by director Steven Spielberg to collect video testimonials from fifty thousand Holocaust survivors. Freddy's bushy black hair was now thin and white, and he wore large, owl-shaped glasses to correct what had been 20/20 vision during the war, but the ear-to-ear grin was unaltered.

The interviewer, Esther Toporek Finder — herself the daughter of Auschwitz survivors — asked Freddy what made him such an effective spy during those remarkable two months in Austria. He flashed his famous smile and summoned a Yiddish word from his childhood in pre-Nazi Germany. "Chutzpah!" he said buoyantly. "I was afraid of absolutely nothing."

Not usually the self-reflective type, Freddy pondered for a moment what it had meant for him to flee Europe for America, then go back to infiltrate the Nazis. Returning to the Reich struck him as both a rare opportunity and a solemn obligation. "I would just like people to realize," he said in a soft voice, "that refugees who got a haven in the US did their best to repay" that debt.

AUTHOR'S NOTE & ACKNOWLEDGMENTS

My research into the OSS mission in Innsbruck relied on thousands of pages of historical documents, including US military records, archival material, and personal letters and emails, as well as extensive interviews that I conducted with people with a range of perspectives, including the last surviving member of the mission (John Billings), family members and friends of the participants, Austrian residents, World War II scholars and researchers, and others. I also took two trips to Innsbruck and Oberperfuss in my research. I spent just one afternoon with Freddy Mayer, unfortunately, before he passed away, in April 2016, but I hope I was able to give readers a full sense of the man and his mission.

Phrases and conversations in quotation marks in the narrative of my book reflect the verbatim accounts of participants and others, as reflected in the endnotes. As with any historical work, the memories of participants can differ on events that occurred many years earlier, and the official military records contain some errors and contradictions on matters of timing and substance. (For instance, some of the cables that Freddy Mayer and Hans Wynberg relayed to OSS in Italy appear to have been dated out of order.) When I found contradictions in the historical records, I included what I believed to be the most credible version in the book, and in a small number of instances where there are contradictions on matters of some significance, I have noted the alternative versions in the endnotes.

I am grateful to many people for their support in this project, beginning with Esther Toporek Finder, an advocate for Holocaust survivors who introduced me to Freddy Mayer in 2016 at the suggestion of Eli Rosenbaum. A three-and-a-half-hour video interview that Esther conducted with Freddy in 1997, one of dozens that she did with Holocaust refugees, was indispensable to me in understanding the arc of Freddy's life, from Germany, to Brooklyn, to Austria, and beyond, and she provided valuable feedback to me through the course of my research.

The work of two other war researchers, Joseph E. Persico and Gerald (Gerd) Schwab, both now deceased, was also particularly valuable. Persico's 1979 book, *Piercing the Reich: The Penetration of Nazi Germany by American Secret Agents During World War II,* provided a groundbreaking look at a number of important OSS missions, including Freddy's, and the taped interviews and papers that Persico left behind at the Hoover Institution at Stanford University were even more valuable to me in my research. Likewise, *OSS Agents in Hitler's Heartland: Destination Innsbruck,* by Schwab, who was a childhood friend of Freddy's in Freiburg, Germany — and even more so the exhaustive records and interviews that Schwab donated to the United States Holocaust Memorial Museum in Washington — were enormously helpful.

I also want to thank John Billings, the pilot of the B-24 who dropped the Gulliver team; Josef Weber and Alois Abenthung in Oberperfuss, Austria; Matthias Breit in Absam, Austria, and Peter Pirker in Vienna; and Richard Breitman in Washington, as well as members of Hans Wynberg's family, including his twin brother, Luke Wijnberg, daughter Audrey Wijnberg, son Jeffrey Wijnberg, and grandson Rob Wijnberg, and Hans's friend and former student Marjorie Bingham. I relied extensively on research assistance from Maria Herd in College Park, Maryland; Diana Fong in Germany and Satu Haase-Webb in Washington as well as translation assistance from Bart Oosterveld in Washington, Lotje Krouwel in Amsterdam, and Simone Kellner in Innsbruck.

I could not have completed this book without the feedback, insight, and unending patience of my wife, Leslie Zirkin, as well as help from others who read early drafts or provided help, including Marty Kanovsky (the fastest reader I know), Anita Lichtblau, John Melissinos, Stephen Meagher, Michael Wolivar, Judy Feigin, Harold and Nancy Zirkin, Holger and Mara Kunst, Jennifer Maisel, Eric Schmitt, and my literary agent, Ronald Goldfarb. Lastly, I am grateful to Bruce Nichols, my wonderful editor at Houghton Mifflin Harcourt, and Ivy Givens, his editorial assistant, for all their help and input. Chronicling the horrors — and heroism — of the Holocaust seems more important today than ever.

NOTES

INTRODUCTION

page

xiii *I did write:* Eric Lichtblau, "Frederick Mayer, Jew Who Spied on Nazis After Fleeing Germany, Dies at 94," *New York Times,* April 20, 2016.

PROLOGUE

2 Gorgeous, *he thought:* Interview with Frederick Mayer, Jewish survivor, by Esther Finder, Visual History Archive, Shoah Foundation, University of Southern California, Los Angeles, 1997.

1. A GERMAN BOY

3 *The signs were subtle:* Author interview with Fred Mayer, February 14, 2016, Charles Town, West Virginia.

4 *place that had once seemed tolerant:* Leslie Maitland, *Crossing the Borders of Time: A True Story of War, Exile, and Love Reclaimed* (New York: Other Press, 2012), 17.

playmate was gone: Interview with Gerald (Gerd) Schwab, United States Holocaust Memorial Museum, Washington, DC, oral history collection, November 18, 1997.

"I was a Frontkaempfer": Interview with Fred Mayer, Gerald Schwab Papers, 1885–2012, United States Holocaust Memorial Museum; and author interview with Fred Mayer.

5 *"a stinking Jude":* Mayer interview, Shoah Foundation.

Friedrich Ludin: Freddy viewed Friedrich Ludin as a benign figure, despite his official Nazi ties, but Ludin's son, Hanns Ludin, became a notorious Nazi SA leader in Slovakia who was ultimately executed for war crimes in 1947. Because of Hanns's notoriety, his father's school, the Rotteck Gymnasium in Freiburg, Germany, removed Friedrich Ludin's portrait from a gallery of former school directors.

6 *boys from a Jewish fraternity:* Photo, United States Holocaust Memorial Museum, "Group portrait of members of the KC Jewish fraternity and their girl friends on an excursion to a mountain in the Black Forest near Freiburg," circa 1930–33, https://collections.ushmm.org/search/catalog/pa1157640.

It was an idyllic childhood: Mayer interview, Shoah Foundation.

8 *"a gentle Gentile":* Ibid.

"Other suppliers": Letter from Mathilde Kinzle to Baden State Office for Restitution Claims, Freiburg, Germany, in support of Heinrich Mayer's application for restitution, March 1, 1955.

At his core: Wolfram Zimmer, close friend of Fred Mayer; interview by researcher Diana Fong on behalf of author, Freiburg, Germany, May 30, 2018.

not because of any deep: Mayer interview, Shoah Foundation.

9 *Heinrich and Hilda reached:* Ibid.

The experiment: Gerald Schwab, *OSS Agents in Hitler's Heartland: Destination Innsbruck* (Westport, CT: Praeger, 1996), 7.

he managed to start: Ibid.

10 *Freddy would parade:* Mayer interview, Shoah Foundation.

11 *Tens of thousands:* Erik Larson, *In the Garden of Beasts: Love, Terror, and an American Family in Hitler's Berlin* (New York: Broadway, 2011), 84. Estimates have varied on how many Jews immediately fled Germany. Larson placed the number at fifty thousand "within weeks of Hitler's ascension to chancellor," while some scholars place the number lower.

12 *His brother, Julius:* Mayer interview, Shoah Foundation.

For a Nazi: Ibid.; Zimmer interview.

13 *the Ford auto dealer:* Mayer interview, Shoah Foundation.

14 *177 marks:* Heinrich Mayer's application for restitution to Baden State Office for Restitution Claims, Freiburg, Germany, August 23, 1954.

"Look, we better prepare": Mayer interview, Shoah Foundation.

He offered to manage: Zimmer interview.

15 *the ambassador met:* Larson, *In the Garden of Beasts,* 232.

President Franklin D. Roosevelt: Richard Breitman and Allan Lichtman, *FDR and the Jews* (Cambridge, MA: Belknap Press, 2013), 94.

A giant swastika banner: "20,000 Nazi Friends at a Rally Here Denounce Boycott," *New York Times,* May 18, 1934. Another massive pro-Nazi rally was held at Madison Square Garden five years later, in February 1939, organized by the German American Bund and also attended by an estimated twenty thousand people.

16 *Nearly eleven thousand:* Breitman and Lichtman, *FDR and the Jews,* 95.

just before a crush: Ibid., 102.

How they had managed: Many of the federal immigration records from this period were destroyed, and it is not clear who sponsored the Mayers' visa applications to the United States. Fred Mayer said he was not certain. As part of the temporary easing of restrictions, the United States began allowing more distant relatives to provide affidavits of support, in addition to close relatives.

17 *A rambling Hitler:* Lois G. Schwoerer, "Lord Halifax's Visit to Germany: November 1937," *Historian* 32, no. 3 (May 1970): 363, https://www.jstor.org/stable/24440688.

"I was not blind": The Earl of Halifax, *Fullness of Days* (London: Collins, 1957), 185.

After years of letting: Letter from Heinrich Mayer to Baden State Office for Restitution Claims, Freiburg, Germany, August 23, 1954, seeking restitution for the financial damages caused when the Nazis forced him to flee the country and abandon his home and business. Heinrich Mayer wrote to the restitution office: "Money alone can never compensate for my suffering. Instead of being a good-standing citizen, I am an unemployed nobody and that is something that cannot be changed anymore. However, money can help me in old age and help prolong my life, money that is due to me and due to losses I suffered under a previous German regime, in which Jews were deprived of all their rights. Even though money and property had not been directly seized, the former NS [Nazi] regime had created impossible circumstances in which a Jew had to pay the price of giving up ownership of all assets for the sake of basic survival." The state restitution office, after demanding documentation of Heinrich's business losses in Germany, agreed to pay a total of $1,103.39 — with the first payment coming before he died, in 1955, and the second payment a year later to his widow, Hilda. The payments were a small fraction of the money Heinrich said he had lost to the Nazis. The government also agreed to pay part of the widow's pension that Hilda said she was due because of Hein-rich's service in the war.

Cobbling together money: Letter from Heinrich Mayer to Baden State Office for Restitution Claims.

18 *had allowed them to leave:* John V. H. Dippel, *Bound Upon a Wheel of Fire* (New York: Basic Books, 1996), 160, 174–75.

bid farewell: Peter Pirker, *Codename Brooklyn: Jüdische Agenten im Feindesland. Die Operation Greenup 1945* (Innsbruck: Tyrolia Verlag-sanstalt, 2019), 50.

making sure: Mayer interview, Schwab Papers; and Mayer interview, Shoah Foundation.

2. ENEMY ALIEN

20 *"Stupid son-of-a-bitch":* Mayer interview, Shoah Foundation.

"fateful year": "1938 — 'The Fateful Year,'" Yad Vashem, World Ho-locaust Remembrance Center, https://www.yadvashem.org/holo caust/about/nazi-germany-1933-39/1938.html.

21 *let out a sigh:* Mayer interview, Shoah Foundation.

all designated: Ship manifest, SS *Manhattan,* March 10, 1938, Le Havre, France, to New York City.

rumors flowed back: Mayer interview, Shoah Foundation.

22 *"saved many lives":* Guido Enderis, wireless, "Hitler in Defense: He Tells Reichstag That His Action in Austria Saved Many Lives," *New York Times,* March 19, 1938.

23 *he would trudge:* Schwab, *OSS Agents in Hitler's Heartland,* 10.

he considered himself: Letter from Heinrich Mayer to Baden State Office for Restitution Claims, Freiburg, Germany, August 23, 1954.

The Nazis had robbed: Ibid.

just as his teachers: Mayer interview, Shoah Foundation.

When he told them: Ibid.

24 *"the perfect American":* Ibid.

If on a Friday: Ibid.

a terror unlike anything: Dippel, *Bound Upon a Wheel of Fire,* xix; and author interview with Richard Breitman.

25 *authorities had begun:* Maitland, *Crossing the Borders of Time,* 400.

Undetected in the bedlam: Ibid., 401.

"It'll make a hell": Mayer interview, Shoah Foundation.

26 *"Here's the next world war":* Ibid.

had published a series: Neil Baldwin, *Henry Ford and the Jews: The Mass Production of Hate* (New York: PublicAffairs, 2002), 144–45.

"distinguished foreigners": Ibid., 284.

"the Jewish groups": Lindbergh speech in Des Moines, Iowa, September 11, 1941, Jewish Virtual Library, https://www.jewishvirtual library.org/lindbergh-accuses-jews-of-pushing-u-s-to-war.

27 *"unworthy words":* Baldwin, *Henry Ford and the Jews,* 304.

"ruthless dictator": "Ickes Hits Takers of Hitler's Medals," *New York Times,* December 19, 1938; and Baldwin, *Henry Ford and the Jews,* 289.

he wanted to run: Mayer interview, Shoah Foundation.

"fight the Japs": "Volunteers Rush to Enlist Lets Up," *New York Times,* December 13, 1941.

28 *"enemy alien":* Speech by Fred Mayer, OSS Society Dinner, Washington, DC, October 27, 2012, https://www.youtube.com/watch?feature=youtu.be&v=ykzxwrFk3tQ&app=desktop.

29 *not only prohibited:* Robert Whitney, "Only 2,971 Enemy Allies Are Held," *New York Times,* January 4, 1942.

Julius could get: Mayer interview, Shoah Foundation. Julius would later enlist as well and serve in the Philippines.

30 *"You, you, and you":* Ibid.

pay a dime: Ibid.

31 *his restlessness got:* Schwab, *OSS Agents in Hitler's Heartland,* 11.

He seemed to fail: Mayer interview, Schwab Papers; and author interview with Fred Mayer.

"a natural leader": Alfred Ulmer Jr., "Greenup Project," February 10,

1945, OSS Declassified Files, 1945, National Archives and Records Administration, College Park, Maryland.

Camp Horn: Sands of War, season 21, episode 7, aired November 11, 2015, PBS, https://www.pbs.org/video/kvie-viewfinder-sands-war/.

32 *The goal was to capture:* Mayer interview, Shoah Foundation.
"You can't do that!": Patrick K. O'Donnell, *They Dared Return: The True Story of Jewish Spies Behind the Lines in Nazi Germany* (Boston: Da Capo, 2009), 4.

33 *"Would you like to do":* Mayer interview, Shoah Foundation.
"another body": Ibid.

3. THE CLOAK-AND-DAGGER BRIGADE

36 "We will do better": David Kahn, *The Reader of Gentlemen's Mail: Herbert O. Yardley and the Birth of American Codebreaking* (New Haven, CT: Yale University Press, 2004), 98.

The closest the United States came: Joseph E. Persico, *Piercing the Reich: The Penetration of Nazi Germany by American Secret Agents During World War II* (New York: Barnes & Noble, 1979), 5.

37 *Donovan made two:* US War Department, Strategic Services Unit History Project [Kermit Roosevelt], *War Report of the OSS* (New York: Walker, 1976), 5.

"driving the Jewish moneylenders": Richard Dunlop, *Donovan: America's Master Spy* (New York: Skyhorse, 2014), 15.

remarkable call to arms: William J. Donovan, "What Are We Up Against? There Is a Moral Force in Wars," speech from "1941 Documents Relating to World War II," March 26, 1941, http://www.ibiblio.org/pha/policy/1941/Documents_relating_to_World_War_II.html.

"Says Nazis Seek": "Says Nazis Seek to Rule the World," *Montana Standard,* March 27, 1941.

38 *"play a bush-league game"*: Dunlop, *Donovan: America's Master Spy*, 275.

for the colorful public: Douglas Waller, *Wild Bill Donovan: The Spymaster Who Created the OSS and Modern American Espionage* (New York: Free Press, 2011), 75.

"I have greater enemies": Ibid., 113.

a scaled-back version: [Roosevelt,] *War Report of the OSS*, 7–9.

39 *"It's a good thing"*: Dunlop, *Donovan: America's Master Spy*, 334.

"We might have had": Henry Clausen and Bruce Lee, *Pearl Harbor: Final Judgement* (Boston: Da Capo, 2001), 47.

"one of the greatest": Walter Laqueur, *A World of Secrets: The Uses and Limits of Intelligence* (New York: Twentieth Century Fund/Basic, 1985), 16.

40 *One favorite mantra:* Central Intelligence Agency, "A Look Back... Gen. William J. Donovan Heads Office of Strategic Services," December 31, 2009, CIA.gov.

41 *veneer was fading:* Anne Reilly Dolan, *Congressional Country Club: 1924–1984* (Baltimore, MD: Wolk, 1984), 26.

"compass runs": Roger Hall, *You're Stepping On My Cloak and Dagger* (Annapolis, MD: Naval Institute Press, 2003), 29.

42 *secret weapons:* Ibid., 25.

sci-fi ideas: Louis Menand, "Wild Thing: Did the OSS Help Win the War Against Hitler?" *New Yorker*, March 14, 2011.

Donovan would stop: Dolan, *Congressional Country Club: 1924–1984*, 29.

"to make young Americans": Ibid., 28.

A brand-new, pristine: Author telephone interview with former OSS agent Henry Sonagere, March 2, 2018.

43 *baby-faced innocence:* Dyno Lowenstein audio interview, Joseph E. Persico Papers (1943–1980), Hoover Institution Library & Archives, Stanford University.

"Young and requires direction": Alfred Ulmer Jr., "Theater Service Record of Hans Wynberg," January 21, 1946, National Archives, In-

teragency Working Group (IWG), Records of the Office of Strategic Services 1940–1946 (RG 226), https://www.archives.gov/iwg/declassified-records/rg-226-oss.

A prodigy: Author telephone interview with Jeffrey Wijnberg, August 6, 2018; and author telephone interview with Audrey Wijnberg, December 4, 2018.

44 *"the greatest time":* Author interview with Jeffrey Wijnberg.

"Hark, hark!": Wynberg emails, from Hans Wynberg to Marjorie Bingham, May 4, 2005.

45 *he came to adore:* Wynberg emails, from Hans Wynberg to Marjorie Bingham, February 24, 2009.

"more American": Interview with Hans Wynberg, Schwab Papers; and Hans Wynberg interview, *Een Leven Lang,* radio show, Netherlands, May 25, 1998. Translated from Dutch.

found a restaurant: Wynberg emails, from Hans Wynberg to Marjorie Bingham, February 24, 2009.

The sergeant: Wynberg emails, from Hans Wynberg to Marjorie Bingham, March 9, 2009. He and Elly, engaged during the war and wed a week after Hans's return to the United States, were married for sixty-five years.

Hans revered him: The Real Inglorious Bastards, directed by Min Sook Lee (New York and Washington, DC, XiveTV, 2015), DVD.

46 *"a windbag":* Security Officer Lester Y. Baylis, "Investigation Report MAYER, Frederick (Pvt. U.S.A.)," February 1944, OSS Records.

Many of the agents: The three other future CIA directors from OSS were William Casey, Allen Dulles, and Richard Helms.

Oh-So-Social: Menand, "Wild Thing."

47 *the dreaded Fifth Column:* [Roosevelt,] *War Report of the OSS,* 5, 6. Donovan cowrote a series of articles distributed nationally in 1940 on the Fifth Column threat.

"skilled in methods": Ibid., 223.

48 *wasn't an army grunt:* Wynberg emails, from Hans Wynberg to Marjorie Bingham, May 9, 2005.

the whole notion: Wynberg interview, *Een Leven Lang.*

He often thought: Ibid.

The lanky kid: Wynberg interview, Schwab Papers; and Wynberg emails, from Hans Wynberg to Marjorie Bingham, May 9, 2005.

"do you want to liberate": Wynberg interview, Schwab Papers.

49 *Gek, they called him:* Wynberg interviews, Schwab Papers and *Een Leven Lang.*

"a maniac": Wynberg interview, *Een Leven Lang.*

50 *he went door-to-door:* Ibid.

He mortgaged: Marien Abrahamse, "Hollander die in Amerikaanse geheime dienst verzetsgroepen steunde: 'Bijna Himmler nog te pakken gehad,'" *Nieuwe Rotterdamsche Courant,* May 4, 1985, translated from Dutch; Wynberg interviews, Schwab Papers and *Een Leven Lang.*

Leo would be taking: Author interview with Luke Wijnberg, Chapel Hill, North Carolina, January 4, 2019. The family name was spelled "Wijnberg" in the Netherlands. In America, Hans changed it to "Wynberg," while his brother and others maintained the original spelling.

Leo chronicled: 1939 family film provided to author by Audrey Wijnberg.

51 *Hans unfolded a giant map:* Ibid.

"the people who can": Wynberg emails, from Hans Wynberg to Marjorie Bingham, August 15, 2009.

Leo assured the twins: Abrahamse, "Hollander die in Amerikaanse geheime dienst verzetsgroepen steunde."

dutifully updating them: Letter from Leo Wijnberg to Hans and Luke Wijnberg, October 18, 1939.

52 *"the most important defense":* Ibid.

"Kisses and all": Ibid.

53 *"But the Dutch":* Letter from Leo Wijnberg to Hans and Luke Wijnberg, November 16, 1941.

"the chess players": Ibid.

54 *"Thankfully I'm still"*: Ibid.

everyone was healthy: Letter from Leo Wijnberg to Hans and Luke Wijnberg, February 17, 1942.

It was too painful: Abrahamse, "Hollander die in Amerikaanse geheime dienst verzetsgroepen steunde."

55 "believed to be living": "Investigation Report WYNBERG, HANS (Pvt.)," December 30, 1943, OSS Records.

Hans hoped that: Wynberg emails, from Hans Wynberg to Marjorie Bingham, July 30, 2009.

56 *difficult to believe:* Wynberg emails, from Hans Wynberg to Marjorie Bingham, May 4, 2009. Hans wrote that "I more or less completely turned away from the Jewish religion when I arrived in the USA." He explained that as a scientist, it became difficult to debate religion with people because "a belief is not swayed by facts."

wireless radio-transmission: William Casey, *The Secret War Against Hitler* (London: Simon & Schuster, 1990), 186–87.

He broke into: Mayer interview, Shoah Foundation.

57 *posed shirtless:* Ibid.

"piss poor": Mayer interview, Schwab Papers.

"wasting our time": Mayer interview, Shoah Foundation.

"another body": Ibid.

58 *His spy agency:* [Roosevelt,] *War Report of the OSS*, 114.

59 *was unclear:* Wynberg interview, Schwab Papers.

4. THE THIRD MAN

62 *"It's still 'Heil Hitler!'"*: Mayer interview, Shoah Foundation.

had become disillusioned: Interview with Franz Weber, Schwab Papers.

some of his Spam: Mayer interview, Schwab Papers.

63 *"son of a bitch":* Mayer audio interview, Persico Papers.

small town in Tyrol: Ibid.

64 *"He was very anti-Nazi":* Mayer interview, Schwab Papers.
"an obsession": Rodney Minott, *The Fortress That Never Was: The Myth of Hitler's Bavarian Stronghold* (New York: Holt, Rinehart and Winston, 1964), xv.
an enormous network: Harry Vosser, "Hitler's Hideaway," *New York Times,* November 12, 1944.

65 *"a German resistance army":* Dunlop, *Donovan: America's Master Spy,* 365.

66 *they didn't even seem:* Wynberg interview, Schwab Papers.
They would have to go: Ibid.

67 *resigned to reading about:* Wynberg emails, from Hans Wynberg to Marjorie Bingham, June 7, 2009.
as silly: Wynberg interview, Schwab Papers.
"the only thing": Ibid.
They played in craps: Mayer interview, Schwab Papers.

68 *"missing in action":* Ibid.
Freddy wasn't sure: Mayer interview, Shoah Foundation.

69 *They readied themselves:* Wynberg interview, Schwab Papers.
"an absolute ass": Ibid.
"I've had enough": Mayer interview, Schwab Papers.
to Hans and three other: The other three Jewish refugees at OSS who went with Freddy and Hans to demand assignments were George Gerbner, Alfred Rosenthal, and Bernie Steinitz. Gerbner and Rosenthal, in a separate OSS mission code-named Dania in early 1945, were supposed to land in southeastern Austria but were dropped off course in Yugoslavia instead. They barely escaped capture by the Gestapo and survived the war. In a third mission, Dillon III, Steinitz was captured and sentenced to death by the Nazis — but was rescued by American soldiers at the end of the war and also survived.

70 *Hans realized as he followed:* Wynberg interview, Schwab Papers.
he was imprisoned: Persico, *Piercing the Reich,* 145. The orthodontist was named Jack Taylor. He survived Mauthausen.
The leader of another: Persico, *Piercing the Reich,* 145.

71 *"Our talents and time"*: Mayer interview, Schwab Papers.
    "This has now gone on": Wynberg interview, Schwab Papers.
    "I'm very familiar": Mayer interview, Schwab Papers.
    "special reconnaissance": [Roosevelt,] *War Report of the OSS*, 225.

72 *"brown offs"*: Lt. Alfred C. Ulmer Jr., "The Gulliver Mission," *Blue
    Book Magazine* 82, no. 6 (April 1946), 65.
    Breaking the rules: Ibid., 58.

73 *the only thing they lacked*: Mayer and Wynberg interviews, Schwab
    Papers.
    "a bunch of idiots": Lowenstein audio interview, Persico Papers.

74 *"going to start"*: Ibid.
    a few months earlier: Breitman and Lichtman, *FDR and the Jews*, 283–
    84.
    One member of Roosevelt's: Ibid., 285.
    Dyno didn't know: Lowenstein audio interview, Persico Papers.
    "Why don't you jump": Ibid.; and Persico, *Piercing the Reich*, 219.
    "spectacular" mission: Walter Haass audio interview, Persico Papers.

75 *"Honest guys versus"*: Henry Fleischer audio interview, Persico Pa-
    pers.
    He hitched a ride: Ibid.
    one bleak topic: Author interview with Luke Wijnberg.

76 *Luke mentioned them*: Ibid.
    "mostly Austria": Lowenstein audio interview, Persico Papers.
    The Brenner line: Ulmer, "The Gulliver Mission," 60.
    "Completely loyal": Schwab, *OSS Agents in Hitler's Heartland*, 62.

77 *"DVs," he called them*: Haass audio interview, Persico Papers.

78 *practically anything short*: Lowenstein audio interview, Persico Pa-
    pers. "At the time we had sort of papers signed by General Eisen-
    hower that said we could do anything short of, I don't know, killing
    our own troops or something."
    "hyphenated American": Alfred Ulmer Jr. audio interview, Persico
    Papers.
    "You know what": Haass audio interview, Persico Papers. Haass ac-

companied Dyno Lowenstein on a number of the recruiting trips seeking Nazi deserters.

"*What do you think*": Lowenstein audio interview, Persico Papers.

80 "*Who are these people?*": Radio interview with Franz Weber, "Desertion aus der Wehrmacht," ("Desertion from the Wehrmacht"); ORF (Austrian Broadcasting Corporation), April 12, 1984.

"*It was a terrible scene*": Franz Weber interview, Schwab Papers.

"*typical, clean-cut*": Mayer audio interview, Persico Papers.

81 "*a circus*": Ulmer audio interview, Persico Papers.

One team of commandos: Ulmer, "The Gulliver Mission," 64.

"*a fiasco*": Ulmer audio interview, Persico Papers.

"*We had no transportation*": Mayer audio interview, Persico Papers.

82 "*A good anti-Nazi*": Wynberg interview, Schwab Papers.

A Nazi victory: Franz Weber audio interview, Persico Papers.

"*you go with us*": Lowenstein audio interview, Persico Papers.

"*the Nazi redoubt*": Ulmer audio interview, Persico Papers.

83 "*has expert local*": Alfred Ulmer Jr., Teletype conference, January 26, 1945, OSS Records; and Schwab, *OSS Agents in Hitler's Heartland,* 55.

84 "*Why are you sending*": Ulmer, "The Gulliver Mission," 60.

85 *package of condoms:* OSS memo, "List of Supplies to Brindisi for Packaging," January 27, 1945, OSS Records.

Hans packed up: Henry Fleischer audio interview, Persico Papers.

"*I'm going to have to lie low*": Ulmer, "The Gulliver Mission," 61.

86 "*Tell Elly*": Ibid.

"*superhuman courage*": Ibid., 59.

"*and damn few*": Ulmer audio interview, Persico Papers.

"*Tyrol would have to be*": Ulmer, "The Gulliver Mission," 56.

87 *gruesome story:* Ibid., 59.

"*You fellows are Jewish*": Persico, *Piercing the Reich,* 219.

"*This is our war*": Ulmer audio interview, Persico Papers.

5. THE DROP

90 *In the pilot's chair:* Author interviews with John Billings, Woodstock, Virginia, April 19, 2017; September 24, 2017; November 13, 2018.

"At this time of year": H. F. Brown, "Proposed Operation," January 16, 1945, OSS Records.

he had wanted to be a pilot: Author interviews with John Billings.

He was just glad: Ibid.

91 *OSS was so worried:* Ibid.

"could see nothing": Haass, "Greenup Drop," February 28, 1945, OSS Records.

Billings wrote later: Author interviews with John Billings; and John Billings, personal master logbook: 1943–57, privately held.

92 *The Allies had set up:* Monro MacCloskey, *Secret Air Missions: Counterinsurgency Operations in Southern Europe* (New York: Richards Rosen, 1966), 125.

Billings and his flight crew: Author interviews with John Billings.

93 *"Joe," he said:* Ibid.

"He's the German": Ibid.

they planned to ski down: Ibid.

Pure foolishness: Wynberg interview, *Een Leven Lang.*

94 *Billings gathered:* Author interviews with John Billings.

"We'll go down": Ibid.

"This is just a 'scare' pistol": Ibid.

He told Billings: Ibid.

95 *"Last night's flight":* Ulmer, "The Gulliver Mission," 62.

"Love Freddy": Ibid.

"We got your pictures": Ibid.

96 *circled for Freddy:* Ibid.

Freddy relayed word: Mayer interview, Schwab Papers.

"Bad weather": Author interviews with John Billings; and John Billings, personal master logbook: 1943–57.

97 *Freddy and the whole crew:* Haass, "Greenup Drop," OSS Records.
   "Do you want to fly": Author interviews with John Billings.
   Freddy grabbed the control-wheel: Ibid.

98 *The plane's belly:* Ibid.
   This kid really is: Ibid.
   he wished he could crank: Mayer interview, Schwab Papers.
   The two OSS men: Haass, "Greenup Drop," OSS Records.

99 *An apologetic Billings:* Author interviews with John Billings.
   "We're going to do it": Mayer interview, Schwab Papers.
   as the plane dipped: Author interviews with John Billings.

100 *One thousand feet down:* Ibid.
    Slammed downward: Billings's flight records and his own account in interviews put the near-crash on February 25, just prior to the actual drop. Some accounts have placed it several days earlier. Billings's account appears to be the most credible.
    "Turn, turn!": Author interviews with John Billings.

101 *Billings could finally manage:* Ibid.

102 *"I'll give you three hundred":* Ibid.

103 *"The slightest hesitation":* Haass audio interview, Persico Papers.
    "Here we go!": Ulmer, "The Gulliver Mission," 63.

104 *He was two hundred miles:* Ibid.

105 *With no hint:* Mayer interview, Shoah Foundation.
    As cold as the snow felt: Ibid.
    One second passed: Haass, "Greenup Drop," OSS Records.
    this wasn't the place: Wynberg interview, *Een Leven Lang.*

107 *"skis are hard":* Haass, "Greenup Drop," OSS Records.
    "We never dropped": Ulmer, "The Gulliver Mission," 63.

6. THE GLACIER

110 *"dropped almost on top":* Ulmer, "The Gulliver Mission," 63.

112 Just as well: Mayer interview, Shoah Foundation.

113 *They couldn't fit everything:* "Greenup Debriefing Report," OSS Records.

The thin air: Wynberg interview, Schwab Papers.

Freddy slapped him: "Absprung nach Tirol — Von den Finstertaler Seen auf den Lachhof," *Das Fenster* 46 (Autumn 1989). Based on 1960 interview with Fred Mayer. Translated from German.

114 *"fairy tale":* Weber interview, Schwab Papers.

116 *"light, compact":* Spy Radio in World War II: "Strategic Service Transmitter-Receiver Number 1" SSTR-1 OSS. OSS instructional film, circa 1943.

He tried again: "Greenup Debriefing Report," unsigned, summer 1945, OSS Records; and Ulmer, "The Gulliver Mission," 63.

he began taking: Schwab, *OSS Agents in Hitler's Heartland,* 67.

He went to swap: Ibid.

went unanswered: Ibid., 63; and "Greenup Debriefing Report," OSS Records.

The canned tomatoes: "Absprung nach Tirol," *Das Fenster.*

118 *"Ja, Herr Oberleutnant":* Ulmer, "The Gulliver Mission," 64.

he would be treated: Wynberg interview, Schwab Papers.

119 *Franz was struck:* "Greenup Debriefing Report," OSS Records.

Franz thanked the farmer: Ibid.

The huge sled: O'Donnell, *They Dared Return,* 72.

120 *the most hair-raising:* Mayer interview, Shoah Foundation.

More than three hours: "Greenup Debriefing Report," OSS Records.

That was the extent: Weber audio interview, Persico Papers.

Waiting for their train: Schwab, *OSS Agents in Hitler's Heartland,* 70.

121 *a few passengers:* "Greenup Debriefing Report," OSS Records.

"These two are foreigners": Weber interview, Schwab Papers.

"This can happen": Wynberg interview, Schwab Papers.

Freddy gripped: Ibid.

Hans struggled to maintain: Ibid.

the Gestapo officer: Ibid.

122 *Hans played with:* "Greenup Debriefing Report," OSS Records; Mayer interview, Persico Papers; Mayer audio interview, Schwab Papers.

"Is that you?": Author interview with Dr. Josef Weber, Oberperfuss,

Austria, July 31, 2018. At the time of the OSS mission, Dr. Weber (no relation to Franz) was a boy of four and a half years old growing up in Oberperfuss next door to Franz's family home. He has studied the OSS operation extensively over the years since then.

7. "FRANZ WEBER SENT ME"

123 *Fathers and sons:* Horst Schreiber, *1938 — Der Anschluss in den Bezirken Tirols* (Innsbruck: Studien Verlag, 2018). Translated from German.

124 *She knew Franz:* Author interview with Dr. Josef Weber.

125 *"Imagine who we met":* Ibid.
forcing him to transfer: Schreiber, *1938 — Der Anschluss in den Bezirken Tirols,* 83.

126 *"You keep quiet":* Author interview with Dr. Josef Weber. (KZ is an abbreviation in German for *Konzentrationslager.*)
They stopped: "Absprung nach Tirol," *Das Fenster.*

127 *Without help:* Mayer interview, Schwab Papers.
"flourishing new life": Adolf Hitler, "Proclamation for the Anschluss of Austria to the Great German Reich," radio broadcast speech, March 12, 1938.
"simple and modest": Franz Weber audio interview, Persico Papers.

128 *"all sorts of grandiose":* Ibid.
Almost overnight: Weber interview, Schwab Papers.
Nearly 120,000 people: Yad Vashem, "Mauthausen," yadvashem.org.

129 *"Do that again":* Author interview with Dr. Josef Weber.
a three-year-old-boy: Ibid. Weber's wife was a cousin of the boy.
For thirty reichsmarks: Ibid.
"playing with life": Weber interview, Schwab Papers.
he escaped capture: "Debriefing Report of Operation Dania," 1945, OSS Records.

130 *a bitter topic:* Author interview with Alois Abenthung (grandson

of Alois Abenthung), in Oberperfuss, Austria, July 31, 2018; and by email, January 18, 2019.

a political opposition: Schreiber, *1938 — Der Anschluss in den Bezirken Tirols,* 82.

"prohibiting the formation": Judgement Against Alois Abenthung, Regional Court of Innsbruck, Docket No. 8034, File KL 15/44 (April 12, 1944). Court document provided to author by Matthias Breit, researcher and historian in Tyrol.

131 *"never heard":* Mayer interview, Shoah Foundation.

"Oh, my God": Ibid.

"Go back": Ibid.

132 *Alois went upstairs:* "Absprung nach Tirol," *Das Fenster.*

"all possible assistance": "Greenup Debriefing Report," OSS Records.

133 *"my first and most reliable":* Fred Mayer to Alois Abenthung, letter for medical clearance, May 5, 1945. Provided to author by Abenthung's grandson of the same name.

"He came with two": Annie Weber audio interview, Persico Papers.

134 *"Where are you going?":* Ibid.

He had done: The Real Inglorious Bastards, DVD.

The Gestapo would hang: Weber interview, Schwab Papers.

"This is not a good idea": Persico files, Annie Weber audio interview.

136 *He imagined:* Wynberg interview, Schwab Papers.

137 *"You've had no message":* Ulmer, "The Gulliver Mission," 64.

"Not necessarily, sir": Ibid., 65.

"Within four days": Ibid.

ALL WELL: OSS cable, March 8, 1945, OSS Records.

an expensive bottle: Ulmer, "The Gulliver Mission," 65.

8. THE FÜHRER'S BUNKER

140 *he told himself:* Mayer audio interview, Persico Papers.

"I need temporary": Mayer interview, Shoah Foundation.

The only explanation: Ibid.

141 *A handful of combat:* Mayer interview, Schwab Papers.

142 *He was drinking:* Ulmer, "The Gulliver Mission," 67.

must have felt: O'Donnell, *They Dared Return,* 87.

143 *Freddy sat frozen:* "Greenup Debriefing Report," OSS Records.

"Are you all right?": Author interview with Dr. Josef Weber.

144 *the stranger slipped:* Mayer interview, Schwab Papers.

"the first link": "Greenup Debriefing Report," OSS Records.

"I no longer believe": Annie Weber interview, Schwab Papers.

145 *let Freddy use:* Mayer interview, Shoah Foundation.

"a perfect fit": Mayer audio interview, Persico Papers; Mayer and others credited Alouisa, a nurse, with getting the uniform for him at the hospital. The Greenup Debriefing Report noted that Annie Weber's brother, an orderly at the hospital, was partly involved in getting the uniform.

"I lost everything": Mayer interview, Shoah Foundation.

"genuine anti-Nazi": Franz Weber interview, Schwab Papers.

Her father had agreed: "Greenup Debriefing Report," OSS Records.

146 *They soon decided:* Author interview with Dr. Josef Weber.

"an absolutely wonderful": Mayer audio interview, Persico Papers.

once again rigged: Ulmer, "The Gulliver Mission," 68.

147 *She taught him:* Wynberg interview, Schwab Papers.

148 *"air warning tower":* "Locomotives in Innsbruck," March 27, 1945, OSS Records.

149 *"a ten-strike":* Ulmer, "The Gulliver Mission," 67.

The other branches: Ibid.

9. THE BIRTH OF A FRENCHMAN

151 *"my biggest coup":* Mayer interview, Schwab Papers.

152 *He even heard:* "Greenup Debriefing Report," OSS Records. "Diane" was an actual American agent, Virginia Hall, who did important espionage work for OSS in Europe during the war, although

Freddy did not know of her existence. She did have a wooden leg.

153 *"Each individual contacted":* "Report on Mission to Innsbruck," unsigned, May 26, 1945, OSS Records.

"alive and working": Mitchell's real name was Paul Kroeck. He was a Nazi deserter from Austria who became an OSS agent; he was the third member of the error-plagued Dania mission, along with George Gerbner and Alfred Rosenthal. Kroeck, too, managed to survive the war.

154 *Three French allies:* Ulmer, "The Gulliver Mission," 71, and OSS cable of March 30, 1945, which specifically mentioned French resister Édouard Daladier, imprisoned by the Nazis at a castle known as Schloss Itter east of Innsbruck. Fred also relayed information on the Nazis' imprisonment at the castle of Marie-Agnès Cailliau, the eldest sister of de Gaulle; and François de La Rocque, accused at various times of helping both the Allies and the Nazis. Stephen Harding, *The Last Battle* (Boston: Da Capo, 2014), 164–68.

purportedly in hiding: It is not clear whether Mussolini was at the Austrian hotel at the time; weeks later, Italian opponents captured and executed him after he was discovered in a Nazi caravan in northern Italy.

"usually reliable": Ulmer, "The Gulliver Mission," 67.

155 *force at his back:* Mayer interview, Shoah Foundation.

156 *"the realities of a world war":* Wynberg interview, Schwab Papers.

What real courage: Ibid.; and Wynberg emails, from Hans Wynberg to Marjorie Bingham. Hans downplayed the risk he faced in his "passive" role as radio man in the attic, telling Schwab: "You have to remember I never shot at anybody. I was not front-line troop like my twin brother. I had never been involved in any action."

157 Eastern Front Collapsing: Wynberg interview, Schwab Papers.

"Do You Know?": Ulmer, "The Gulliver Mission," 71.

"His little paper": "Greenup Debriefing Report," OSS Records.

158 *$10 or $20 per:* Ibid.

two men soon: Ibid.

159 *"Three trains of paratroops":* OSS cable, April 2, 1945, OSS Records.
"the Krauts had devised": Ulmer, "The Gulliver Mission," 60.

160 *the man's body language:* "Greenup Debriefing Report," OSS Records.

161 *asked the yardmaster: The Real Inglorious Bastards,* DVD.
"These twenty-six trains": Ibid.
"loaded with ammo": OSS cable, April 2, 1945, OSS Records. Punctuation in the cable has been edited for clarity.

162 *heavy-bomber operation:* Ulmer, "The Gulliver Mission," 67.

163 *"destroyed virtually":* Ibid., 68. The bombing mission appears to have taken place April 4, 1945.
the wreckage: Mayer interview, Shoah Foundation.
They bombed the hell: Mayer audio interview, Persico Papers.
"destroy completely": OSS memo from Col. Howard Chapin recommending award, September 17, 1945, OSS Records.
he had made: Mayer interview, Shoah Foundation.
Freddy took off: The formal OSS review of the mission stated that Freddy switched his cover story from Nazi officer to French laborer "around the first of April," but other OSS records suggest the switch occurred at least four days after that.

164 *An ally of Alois's:* "Greenup Debriefing Report," OSS Records.

165 *Freddy had run through:* Ibid.
As a boy growing up: Mayer interview, Shoah Foundation.
about as much rehearsal: Mayer audio interview, Persico Papers.
"Born 19 February, 1920": Heinz Weibel-Altmeyer and Joachim Murat, "Unternehmen Alpen-Festung" (Operation Alpine Fortress), *Neue Illustrierte* magazine, January 1961 (Germany; defunct). Translated from German.
He couldn't get over: Mayer audio interview, Persico Papers.

166 *liked to drink:* Ibid.
"trustworthy worker": Ulmer, "The Gulliver Mission," 65.
the first jet-propelled: Smithsonian National Air and Space Museum, Messerschmitt Me 262 A-1a Schwalbe (Swallow), https://

airandspace.si.edu/collection-objects/messerschmitt-me-262-1a-schwalbe-swallow.

167 *The Luftwaffe had managed:* Ibid.

   doubled the number: Daniel Uziel, *Arming the Luftwaffe* (Jefferson, NC: McFarland, 2011), 130.

   "I blew more fuses": Mayer interview, Schwab Papers.

   "one hour building": Ibid.

168 *acts of sabotage:* Eric Lichtblau, *The Nazis Next Door* (Boston, New York: Houghton Mifflin Harcourt, 2014), 164.

169 *Freddy never saw:* Mayer interview, Schwab Papers.

170 *"I got whipped cream":* Mayer interview, Persico Papers.

   "tech corporal": Under the army rankings in place at the time, Freddy was a "Technician fifth grade/T-5," the equivalent of a corporal.

   he was still in Italy: Mayer interview, Shoah Foundation.

   "Definite answer expected": OSS cable, Incoming Message report from "Gadsen" cable #346, OSS Records.

171 *"Hold your horses":* OSS cable, Incoming Message report for "Gadsen" cables "#5 to #17," OSS Records.

   "he is alive": Schwab, *OSS Agents in Hitler's Heartland,* 95. The letter spelled his first name as "Freddie."

10. "TAKE INNSBRUCK"

173 *"grandiose ideas":* Wynberg interview, Schwab Papers.

174 *"good enough":* Ibid.

   on the way: Ibid.

   "play war": Franz Weber interview, Schwab Papers.

   he had been one of them: Ibid.

175 *"just sitting there":* Mayer interview, Shoah Foundation.

   "If desired can take": OSS cables, Incoming Message report from "Gadsen," cable #346, OSS Records.

   "the highest proportion": Peter Pirker, "'Ich verstehe nicht, warum ich Menschen erschiessen gehen soll...' Die Deserteursgruppe im Tiroler Vomperloch und die Zerstörung von Erinnerung," in *Da*

machen wir nicht mehr mit . . . : Österreichische Soldaten und Zivilisten vor Gerichten der Wehrmacht, eds. Thomas Geldmacher et al. (Vienna, Austria: Mandelbaum Verlag, 2010), 155–66. Article translated from German.

Wehrmacht deserters began: Ibid., 156.

scattered pockets: One of the leading resisters, Karl Gruber, went on to become both governor of Tyrol and Austrian foreign minister after the war. At times after the war, he and Freddy would vie for credit over their roles in the resistance.

one loosely formed: Harding, *The Last Battle,* 74.

176 *motivated mainly:* Weber interview, Schwab Papers.

holed up somewhere: "Greenup Debriefing Report," OSS Records.

Freddy dismissed him: Ibid.

177 *using the alias:* "Absprung nach Tirol," *Das Fenster.*

destroyed the internal: "Greenup Debriefing Report," OSS Records.

seemed genuine: Ibid.

178 *"an intelligence mission":* Casey, *The Secret War Against Hitler,* 210.

"nothing he could do": Cable #293 of April 15, 1945, OSS Records.

didn't seem well thought out: Ulmer, "The Gulliver Mission," 67.

179 *"Otherwise continue":* OSS cable, Incoming Message report for "Gadsen" cables "#5 to #17," OSS Records.

Stick to your first: Mayer interview, Shoah Foundation.

"one thousand partisans": Schwab, *OSS Agents in Hitler's Heartland,* 100.

slammed repeatedly: Ulmer audio interview, Persico Papers. Ulmer did not name the agent who was killed, but he said the episode "really created a morale problem" within OSS in the war's final stage.

180 *He considered many:* Ulmer audio interview, Persico Papers.

"He was magnificent": Ibid.

"keep aloof": Ulmer, "The Gulliver Mission," 68.

"Fifty fighter planes": OSS cable, April 14, 1945, OSS Records.

"67 four-ton trucks": "Artillery: Innsbruck Area," April 14, 1945, OSS Records.

181 *"one hundred duds":* OSS cable, April 15, 1945, Schwab Papers.

the names of many: Mayer interview, Schwab Papers; Ulmer, "The Gulliver Mission," 66.

Bari was scrambling to arrange: Ibid.

"plus special stuff": OSS cable, April 16, 1945, OSS Records.

to bribe a diabetic: Ibid.

182 *He knew his mother:* Ulmer, "The Gulliver Mission," 68.

They drove out: "Gadsen Team," OSS cable, March 9, 1945, OSS Records.

two-and-a-half-ton German truck: "Greenup Debriefing Report," OSS Records.

183 *about using flares:* Ibid.

a special "Eureka": Ibid.

184 *to jettison all eight:* Ibid.

"A great screw-up": Schwab, *OSS Agents in Hitler's Heartland,* 105.

scattered somewhere high: "Greenup Debriefing Report," OSS Records.

"The whole area": Ibid.

185 *All hell has broken loose:* Mayer audio interview, Persico Papers.

cold and hungry: Ibid.

Weren't the Brits: The British plane and the flares shooting from it remained a mystery. OSS theorized that the UK special forces were running a spy mission nearby that night, perhaps even parachuting their own agents down into Tyrol.

The idea: "Greenup Debriefing Report," OSS Records.

186 *A stove was burning:* Ulmer, "The Gulliver Mission," 69.

"What newspaper": OSS cable, April 20, 1945, Persico Papers.

187 *the late-night callers:* Mayer interview, Shoah Foundation.

What can they do: Ibid.

hard labor: Mayer audio interview, Persico Papers; Mayer interview, Schwab Papers.

threw the Gestapo papers: Ulmer, "The Gulliver Mission," 69.

grabbed his gun: Mayer interview, Schwab Papers. An OSS report, based partly on the statements of Nazi interrogator Walter Güttner, later said that the Nazis seized the money belt and the cash from

Freddy when he was arrested. Freddy said that was untrue and that "I'm upset that they took Güttner's word." He said he later retrieved the money belt from under the sofa and returned the gold coins to OSS.

188 *he stood no chance:* Mayer interview, Shoah Foundation.

"*Oui," he answered:* Ulmer, "The Gulliver Mission," 69.

"*You're under arrest":* Mayer interview, Shoah Foundation.

11. THE WATER TREATMENT

190 "*little rat":* Mayer audio interview, Persico Papers.

almost fatherly: "Absprung nach Tirol," *Das Fenster.*

Austrian resisters: Walter Güttner, "Treatment of Fred Maier," June 7, 1945, OSS Records. (Mayer's last name was misspelled.)

191 *the interpreter translated:* Mayer interview, Shoah Foundation.

home long ago: Güttner, "Treatment of Fred Maier," OSS Records.

"*extreme, severe":* Ibid.

"*mass of raw flesh":* Larson, *In the Garden of Beasts,* 4. The physician, Joseph Schachno, was beaten June 21, 1933, when Nazi officers suspected him of engaging in subversive activity.

Knives, sticks, whips: Nikolaus Wachsmann, *KL: A History of the Nazi Concentration Camps* (New York: Farrar, Straus and Giroux, 2016), 105, 429.

192 *Down the hall:* Interview report, "Busch, Friedrich, German National, Assistant Gestapo Chief of Innsbruck, SS Hauptsurmfuehrer," 307th Counter Intelligence Corps Detachment, Headquarters Seventh Army, APO 758, September 15, 1945, Internet Archive.

"*Are you a spy?":* Mayer interview, Shoah Foundation.

one of the SS men: Güttner, "Treatment of Fred Maier," OSS Records.

193 *information they could extract:* Mayer interview, Shoah Foundation.

becoming woozy: Mayer interview, Schwab Papers.

the suicide pill: Mayer interview, Shoah Foundation.

"Ach Quatsch": Güttner, "Treatment of Fred Maier," OSS Records.
They underestimated me: Mayer interview, Shoah Foundation.
stripping off his clothes: Güttner, "Treatment of Fred Maier," OSS Records.
he could take down: Mayer audio interview, Persico Papers.
"my arms were sore": Güttner, "Treatment of Fred Maier," OSS Records.

194 *The prisoner's strength*: Ibid. Güttner said in the interrogation that "since MAIER was very strong and evaded further beatings, handcuffs were put on him." (Again, Mayer's last name was misspelled.)
"wherever he could": Testimony of Erna Schmid, Gestapo employee, in 1955 in court proceedings in Innsbruck against Güttner over the beating (Schwab Papers). Freddy himself said that he "was struck, with a bull whip, by his own count, at least 180 times." Memo from Judge Advocate General's office, "Investigation of Alleged War Crime," September 10, 1945, OSS Records.
"We don't do it that easy": Mayer interview, Persico Papers.
gold threads: "Absprung nach Tirol," *Das Fenster.*

195 *come to rely heavily*: "Greenup Debriefing Report," OSS Records. Some alternate accounts have identified the prisoner who "squealed" on Freddy as "Leo," a second black-market operator who helped him in Innsbruck. The debriefing report from OSS and Freddy's own accounts, however, have said that it was Fritz Moser. Peter Pirker, the Vienna researcher and author, suggested that Fritz Moser and "Leo" could have been the same person.
"Tell them the truth": Mayer interview, Shoah Foundation.
Fritz had talked: Mayer interview, Schwab Papers. "I got into trouble when someone squealed — Fritz Moser," Freddy said.
never have been captured: Mayer audio interview, Persico Papers. "If he hadn't opened his stupid mouth, I don't think we ever would have gotten captured," Freddy said.
the urge to spit: Ulmer, "The Gulliver Mission," 70.
"I don't even know": Mayer interview, Shoah Foundation.

196 able to be whatever: Lichtblau, "Frederick Mayer, Jew Who Spied on Nazis After Fleeing Germany, Dies at 94."

the Swabian accent: Güttner, "Treatment of Fred Maier," OSS Records. "I noticed that he had a Schwaebisch dialect," Güttner said. "I told him that I did not believe that he was an American, but that because of his dialect, I took him for a German."

"I refuse to answer": Mayer interview, Shoah Foundation.

"the sticks": Güttner, "Treatment of Fred Maier," OSS Records. In some accounts, Mayer said that the Gestapo thrust a long rifle beneath his legs and used that to hoist him toward the ceiling. In his beaten state, he may not have known whether it was a stick or a rifle.

197 *dunked his head:* "Greenup Debriefing Report," OSS Records; and Mayer interview, Shoah Foundation.

tried to force himself: Ulmer, "The Gulliver Mission," 70.

a gruesome six hours: "Greenup Debriefing Report," OSS Records.

198 *"Better stop":* Mayer interview, Shoah Foundation.

Hofer would need to know: Weibel-Altmeyer and Murat, "Unternehmen Alpen Festung."

wanted to find: Güttner, "Treatment of Fred Maier," OSS Records.

199 *"If you are captured":* Ulmer, "The Gulliver Mission," 60.

"weren't smart enough": Ulmer audio interview, Persico Papers.

didn't need any warnings: Ulmer, "The Gulliver Mission," 70.

"A Mississippi steamboat": Ulmer audio interview, Persico Papers.

200 *"I know you bastards":* Persico, *Piercing the Reich*, 285.

to see a girlfriend: Güttner, "Treatment of Fred Maier," OSS Records.

smoking American cigarettes: Ibid.

updates on his "mission": Schwab, *OSS Agents in Hitler's Heartland*, 132.

201 *"already declared himself":* Güttner, "Treatment of Fred Maier," OSS Records.

talk to Max earlier: Ibid.

"big catch": Ibid.

part of his sandwich: Ulmer, "The Gulliver Mission," 70.

a handkerchief: Mayer interview, Shoah Foundation.

202 *His whole face:* Ulmer, "The Gulliver Mission," 70.

"Lieutenant Fred": Güttner, "Treatment of Fred Maier," OSS Records.

"a happy and friendly face": Ibid.

the grassy quarters: "Greenup Debriefing Report," OSS Records.

Freddy remained quiet: Güttner stated in his interrogation by OSS after the war that Freddy admitted working for OSS in Italy, but this claim, along with other admissions that Güttner claimed Freddy made, is contradicted by a wealth of other documents and accounts.

"We also have our agents": Güttner, "Treatment of Fred Maier," OSS Records.

"another man": Mayer interview, Shoah Foundation.

203 *the air-raid sirens*: "Absprung nach Tirol," *Das Fenster.*

204 *gone to the Nazis*: Interview report, "Busch, Friedrich, German National, Assistant Gestapo Chief of Innsbruck, SS Hauptsurmfuehrer."

a self-proclaimed "resister": Ibid.

he badly injured: Mayer interview, Schwab Papers.

205 *"animal-like manner"*: Pirker, *Codename Brooklyn*, 233. A plaque in memory of Robert Moser is now displayed outside the Innsbruck building that housed the Gestapo headquarters and jail during the war.

five thirty in the morning: Güttner, "Treatment of Fred Maier," OSS Records.

thought confounded him: Mayer audio interview, Persico Papers. "I was amazed at how they knew we had to go to Oberperfuss of all places."

206 *Güttner was cunning*: It was never clear how the Gestapo traced Freddy to Oberperfuss. The OSS debriefing report said that a Kripo police officer arrested with Kuen "broke under pressure" and told the Gestapo that Hans, the radio man, was in Oberperfuss. But Freddy and others disputed that account, saying that none of the Kripo officers had that information.

a Sunday morning: Annie Weber interview, Schwab Papers.

207 *hiding in the attic*: "Greenup Debriefing Report," OSS Records.

The report refers to the Kirchebners' farm by their local name of Klaxner.

out by the stables: Author interview with Dr. Josef Weber.

Güttner slapped him: Schwab, *OSS Agents in Hitler's Heartland,* 136.

fled the night before: "Greenup Debriefing Report," OSS Records.

The two of them packed: Franz Weber interview, Schwab Papers; and author interview with Dr. Josef Weber.

208 *"We have to do something":* Franz Weber interview, Schwab Papers.

church bells rang: Schreiber, *1938 — Der Anschluss in den Bezirken Tirols,* 84.

12. A WHITE FLAG

210 *"This is Kreisleiter":* Schwab, *OSS Agents in Hitler's Heartland,* 138.

found it astonishing: "Greenup Debriefing Report," OSS Records.

211 *"a fine boy":* Güttner, "Treatment of Fred Maier," OSS Records.

husky build: Ulmer, "The Gulliver Mission," 71.

"100% pro-Hitler": Mayer audio interview, Persico Papers.

"remembered by all": United States Holocaust Memorial Museum photo archives, "Portrait of Gauleiter Franz Hofer," 1939.

212 *"first Jew-free region":* "Ainzeige Gegen Ex-Gauleiter Hofer," *Die Tat* (Switzerland), February 11, 1961.

ordering the roundups: Criminal filing in war-crimes proceedings by Upper Prosecutor Düsseldorf, Germany, Against Hofer; August 10, 1965.

"the German victory": Franz Hofer, "Bereit zu jedem Einsatz!" ("Ready for Any Assignment!"), *Voralberger Tagblatt,* December 30, 1944; reprinted in German Propaganda Archive at Calvin College, Grand Rapids, Michigan.

beautiful home: Mayer interview, Shoah Foundation.

213 *"what do you think":* Ulmer, "The Gulliver Mission," 71.

"It will be over": Mayer audio interview, Persico Papers.

a four-course meal: "Absprung nach Tirol," *Das Fenster.*

had not been poisoned: Ibid.; and Mayer interview, Schwab Papers.

a carrot-and-stick strategy: "Absprung nach Tirol," *Das Fenster.*

214 *join forces with the Germans:* Ibid.

What made anyone think: Ibid.

Eisenhower and his top generals: Minott, *The Fortress That Never Was,* 88.

"the Redoubt will hold": Persico, *Piercing the Reich,* 289.

"Operations in Berlin": Minott, *The Fortress That Never Was,* 92.

215 *"Gauleiter Hofer's behavior":* Albert Kesselring, *The Memoirs of Field-Marshal Kesselring,* (Novato, CA: Presidio, 1989), 284.

he might be willing: "Greenup Debriefing Report," OSS Records.

"I suggest you surrender": Mayer interview, Shoah Foundation.

Hofer quickly assented: "Greenup Debriefing Report," OSS Records.

216 *"Am at present":* Ulmer, "The Gulliver Mission," 71.

unlocking Freddy's handcuffs: Güttner, "Treatment of Fred Maier," OSS Records.

"with his life": Persico, *Piercing the Reich,* 290–91.

217 *there was no reason for alarm:* "Absprung nach Tirol," *Das Fenster.*

hauled to Reichenau: B. A. "Jimmy" James, *Moonless Night: The Second World War Escape Epic* (Barnsley, South Yorkshire, UK: Pen & Sword Military, 2001), 179.

218 *announced a metal sign:* Ibid., 178.

which of the Nazis: "Absprung nach Tirol," *Das Fenster.*

hanged three Austrian resisters: James, *Moonless Night,* 181.

thought of himself: Mayer audio interview, Persico Papers. "I always had a feeling that at Reichenau they were . . . going to shoot me and ask no questions so there would be no witnesses," Freddy said.

219 *before giving up the fight:* "Absprung nach Tirol," *Das Fenster.*

"a last-ditch stand": "Greenup Debriefing Report," OSS Records.

220 *"to save German":* Schwab, *OSS Agents in Hitler's Heartland,* 150.

"to surrender unconditionally": Ulmer, "The Gulliver Mission," 71.

221 *begin his radio broadcast:* Ibid.

his word "as an officer": "Greenup Debriefing Report," OSS Records.

not mentioning: Ibid.

223 *told the major everything:* Memo from Maj. Bland West, May 6, 1945, in support of commendation for Fred Mayer.

"Heil Hitler!": Memo from 103rd Army Division, OSS Records.

224 *inside Güttner's wallet:* Ulmer, "The Gulliver Mission," 70.

225 *"What do you think we are":* Mayer audio interview, Persico Papers.

EPILOGUE: AFTER THE FALL

227 *"to arrange the surrender":* "Report on Mission to Innsbruck," nomination of Frederick Mayer for officer's commission, May 26, 1945, 2677th Regiment headquarters.

"by far the most successful": Casey, *The Secret War Against Hitler,* 209.

228 *"without a drop of blood":* Ibid., 210.

"the most productive": Anthony Cave Brown, *The Secret War Report of the OSS* (New York: Brandt and Brandt, 1976), 557.

"destroy completely": OSS memo from Col. Howard Chapin recommending award for Frederick Mayer, September 17, 1945, OSS Records.

"The front died": "U.S. Tactical Air Power in Europe," *Impact* 3, no. 5 (May 1945): 62–66.

229 *"severe" cuts:* Description of medical examination conducted in Salzburg, Austria, on May 14, 1945, included in OSS citation nominating Mayer for Purple Heart award on July 26, 1945, OSS Records.

"outstanding performance": Memo to 2677th Regiment/OSS, May 26, 1945, from Lt. Col. William P. Maddox, OSS Records.

shined shoes: Mayer interview, Shoah Foundation.

You look as though: Ulmer audio interview, Persico Papers.

230 *"actual conflict":* Memo from Army Lt. Gen. John C. H. Lee, April 8, 1946, rejecting recommendation for Medal of Honor, OSS Records.

"one of the great unsung heroes": Lichtblau, "Frederick Mayer, Jew Who Spied on Nazis After Fleeing Germany, Dies at 94," *New York Times,* April 20, 2016.

"supports the original decision": Army Board for Correction of Mil-

itary Records, record of proceedings in case of Frederick Mayer, May 9, 2013, Schwab Papers.

"the residue of human misery": Mayer interview, Shoah Foundation.

"wasted so much time": Ibid.

231 *He would like to see that:* Ibid.

"not *suitable for staff":* "Theater Service Report" on Mayer written by Ulmer, November 16, 1945, OSS Records.

"Torture Endured by Brooklynite": New York Times, October 5, 1945.

beaming with pride: Mayer interview, Shoah Foundation.

a pair of silk stockings: Mayer intervew, Schwab Papers.

232 *salvaged two paintings:* Wynberg emails, from Hans Wynberg to Marjorie Bingham, July 30, 2009.

seized the family bike-tire factory: Hans said that he and his brother, Luke, were able to regain ownership of the family factory after the war and sold it in about 1950 to pay for tuition at Cornell University. Wynberg interview, Schwab Papers; author interview with Luke Wijnberg.

"Your parents and their son": Letter from the Red Cross in the Netherlands to Hans Wynberg, dated August 15, 1985. Translated from Dutch. The letter apparently confirmed details Hans had received years earlier from the Red Cross and other sources.

233 *"this part of your life":* Wynberg interview, *Een Leven Lang.*

never willing to move: Author interview with Luke Wynberg.

"Never forget": Wynberg emails, from Hans Wynberg to Marjorie Bingham, July 30, 2009, regarding what he might say at a Holocaust memorial.

He placed a gravestone: Wynberg interview, *Een Leven Lang.*

234 *tried to teach his children:* Author interview with Audrey Wijnberg.

one of the many books: Ibid.

"Too much about that past": Wynberg interview, *Een Leven Lang.*

"I just tagged along": Author interview with Jeffrey Wijnberg.

Annie made her wedding dress: Franz and Annie Weber interview, Persico Papers.

"a great problem": Weber interview, Persico Papers.

235 *"under duress"*: Ulmer interview, Persico Papers.

236 *as a "respected businessman"*: "German Catholic Organ Identified Nazi Who Killed 300,000 Jews," *Daily News Bulletin* (Jewish Telegraphic Agency), March 30, 1965. The figure in the headline appears to be a typo; the item itself said that Hofer was accused of ordering the murders of 30,000 Jews.

charges were dropped: Schwab, *OSS Agents in Hitler's Heartland*, 159.

237 *"Chutzpah!"*: Mayer interview, Shoah Foundation.

PHOTO CREDITS

INDEX